Abortion
&
Dialogue

Abortion & Dialogue

PRO-CHOICE, PRO-LIFE, AND AMERICAN LAW

RUTH COLKER

INDIANA UNIVERSITY PRESS
Bloomington & Indianapolis

The paper used in this publication meets the minimum requirements of
American National Standard for Information Sciences—Permanence of
Paper for Printed Library Materials, ANSI Z39. 48-1984.

∞™

Manufactured in the United States of America

Library of Congress Cataloging-in-Publication Data

Colker, Ruth.
    Abortion and dialogue : pro-choice, pro-life, and American law /
  Ruth Colker.
        p.   cm.
    Includes bibliographical references and index.
    ISBN 0-253-31393-7 (cl). — ISBN 0-253-20738-X (pa)
      1. Abortion—Law and legislation—United States.   2. Abortion—
  United States—Moral and ethical aspects.   3. Feminism.
  4. Theology.   I. Title.
  KF3771.C65   1992
  344.73'0546—dc20
  [347.304546]   91-46603

1 2 3 4 5   96 95 94 93 92

For Cara Colker-Eybel

*May her life be filled with
love, compassion, and wisdom.*

CONTENTS

Acknowledgments

This book is the result of many genuine dialogues. I decided to write this book after reading Michael Perry's book *Morality, Politics, and Law*, in which he cryptically mentioned that religious feminists might offer the most insight on "what it means to be authentically human."[1] Quickly devouring the one book he cited for that proposition, Catherine Keller's *From a Broken Web: Separation, Sexism, and Self* (1986), I then searched for more books from a feminist-theological perspective. Christine Gudorf made that search possible by responding to my quite broadranging request for bibliographic assistance in feminism and theology.

As I then began to write a series of pieces on feminism and theology, I had the fortunate opportunity to deliver earlier drafts and parts of this book at various conferences. Without exception, the conversations that I had with the people attending these conferences and workshops were extremely helpful to me as I wrote and revised this book. Thus, I would like to thank the organizers and participants at the following conferences at which I presented versions of this book: the University of Toronto Legal Theory and Clara Brett Martin Workshops; Celebration 35 at Harvard Law School; the South Central Women's Studies Association; the Feminism and Legal Theory Conference held at the University of Wisconsin–Madison; the Frontiers of Legal Thought Conference held at Duke Law School; the International Congress of the International Academy of Law and Mental Health held in Toronto, Ontario; the Faculty Workshop at Osgoode Hall Law School in Toronto, Ontario; the Theology Workshop at the Critical Legal Studies Conference in Washington, D.C.; and the Conference on the United States Constitution sponsored by the Institute of American Culture in Taipei, Taiwan.

In addition, numerous colleagues have provided me with comments on earlier drafts of parts of this book. I am sure that I will unintentionally omit some of them from this list but I would like to thank them each publicly. Even when they disagreed with my conclusions or perspectives, they managed to communicate with me in a way that facilitated my project greatly. For their generous conversations, letters, and telephone calls, I therefore wish to thank: Adeno Addis, Paul Barron, Larry Beyer, Rebecca Cook, Mary Coombs, Richard Delgado, Nitya Duclos, Martha Fineman, Lucinda Finley, Emily Fowler Hartigan, Alison Jaggar, Sylvia Law, Catharine MacKinnon, Sabrina McCarthy, Martha Minow, Connie Mui, Michael Perry, John Stick, Cathy Wessinger, and Ann Wooldridge. My many research assistants, particularly Joyce Cain, Lorena Dumas, Jan Dyer, and Roxanne Newman, have provided me with excellent research and support; this book would not have been possible without their assistance. Finally, I thank my secretary, Brenda Du Faur, for her patience during the many times that I sneaked onto her computer to work and disrupted her busy work schedule.

I would also like to thank Tulane Law School for its generous support of my research through summer writing grants and the funds made available through the C. J. Morrow Research Professor of Law. By being able to teach and conduct research in a supportive and compassionate environment, I was able to devote myself selfishly. I wish that the women whose stories I tell in this book could have been as fortunate as myself in experiencing a life full of love, compassion, and respect. I thank them, however, for the wisdom that they were kind enough to share with me.

Note

1. Michael Perry, Morality, Politics, and Law: A Bicentennial Essay 183 (1988).

Introduction: Abortion and Dialogue

> Love is at the same time the foundation of
> dialogue and dialogue itself.[1]

> We still have to be born as human beings;
> that is the great task that lies before us.[2]

I began writing this book in May 1987. It was a very confusing period of my life, because I was trying to rediscover my sexual identity and a set of ethics upon which I could lead my life. I wanted to discover and experience my *authentic self*. What I soon learned, through a study of theology and feminism coupled with meditation, was that I had no one authentic self. I learned that we are selves who discover, construct, and experience our authenticity as part of a web of selves with others.

Although this project did not begin as an investigation of the abortion issue, it soon led to an examination of that issue since the abortion issue raised complex questions about our relationship to our selves and others. Eventually, this investigation of abortion led to a fuller investigation of the topic of reproductive health, a topic that lends context to the abortion issue. During the journey that has led to the writing of this book, I have tried to maintain an openness and curiosity about the world in which we live. Thus, I have found myself changing my opinion many times on various subjects such as abortion and sexuality. During a four-year period, I found myself going from a rigid pro-choice position to a very weak pro-choice position to a moderate pro-choice position on abortion. In this book, I hope to share with the reader some of what I learned in this four-year journey.

Readers may wonder why I decided to investigate feminism and theology to answer my questions about our authentic selves. In general, feminist theory and theology can benefit from dialogue because both disciplines try to assist people in experiencing their aspirations for their authentic selves. They both offer a critique of society and aspirations for a better society, although their emphases are different. Feminist theory does a relatively better job in presenting a critique of society and theology does a relatively better job in exploring the aspirations that we should seek for society.

Specifically, feminist theory explains both how women's lack of awareness of their own oppression (what feminists call a *problem of consciousness*) and how women's experience of nonmutual love (what feminists call *sexual objectification*) create barriers to that journey. Feminist theory emphasizes its critique by focusing on the subordination, weakness, and invisibility of women as part of gender-based society. Feminism (as contrasted with some forms of humanism) believes that a critique of gender socialization must begin from the perspective of women because women's condition has been generally overlooked in analyses of the human condition.[3]

In contrast, theology describes aspirations, such as love, compassion, and wisdom, which we should try to embed in our authentic self, thereby facilitating us to overcome the problems of consciousness and sexual objectification. Theology emphasizes its aspirations. It reflects on the meaning of life and how to live accordingly; it offers a vision of justice. Like feminist theory, it seeks to help people move closer to experiencing their aspirations for their authentic selves. Aspirational thinking has played an important role within spirituality or theology, including religious feminism. As the authors of a collection of essays on feminism and theology explain:

> Feminist spirituality, whether it is an extension of traditional western religions or a revival of Goddess religion, provides a "ground" in which feminists can root their visions of justice for women and a source of energy to struggle for that future. . . . We feminists do not yet have a common language to describe divine being, but we are beginning to mold new images. So, too, feminist ethicists are just beginning the task of describing those actions and habits of life (virtues) which are consistent with our new vision of the Ultimate.[4]

Feminist theory also has aspirations. It suggests that women and men should try to experience their aspirations for their authentic selves. I use the word *suggest* rather than *argue* in describing feminist theory's aspirations because feminist theory has rarely focused on its aspirations; it has mostly concentrated on its critique.

Theology also has a critique. A need to discuss aspirations is embedded in a recognition that our present society suffers from fundamental problems. As contrasted with feminist theory, theology is less concerned with describing the fundamental problems that prevent people from experiencing their aspirations for their authentic selves.

Whereas feminist theory emphasizes a critique of society, theology emphasizes aspirations. Whereas feminist theory focuses on human problems from the perspective of women, theology focuses on human problems from the perspective of all people. Within theology, certain traditions, such as liberation theology, focus more on critique than do other branches of theology. Within feminist theory, certain traditions, such as radical feminism, focus more on aspirations than do other branches of feminist theory. An emerging tradition, which I call *religious feminism*, considers both critique and aspirations in a balanced way. Nevertheless, I think it is fair to generalize that feminist theory has a relatively more sophisticated critique than set of aspirations, and theology has a relatively more sophisticated set of aspirations than critique.

Although I believe that theology has a lot to offer feminism and feminism has a lot to offer theology, neither discipline takes the other very seriously. In doing research for this book, I have been disappointed to see the hostility toward and ignorance of theology often found in feminist theory. For example, Alison Jaggar deliberately disregards that tradition in her survey of feminist theory. She says:

> Among the most obvious omissions from this book are religious and existential conceptions of women's liberation. Such conceptions have been significant his-

torically; indeed, *The Second Sex*, published in 1949 by the existentialist Simone de Beauvoir, must be considered a forerunner of the contemporary women's liberation movement. I have omitted religious and existentialist conceptions primarily because I find them implausible. They are outside the mainstream of contemporary feminist theorizing, and they have little direct connection with socialist feminism, the version of feminist theory that I consider the most plausible.[5]

Jaggar's disregard of religious feminists probably reflects her ignorance of that branch of feminist theory.[6] To group de Beauvoir with religious feminists is like saying that both Franklin Roosevelt and George Wallace were Democrats. Not only is there a wide range of views within feminist theory written by theologians but there are sharp differences between the existentialists and the theologians. It is disappointing to see an entire branch of feminist theory dismissed because it is outside the mainstream of contemporary feminist theory and considered "implausible." Clearly, religious feminism is outside mainstream feminist theory through its absence from such works as Jaggar's survey of feminist theory. As for its being implausible, that is not a very helpful statement without further exposition. Given that theology is one of our oldest philosophical traditions and one of many people's most deeply held philosophies, it is not helpful for Jaggar to dismiss it as implausible.

I do not mean to suggest that theology is necessarily rendered true because it is old and widely shared. We can obviously think of many beliefs that are old and widely shared, such as racism or sexism, which we feel confident in rejecting today. Nevertheless, the near universality of religious concerns throughout modern history should make us pause and ask whether some of those concerns might offer us insight today.

Similarly, many theologians, even progressive theologians, fail to consider feminist sources. Recently, some theologians have begun to publish articles and books about love and sexuality that challenge the traditional Catholic church's understanding of sexuality.[7] Although these discussions often are compatible with feminist theory, they rarely refer to feminist works or recognize the special problems that women may face in experiencing mutual love.

Some feminists have criticized theology for focusing on men's needs rather than all people's needs. Many of these criticisms are well founded. Nevertheless, it is true that theology aspires to consider how all people can move closer to experiencing their aspirations for their authentic selves. Similarly, some people have criticized feminists for focusing only on problems of white middle-class women. Nevertheless, feminism aspires to consider the problems of all women. I am, therefore, describing feminism and theology at their best.

In sum, theology has been very helpful to me in enhancing my understanding of appropriate aspirations for us, as feminists. Because I believe that a lack of discussion of aspirations is one shortcoming within feminist theory, I have structured this book to emphasize the development of those aspirations. In the first chapter, for instance, I defend the importance of speaking aspirationally and then develop three aspirations that I believe can contribute to feminist theory—love, compassion, and wisdom. As I develop these aspirations, I will also show how they can be applied concretely to the abortion issue.

Because I do not believe that we can develop a feminist-theological perspective that is entirely abstract, I have chosen to explore my feminist-theological perspective within the concrete topic of reproductive health, including abortion. I have chosen the abortion issue because it is such a difficult issue, one that raises deeply religious as well as feminist questions about the meaning of life in all of its various forms. I have also tried to bring the stories of women's sexuality and pregnancies to the forefront through the use of experiential and empirical literature.

My feminist-theological journey has led me to the following observations about the pro-choice and pro-life movements: Although I still consider myself to be a pro-choice feminist, I am troubled by three common pro-choice arguments. First, I am disappointed that pro-choice arguments often seem disrespectful of the seriousness of the pro-life position. Second, I am disappointed that pro-choice arguments tend to focus almost exclusively on the abortion issue while losing sight of the larger context of reproductive health. Third, I am disappointed that the pro-choice position is usually defended on privacy grounds rather than on equality grounds. In my own pro-choice position, I have tried to develop an equality perspective that is respectful to all of the lives involved in the abortion decision, especially those of the women who are socialized to bear the disproportionate burdens of childbirth and childcare. I have tried to examine the abortion issue in the broader context of reproductive health, emphasizing the impact on women of not being able to control their reproductive capacity. I do not try to pretend, however, that the abortion decision is a private decision that only affects the lives of women.

I am also troubled by three common pro-life positions: First, I am disappointed that pro-life advocates are often willing to use the criminal law to regulate abortion. Second, I am disappointed that pro-life advocates also ignore the context of reproductive health; hence, they are often willing to provide virtually no public funding for reproductive health services for poor women even when their health or well-being is substantially threatened by a pregnancy. Third, I am disappointed that pro-life arguments often ignore entirely the lives of the women who bear and raise children, as well as the existing offspring of these women. All of these positions, I will argue, are not tenable to a pro-life perspective that truly respects the lives of women and children.

From a feminist-theological perspective, I will suggest that greater sensitivity to the aspirations of love, compassion, and wisdom would require pro-choice and pro-life advocates to modify their positions. Further, pro-choice and pro-life advocates should examine the abortion issue in the larger context of reproductive health and see the impact of the abortion issue on all women in society. I will use the following chapters to develop these and other arguments:

Part 1 will describe my feminist-theological perspective. In chapter 1, I will defend the need for feminists to speak aspirationally and will suggest three aspirations that can be drawn from theology and which have application to feminist theory—love, compassion, and wisdom. Chapter 2 will describe the feminist critiques of the problems of consciousness and sexual objectification and will try to enhance these critiques by more explicitly considering our aspirations for our authentic selves. Specifically, I will consider the role that participating in dialogue and valuing life (in all of its various forms) can play in overcoming the problems in society identified by feminist theory.

Part 2 will describe reproductive decisionmaking in the lives of women. Chapter 3 will use experiential literature and chapter 4 empirical literature to describe how it is that women find themselves facing unintended pregnancies and the lifelong consequences of whatever reproductive decisions they make. Because I do not agree with some aspects of the feminist critique of objectivity, I believe that we should be making more use of empirical literature. Experiential literature can best capture the emotional impact of women's lives; however, empirical literature can give us a fuller sense of the scope of women's oppression. One major aspect of this part of the book will be to discuss the impact of abortion regulations on the lives of poor, female adolescents who are also often African-American or Hispanic. Aside from articles on the impact of juvenile-specific regulations (such as parental notification laws) on the lives of juveniles, their situation is largely ignored in discussions of abortion. Reference to the empirical literature, however, will show that they face the major burden of any abortion restrictions so that their well-being needs to be at the forefront of our abortion analysis.

Part 3 will apply an equality perspective to reproductive health cases. Chapter 5 will develop a group-based equality perspective and argue that such a perspective is preferable to a privacy approach. Chapters 6 and 7 will apply an equality perspective to some of the major abortion cases. Chapter 6 will discuss *Roe v. Wade*, and chapter 7 will discuss *Webster v. Reproductive Health Services*. I will show how the arguments made by both the plaintiffs and the defendants, as well as the decision rendered by the courts, were not feminist and did not encourage good-faith dialogue on the abortion issue.

In chapter 8, I will apply an equality framework to reproductive health cases outside the abortion area—where the state is trying to coerce women's conduct during the course of their pregnancies. One reason that women of color often say that they feel alienated from the abortion debate is that there is insufficient focus on how we can create the societal conditions so that women can also safely carry their fetuses to term. I will argue that the state falsely views the woman and the fetus as having conflicting needs when it intervenes into women's decisions regarding their pregnancies, such as when the state either tries to coerce a woman to have a cesarean section or tries to punish her for using drugs during her pregnancy. I will argue that this polarized, conflictual model is an outgrowth of the inadequate way we have discussed the abortion issue in privacy terms. By using a group-based, equality perspective on all reproductive decisionmaking, I believe that we can see the commonality between the interests of pregnant women and their fetuses. For example, it benefits both the pregnant woman and the fetus for effective treatment programs to exist to respond to drug abuse by a pregnant woman, but it harms both the pregnant woman and the fetus to throw a pregnant woman into jail during her pregnancy in order to force her to go into immediate withdrawal from drugs.

I hope that this book will help move the entire abortion debate into a more general discussion of effective and respectful reproductive health strategies that can help women truly decide how to make the reproductive decisions that are best for themselves and their community. By focusing our efforts so single-mindedly on the abortion issue without also considering how to effectuate women's decisions to carry their fetuses to term, we have lost sight of the fundamental value of life, a belief which I believe we all share and can all use as the basis for dialogue about abortion and other reproductive matters.

I have often been commended for trying to provide a moderating influence on the abortion debate and thereby encouraging genuine dialogue. I hope that this book can continue this influence by helping pro-life advocates more fully consider all the ways that the value of life is implicated in reproduction discussions and by helping pro-choice advocates more fully consider the ways that they can be both pro-choice and pro-life. Being an optimist, I refuse to believe that there is no common ground for dialogue about abortion, but the privacy framework within which abortion is often discussed makes it difficult for people to see the common ground on broad issues relating to reproduction.

Because our life experience does shape our perspective, I believe that it is appropriate to disclose my own life experiences concerning pregnancy to aid the reader in assessing my observations and arguments. I became pregnant for the first time in mid-1990 and experienced a miscarriage about seven weeks later. Two months later, I again became pregnant and experienced a miscarriage about twelve weeks later. I was very nauseous and exhausted throughout my second pregnancy and experienced a very painful miscarriage (about five hours of painful contractions before the D & C was performed). I shared the fact of both pregnancies with some of my friends, family, and coworkers so that they could share my excitement as well as help me grieve. The fact that I was not alone in my nausea, exhaustion, and ultimate grief helped me deal with each of these life events. As I complete writing this book, I have recently given birth to my first child.

The standard folklore on pregnancy is that a woman is not supposed to disclose to others that she is pregnant during the first trimester. The apparent justification for this view is that she may experience a miscarriage so that it is bad luck to go public. In reality, many women like myself have very difficult first trimesters. Imposed silence causes women to suffer in silence. When a woman does have a miscarriage, if she has suffered in silence, then she must also grieve alone.

This *suffer in silence* perspective devalues the woman's choice as well as the meaning of the life that she is nurturing within her. By imposing silence on women, we do not have to hear about women's pain through pregnancy or miscarriage. Thus, I would argue that a society that is truly pro-choice and pro-life would tell women that it is all right to be public about their pregnancies (if they so choose) and that they will be provided with a helpful hand, if necessary, to assist them in their pregnancies. Individual women may still choose to be silent about their pregnancies (until the physical manifestations make that silence impossible), but at least they would not feel that it was societally inappropriate for them to make the fact of their pregnancies public.

During my various pregnancies, I have also found that many people feel comfortable in advising me to take it easy (stop exercising, stop air travel, cut back working, etc.) In addition, many people feel comfortable assuming that the miscarriages were due to my behavior rather than nature's way of spontaneously aborting a nonviable fetus. I understand the good intentions of the people who make these comments. Nevertheless, I often find their comments exasperating because they don't seem to acknowledge that I have to continue to live my life during my pregnancies. I have been pregnant off and on for two years. As much as I wanted to bear a healthy child, I did not care to be an invalid for nearly two years of my life to achieve that result. I guess that what disturbs me the most about these comments from others is that I am a woman who takes excellent care of herself—I don't smoke, don't drink coffee, eat a low fat diet, and keep fit. Nevertheless, if people feel comfortable telling me how to modify my lifestyle during pregnancy, I worry about how coercively other women might be treated during their pregnancies.

I have also been influenced by the actions of my own state legislature—Louisiana. The Louisiana legislature has recently enacted, over the governor's veto, the most restrictive abortion law in the United States. The law forbids all abortions unless the woman's life is in danger or she was a victim of rape or incest. In addition, the woman must have a medical examination within five days of the alleged rape and report the rape to law enforcement authorities within seven days. Not one of the four women in the Louisiana legislature voted to override the governor's veto. Nevertheless, the women were too few to be decisive. As the governor said in his veto message, the legislation "dishonors women, shows great mistrust of doctors and their professional judgment, and unduly burdens the traumatized victims of rape." I find that the bill angers me—angers me that a predominantly male legislature could tell me, a woman over the age of thirty-five who has already undergone two painful miscarriages and who provides the primary financial support for her family, that I am not entitled to choose whether to continue with my pregnancy. In the eyes of the legislature, I am no more than a baby-making machine whose well-being is irrelevant. As many people have said, the Louisiana legislature's attitude is that life begins at conception and ends at birth.

Witnessing the Louisiana legislature's unresponsiveness to women's well-being has renewed my commitment to the pro-choice position while also strengthening my resolve to work toward good-faith dialogue on abortion. The former governor of Louisiana, Buddy Roemer, has been a model of good-faith dialogue, moving from a rigid pro-life position to a more moderate pro-life position after listening to women's counsel. Sadly, there is much work to do before a genuine good-faith dialogue on abortion can take place. At present, it looks like the state legislatures and state courts may be a more hospitable forum for that dialogue in some states than the federal judiciary. I hope that this book helps us move one step forward to a good-faith dialogue on abortion in whatever sectors of society that is possible.

Notes

1. Paulo Friere, Pedagogy of the Oppressed 77 (Myra Ramos trans. 1970).

2. Etty Hillesum, An Interrupted Life: The Diaries of Etty Hillesum 1941–43 28 (Arnold Pomerans trans. 1983).

3. Because I am writing this book from a feminist perspective, I have chosen to focus on the implications of feminism and theology on women's movement to authenticity. I suspect that many, if not all, of my observations would apply equally forcefully to men. At this time, however, I have not attempted to take the step of speaking more generally, because the gender context of men and women's lives often differs. One crucial difference between feminism and theology is that feminism is embedded in a discussion of women's human nature; theology is embedded in a discussion of all people's human nature. By focusing on women, I have therefore allowed feminism's perspective to dominate the feminist-theological dialogue. Given my greater familiarity with feminism than theology, it makes sense for me to do that. A theologian might properly choose the opposite emphasis. As we participate in feminist-theological dialogue, we may be able to achieve a more balanced discussion which equally respects both traditions.

4. Barbara Andolsen, Christine Gudorf & Mary Pellauer, *Introduction* in Women's Consciousness, Women's Conscience: A Reader in Feminist Ethics xi, xxiii (Barbara Andolsen, Christine Gudorf & Mary Pellauer eds. 1987).

5. Alison Jaggar, Feminist Politics and Human Nature 10 (1983).

6. When Alison Jaggar visited Tulane University in 1988, I asked her why she ignored religious feminism in her book. She said that she hadn't thought about religion since she went to Sunday school as a child and did not know anything about religious feminism. If that is true, I think it would have been far wiser for her to acknowledge her ignorance in her book rather than characterize views with which she was unfamiliar as "implausible."

7. See, *e.g.*, James Nelson, *Reuniting Sexuality and Spirituality*, The Christian Century (Feb. 25, 1987); James Nelson, Between Two Gardens: Reflections on Sexuality and Religious Experience (1983); James Nelson, Embodiment: An Approach to Sexuality and Christian Theology (1978); Dick Westley, Morality and Its Beyond (1984); Dick Westley, Redemptive Intimacy (1981).

Feminism and Theology

CHAPTER ONE

Aspirations

An Authentic Self Embedded in Love, Compassion, and Wisdom

> The light is critical; of me, of this
> long-dressed, involuntary landing
> on the arm of an inland sea.
> The glitter of the shoal
> depleting into shadow
> I recognize: the stand of pines
> violet-black really, green in the old postcard
> but really I have nothing but myself
> to go by; nothing
> stands in the realm of pure necessity
> except what my hands can hold.[1]

I. INTRODUCTION

In this chapter, I will describe what it means to move toward our aspirations for our authentic selves, in particular, the aspirations of love, compassion, and wisdom. But first, I will defend the importance of aspirational thinking, because some feminists are skeptical of the need for such thinking.

Catharine MacKinnon has strongly criticized the necessity of engaging in aspirational thinking. She claims that such thinking is often done instead of political work and often reflects the mistaken assumption that we can change reality through our imagination alone. For example, she says:

> Audiences want to hear about the design of life after male supremacy. Or, after all this negative, what do I have to say positive. This requests a construction of a future in which the present does not exist, under existing conditions. It dreams that the mind were free and could, like Milton, make a heaven out of

hell, or a hell of heaven. The procedure is: imagine the future you want, construct actions or legal rules or social practices *as if* we were already there, and that will get us from here to there. This magical approach to social change, which is methodologically liberal, lives entirely in the head, a head that is more determined by present reality than it is taking seriously, yet it is not sufficiently grounded in that reality to do anything about it.[2]

Sonia Johnson, a feminist whose work has a spiritual base, takes a seemingly different perspective on the role of aspirational thinking in effecting change. She says:

[S]ince reality is only what we give the energy of our belief to, what we feel as real, all systems are *internal* systems; patriarchy does not have a separate existence outside us; it exists only inside us and we project it onto our external screen. It follows, then, that the instant patriarchy ceases to exist inside our hearts and minds, it dies everywhere.

. . . When we seize power in our inner world, the outer world will have to change.[3]

Johnson's statement may reflect exactly the kind of observation within feminist theory that MacKinnon disdains. Johnson suggests that we are changing external reality when we work to move our internal self closer to our aspirations for our self. MacKinnon disdains that kind of statement, because it suggests that we can change reality by only imagining that it be changed.

But that is not what I understand Johnson to mean. Johnson seems to reject the distinction between self and other. As I will discuss later, that is a Buddhist-feminist conception of the self, a self that is connected with others and ever changing. If we view the self in that way—as connected and ever changing—then we see that we are making changes in external reality when we make changes in our self. We move the external world closer to our aspirations for our self as we move our self closer to our aspirations for our self. There is no way to change internal reality without changing external reality since the internal and external are not entirely distinct.

Of course, MacKinnon is correct to observe that neither internal reality nor external reality change through our imagination alone. However, since a part of our self is our mind, our feelings, our understanding of the world, it does make sense to suggest, as does Johnson, that our lives change as we make changes in our consciousness.

Aspirational thinking is also important for another reason: it helps us formulate our critique and decide how to take steps to move from present reality to our aspirations for society. For example, MacKinnon's work might be more convincing if she articulated her vision more clearly. Many feminists question whether they want to accept MacKinnon's critique of sexuality, because they are not sure where she is trying to lead the feminist community.[4] Is she saying that sexual relationships between men and women are impossible, undesirable, ultimately not in the interest of women's well-being? Or, is she saying, that we need to move toward more authentic expressions of our love, which might include sexual relationships between women and men? These are not trivial questions about our feminist vision; they are questions that might affect whether women are willing to identify with feminist theory and also try to join the struggle to move toward its vision for society. By *not* articulating her vision, MacKinnon may be inhibiting some feminists from endorsing her critique. They may assume that MacKinnon holds a vision which is incompatible with their vision for society when, in fact, she may not. By sharing their visions and coming to some common agreement about those visions, feminists might be able to move beyond their distrust of each other and come together to work to make those visions into reality.

For these reasons, I have chosen to share my aspirations with the reader in the hope that we can begin to discuss what these aspirations should be and how best to move toward them.

II. THE AUTHENTIC SELF

Feminists and theologians seem to agree that we should try to discover and experience our authentic self, yet rarely do they define the phrase *authentic self*. I would like to sketch a conception of the authentic self that I find compatible with Buddhism and feminism.

Before sketching a Buddhist-feminist conception of the self, I need to make some methodological observations. Buddhism is embedded in the practice of meditation. It is not a religion that is embedded in the kinds of theoretical written discussions that one often finds in Western religion. The self that I will sketch has therefore been formulated largely through my experience of meditation and my discussions with others who have also experienced meditation. I cannot say with confidence that all other Buddhists or even many other Buddhists would agree with my description of the self. And I suspect that the reader will only be able to agree or disagree with my description of the self if she tries to experience Buddhism through meditation; I doubt that she can respond to my description by reading about Buddhism alone. (The best discussion of Buddhism that I have found is *Zen Mind, Beginner's Mind*, by Shunryu Suzuki, because the reader can experience meditation while reading the book due to its lyrical quality.)

In addition, it is important to understand that it is controversial within Buddhism to speak of the self. Some Buddhists say that it does not make sense to talk about the self, since there is no real distinction between the self and others.[5] Other Buddhists, like Nancy Wilson Ross, say that it is meaningful to talk about the self; we simply have to be careful to recognize that the self and other are deeply connected. Thus, Ross says:

> In Buddhism the idea of the separate self, an "ego," is considered a mere intellectual invention, not a reality but simply a convenient term for designating an ever-changing combination, or bundle, of attributes known as *skandhas*.[6]

I have chosen to adopt Ross's description of the Buddhist self and try to talk about the self while recognizing the importance in Buddhism of speaking of the *no-self*.

From my experience with Buddhism and feminism, this is how I conceive of the authentic self or selves. (Actually, it is misleading to speak of the self in the singular, because we are a bundle of selves. For linguistic reasons, however, I will sometimes refer to the authentic self rather than the authentic selves.) First, the self is a deeply connected self since we are social beings. It makes no sense to describe the self as presocial, entirely isolated from society, because, from (and before) birth, we are deeply connected to others. The distinction between self and other is illusory. We construct the society around us, as it constructs us. We are both other and self. Second, the self is ever changing; it is not a static entity. Since the self is ever changing and subject to our control, we seek to move it toward our aspirations for our selves. Thus, as we move toward experiencing our aspirations for our authentic selves, we approach authenticity—we begin to realize our authentic selves.

This latter aspect of our authentic selves—its relation to our aspirations—is the most important. Because the self is dynamic, it permits us to move toward our aspirations for our selves. In addition, because the authentic self does not embrace a separation between self and others, it permits us to develop those aspirations through our connectedness both with our selves and with others. We can develop aspirations through both meditation (communication with our selves) and dialogue (communication with others).

This conception of the authentic self provides us with a tentative resolution of the feminist paradox of how we can be a socially constructed self and move beyond dominant social norms that contribute to our oppression. Because resolution of this paradox is essential to feminism, and in particular feminist jurisprudence, I will discuss it in some detail.

First, I need to explain the paradox. It can easily be seen in Catharine MacKinnon's work. MacKinnon, like other theorists who believe we have been socially constructed, claims that male domination "is *everywhere* and relatively *invariant*."[7] But if male domination were everywhere and invariant, then feminists would have no access to values other than the values of male domination. We, too, would be part of the invariant fabric of male domination. Thus, feminism needs a way to explain how we can assert values outside of male domination and thereby contribute to our own social construction as feminists. For feminist legal activists, the question becomes even more difficult. How can we persuade others, in particular judges, to reach conclusions that are inconsistent with male domination if male domination is everywhere and invariant? We need a way to explain not only our own feminism but how we can persuade others to hold a feminist perspective despite the power of male domination.

I resolve that dilemma by observing that society is more than male domination, although male domination is certainly a distinct and important aspect of society. There are values present in society that are inconsistent with and in opposition to male domination. Those values that are inconsistent with male domination are what permit us to be feminists. Feminism exists within our current society; it would not be possible for feminism (or any other values presently in existence) to exist outside of society.

On a formal level, it may be true that women cannot stand outside male domination, because male domination permeates, at least in a modest way, all institutions in society. I would suggest, however, that in a real, lived sense women can step outside the *control* of male domination. For example, feminists who engage in consciousness-raising have used their power to create women-only space where the focus of the discussion is women's well-being and the tone is one of respect. Consciousness-raising is possible in that setting because women have the power to acknowledge and control the influence of male domination on their lives. If women did not have that power, then consciousness-raising would not be possible. When women exercise that power, they have stepped outside the control of male domination because male domination is no longer controlling or defining their lives. They may be reacting to male domination, but they are not being controlled by it.

Similarly, feminist legal activists can be successful in a court room to the extent that they can make arguments that are compatible with values held by judges that are outside male domination. Not every judge may hold such values. But by noticing and building on those values when they do exist, feminists can hope to transform law from a system founded on male domination to one which is far less influenced by those values.

Thus, although we are socially constructed, we do have control over that construction. A Buddhist-feminist conception of the self correctly emphasizes that we can control our construction of our self. And the ability to control the construction of our selves is fundamental to feminism and to feminist jurisprudence.

III. RESPONSE TO FEMINIST CRITICS

Although I consider my description of the authentic self to be both feminist and Buddhist, many feminists have suggested to me that my conception of the self is incompatible with feminist theory. I would, therefore, like to respond to the common objections to my description of the authentic self.

Feminists often turn to two premises within feminist theory that they consider incompatible with my conception of the authentic self: group-based theory and social-construction theory. Feminism is embedded in group-based theory because it attempts to describe how women have been treated as a class. In addition, feminism is embedded in social-construction theory because it argues that women have been artificially gendered female; feminism describes gender as a social construct. If the concept of the authentic self is inconsistent with either aspect of feminist theory, then feminists would need to reject that concept.

There is no conflict between my concept of the authentic self and group-based theory. The authentic self, as I have defined it, is both a group-based and an individual-based concept since it recognizes not only our connectedness to others and other commonality as humans but also the meaningfulness of the concept of self. The group-based aspect of experiencing the authentic self should be easy for feminists to incorporate into their theoretical framework. They acknowledge that women may come to understand their situation of subordination by sharing their experiences with other women. Women will realize that they are not alone; that their experience has the name of subordination.

Moving toward the authentic self through consciousness-raising, however, also has an individualistic aspect. Not every woman's story is identical. Each woman must decide for herself which life experiences have been predominantly shaped by her sex and gender and which life experiences may have been shaped by other influences. The anti-essentialism critique that has been articulated by many women of color has forced feminists and others to confront that not all life experiences can be fully described in sex-based terms, that women's experiences are both particular and universal.[8] The particularity of women's experiences offers a challenge to feminism. Can feminism recognize the particularity of women's experiences while retaining its sex-based analysis? My conception of the authentic self would seem to strengthen feminist theory by making it better equipped to respond to the particularities of women's lives. Thus, my conception of the self is anti-essentialist while, as we shall see, it is also postmodern in its recognition of our social construction.

In addition, my conception of the authentic self does not conflict with the understanding that we are socially constructed. The importance of thinking about the authentic self in Buddhist terms is to help us to gain control over that social construction by being more meditative and reflective. Feminists who strongly advocate consciousness-raising as a tool whereby women become more conscious of their self and work to shape that self more authentically should endorse a conception of the self that is similar to the one I have sketched from Buddhism. Thus, Ruth Smith, a feminist theologian, has explained how a dynamic conception of the authentic self is compatible with feminist theory:

[F]eminists recognize that our moral activity includes not only actions, decisions, and loyalties to persons, ideals, and projects. Moral activity includes ourselves. To become a moral subject is itself a moral task, if not the central moral task. The moral subject is not a completed, closed entity but is unfinished and open. The terms and implications of this process are particularly relevant to women and others currently involved in their own liberation struggles. Becoming the subject of one's own actions is a social and historical process key to liberation politically, socially, and psychologically so that we no longer collude in our own oppression and so that we can attempt to change conditions of life negation and alienation into conditions of affirmation and fulfillment.[9]

Feminist theory need not abandon its group-based and socially constructed premises in order to embrace my conception of the authentic self. In fact, embracing my conception of the authentic self may strengthen feminist theory by making women better understand the noninevitability of male domination and their ability to counteract their subordination.

IV. THREE ASPIRATIONS: LOVE, COMPASSION, AND WISDOM

What we need in the United States is not hatred. What we need in the United States is not violence and lawlessness, but is love and wisdom and compassion toward one another.[10]

Because the authentic self is a dynamic, ever-changing concept, we have some control over what aspirations we would like to move it toward. As discussed earlier, we can choose from among the aspirations that exist in society, some of which are inconsistent with male domination. I would like to suggest three aspirations for the authentic self that are inconsistent with male domination: love, compassion, and wisdom.

A. Love

1. A Definition

When I refer to *love*, I am referring to the intimate connectedness that we might experience, including but not limited to, sexual love or *eros*. In the words of the theologian James Nelson, it includes sexual expressions which are "self-liberating, other-enriching, honest, faithful, socially responsible, life-serving and joyous."[11]

Theology speaks aspirationally about love. For example, the Bible says:

> I give you a new commandment:
> love one another;
> you must love one another
> just as I have loved you.
> It is by your love for one another, that everyone will recognize
> you as my disciples.[12]

This biblical love of neighbor has been used as the foundation for political-religious movements such as liberation theology; it can also be found in Judaism.[13]

Secular feminists who have presented probing and deeply spiritual discussions of the role of love and compassion in women's lives include Audre Lorde and Adrienne Rich. Lorde discusses the concept of the *erotic* and asserts that it is an intrinsically dynamic force within women's lives.

> The very word *erotic* comes from the Greek word *eros*, the personification of love in all its aspects—born of Chaos, and personifying creative power and har-

mony. When I speak of the erotic, then, I speak of it as an assertion of the lifeforce of women; of that creative energy empowered, the knowledge and use of which we are now reclaiming in our language, our history, our dancing, our loving, our work, our lives.[14]

Lorde therefore wants to acclaim the importance of women discovering and experiencing the erotic within their lives. She says:

[W]hen we begin to live from within outward, in touch with the power of the erotic within ourselves, and allowing that power to inform and illuminate our actions upon the world around us, then we begin to be responsible to ourselves in the deepest sense. For as we begin to recognize our deepest feelings, we begin to give up, of necessity, being satisfied with suffering and self-negation, and with the numbness which so often seems like their only alternative in our society. Our acts against oppression become integral with self, motivated and empowered from within.[15]

Although Lorde recognizes that the erotic can be synonymous with women's suffering and self-negation, she also believes that it can be transformed into a positive source of women's struggle against oppression. Lorde argues, therefore, that women should try to develop positive erotic expressions within their lives as well as struggle against the subordinating images of women within pornography.

Adrienne Rich has explored the role of love and compassion within women's lives in a variety of contexts. Like Lorde, she recognizes both the destructive and life-building implications of women's love. For example, in her introduction to the tenth-anniversary edition of *Of Woman Born*, she describes the balance that she tried to strike between exploring the negative and positive aspects of motherhood:

I never wished this book to lend itself to the sentimentalization of women or of women's nurturant or spiritual capacity. . . . But what I wrote in 1976 I believed: *Theories of female power and female ascendancy must reckon fully with the ambiguities of our being, and with the continuum of our consciousness, the potentialities for both creative and destructive energy in each of us.*[16]

Despite the difficulties of creating an institution of motherhood that is free rather than oppressive, Rich claims that such a struggle is worthwhile because it can bring women closer to "personhood." She defines the claim to personhood as:

the claim to share justly in the products of our labor, not to be used merely as an instrument, a role, a womb, a pair of hands or a back or a set of fingers; to participate fully in the decisions of our workplace, our community; to speak for ourselves, in our own right.[17]

Thus, Rich connects authentic expressions of love and compassion through motherhood to movement to full personhood or what I call authenticity.

Many religious feminists offer a similar description of the role of love in our lives. For example, Etty Hillesum, a Jewish writer who was influenced by Christianity, used her love as a source of strength to persevere during the Holocaust. She wrote:

> I see no alternative, each of us must turn inwards and destroy in himself all that he thinks he ought to destroy in others. And remember that every atom of hate we add to this world makes it still more inhospitable. . . . If one wants to exert a moral influence on others one must start with one's own morals.[18]

For Hillesum, who was struggling with the daily realities of life in a concentration camp, a focus on the power of her inner love may have increased her strength to fight daily oppression. Hillesum used that love to fight the racism of anti-Semitism as well as to discover herself as a woman. Her work suggests that women can transform their love into a source of power for fighting not only patriarchy but many arenas of oppression.

Similarly, Dorothy Day, who played a significant role in developing the Catholic Worker's Movement, used her love as the foundation of her work to create a more humane world. In a conversation with Robert Coles, she explained how we should question our love and sexuality and try to use our authentic love to move to a higher moral plane:

> God put us here to go through this kind of mental gymnastics, and He certainly put us here to enjoy our sexual lives. He put us here to *ask*, to try to find out the best way possible to live with our neighbors. Of course, you can go through a life not asking, and that's the tragedy: so many lives lived in moral blindness.[19]

Finally, Simone Weil used her fundamental belief in equality through love and compassion to work to improve the conditions of workers in France during the 1940s. She wrote:

> Not only does the love of God have attention for its substance; the love of neighbor, which we know to be the same love, is made of this same substance. Those who are unhappy have no need for anything in this world but people capable of giving them their attention. The capacity to give one's attention to a sufferer is a very rare and difficult thing; it is almost a miracle; it *is* a miracle. Nearly all those who think they have this capacity do not possess it. Warmth of heart, impulsiveness, pity are not enough.[20]

Each of these religious feminists considers love to be a part of a person's most complete and morally uplifting life on this earth. Rather than ask what Judaism or Christianity has to say about love, they ask how love can lead one to a more spiritual life.

2. Response to Feminist Critics

Many feminists appear reluctant to embrace the aspiration of love, especially sexual love, because they recognize that what has been called love has not served women's well-being. For example, Celia Kitzinger has surveyed this reluctance to embrace the aspiration of love and concluded that "the various feminist critiques of romantic love present it as an objectifying and individualistic construction of the patriarchy which functions as a means whereby men have justified their dominance over women."[21] As Kitzinger notes, however, other feminists insist upon the importance of "ardent" and "fervent" love, claiming that it is essential to healthy functioning.[22]

Catharine MacKinnon's work exemplifies the feminist position that is skeptical of love. She is reluctant to consider the positive potential of love for fear that women would then misunderstand the critique of existing sexual arrangements within radical feminism. She has said:

> Sex feeling good may mean that one is enjoying one's subordination; it would not be the first time. Or it may mean that one has glimpsed freedom, a rare and valuable and contradictory event. Under existing conditions, what else would freedom be? The point is, the possible varieties of interpersonal engagement, including the pleasure of sensation or the experience of intimacy, does not, things being as they are, make sex empowering for women.[23]

MacKinnon is correct to note that women's reported pleasure in sexual love does not make that kind of love empowering for women. The problem of consciousness must make us skeptical of women's claims of empowerment within sexual expressiveness. To say that sexual expressiveness has been problematic for women, however, is not to say that it has no positive potential. An instrument of oppression can also be an instrument of liberation. As Adrienne Rich has noted in describing the oppressiveness and empowerment of women through the act of child bearing: "Theories of female power and female ascendancy must reckon fully with the ambiguities of our being, and with the continuum of our consciousness, the potentialities for both creative and destructive energy in each of us."[24] Similarly, theories of female love must consider love as both a creative and destructive aspect of women's lives.

Although MacKinnon may worry that such aspirational conceptions of love are apolitical or nonpolitical, I believe that the lives of the women whom I have quoted above demonstrate the political dimensions of love. Hillesum was able to use her love to retain control over her own feelings and inner strength. Rather than allow the Nazis to define her as less than human, to deny the value and significance of her life, she persisted in living a life that gave her meaning and satisfaction. In Hillesum's words:

> Does that mean that I am never sad, that I never rebel, always acquiesce, and love life no matter what the circumstances? Far from it. I believe that I know and share the many sorrows and sad circumstances that a human being can experience, but I do not cling to them, I do not prolong such moments of agony. They pass through me, like life itself, as a broad, eternal stream, they become

part of that stream, and life continues. And as a result all my strength is preserved, does not become tagged on to futile sorrow or rebelliousness.[25]

In addition, the strength from her love enabled her to act as a source of inspiration for others who were struggling with feelings of despair and to help transform the world into a freer society. Similarly, Dorothy Day's and Simone Weil's love were the foundation of their struggles on behalf of working people.

Our consideration of the positive potential of love, of course, is not going to make the problem of sexual objectification disappear tomorrow. Women's consideration of their highest aspirations for love might move them away from sexual relationships with men because the reality of those relationships may be so far from what those relationships should be capable of. Rejecting particular relationships because they do not meet one's aspirations for love, however, is far different than rejecting the possibility of loving relationships in one's life. I therefore suggest that feminist theory needs to express openly its aspiration for love as between all people in society (including men and women) while acknowledging how far present reality is from that aspiration. With that combination of aspiration and critique, women may be more willing to come together and work for their shared aspirations.

Even more importantly, feminists' embrace of the aspiration of love may serve as a bridge to the outside community which also embraces this aspiration. Later in this book, I will talk about how the pro-life movement is often inconsistent in its desire to protect life. Similarly, pro-choice advocates may not sufficiently consider the value of pro-life arguments, falsely assuming that there is a conflict between valuing fetal life and women's life. We may be able to encourage dialogue on abortion if both sides of this polarized debate recognized their common interest in life and love. Criminalizing abortion when a woman faces an unintended pregnancy in a society that offers little or no support for women during their pregnancies or for mothers during their many years of child care is not, I will argue, a loving response to the problem of unintended pregnancies. Similarly, ignoring the trauma that some women may experience when they make an abortion decision is also not a loving response to the abortion issue. By seeking commonality rather than divisiveness on the abortion issue, we may see that some common ground is possible.

B. Compassion

One confusing aspect of the aspiration of love is that there are so many kinds of love, including sexual or erotic love. When we talk about love it can therefore be confusing if we do not specify the particular type of love to which we are referring. For women, this problem is especially troubling since sexual love with men has often been such a troubling experience. Feminists might reject love as an appropriate aspiration out of their distrust of the potential for sexual love with men without recognizing the many positive dimensions of other kinds of love. I therefore suspect that many feminists have turned to other similar aspirations that contain many of the strengths of the aspiration of love without the confusing sexual dimension. These other aspirations include what has often been termed "caring"[26] or what I prefer to call *compassion*.

Compassion requires a fully empathetic attitude where we try to understand another person's life from their perspective. Buddhism is based on the aspiration of universal compassion. Theravada Buddhism, for example, includes an exercise called *metta*, in which one suffuses one's whole being with active love and benevolence. One creates that state of being and sends it forth from one's innermost center with concern and loving-kindness.[27] The strength of this conception of compassion is that it connects the self to other and makes it clear that compassion is an *activity*, not just an intellectual state.

Various Western writers have also described the aspiration of compassion in a way similar to Buddhism. For example, Simone Weil argued that a compassionate attitude is good both for our self and others. It is a rare and special gift:

> The capacity to give one's attention to a sufferer is a very rare and difficult thing; it is almost a miracle; it *is* a miracle. Nearly all those who think they have this capacity do not possess it. Warmth of heart, impulsiveness, pity are not enough.[28]

Weil believed that we become a better society as we learn to have a more compassionate attitude towards others. It is not only for the *other* that we need to learn to be more compassionate; it is also for *our self*. As an ethical principle, compassion therefore helps move us towards our aspirations for our self and others as persons.

One challenge of the aspiration of compassion is that it insists that we can understand others' lives from their perspective, irrespective of our differences from others. Feminist conceptions of caring or responsibility often seem to suggest that we should only be compassionate to those whom we are close to and can readily understand.[29] The conception of compassion that I have sketched takes quite a different approach. It insists that we should aspire to understand the life of anyone, no matter how different he or she appears to be. This conception of compassion has no patience with the feminist claim that is sometimes made that men, for example, cannot understand what it means to give birth or to have an abortion.[30] Instead, compassion would insist that we should aspire to be a society in which we can each understand each other across our differences.

The fact that we decide to aspire to understand each other across our differences does not, of course, mean that we know or even think that we will succeed. We may agree that we will be a better society through our efforts to understand each other across our differences even if our efforts are not totally successful. Thus, although Martha Minow takes the position that "we cannot really know what another sees," she also rejects the position that "we can never glimpse another's world." Coupling both observations, she insists "that we must take the perspective of another . . . and must put our own categories up for challenge, without ceding the definition of reality over to others."[31] So long as we reject the pessimistic view that we can never even *glimpse* another's world, it is worthwhile to attempt to know others across differences.

Andreas Teuber, relying on Weil's work, has further explained the concept of compassion and tied it to the concept of equality, which has jurisprudential implications. He says:

> Compassion sees the rights of others from the "inside," as it were, and takes the interests others have in their right to heart. Although it does not in itself define any rights, compassion does this much: conveying certain attitudes without which we would lose sight of the values expressed by these rights. It is not a very strong claim but we can see in it at least the value of cultivating this sense of equality. Compassion works in relationship to the obligations and rights we already have in much the same way self-acceptance works for an individual who is punished by a law he has broken. . . . If we lose sight of the human interest and values that a right is designed to secure and protect, we shall see that right only as a barrier which insulates and isolates others from us. A compassionate attitude "sees" a person on the other side of this boundary with a definite interest in the values which the right is designed to protect. Rights are not just abstract creations; they have a context. In this sense, compassion urges us to respect not this particular person who (among other things) has these rights. To regard this particular person who (among other things) has these rights, it is necessary to look "behind" his interests to the interests of his they are designed to secure and protect. Indeed, without the cultivation of such an attitude, a system of rights is unlikely to be very effective.[32]

Teuber's interpretation of Weil connects the principle of compassion with the principles of equality and respect. Rather than consider equality as a right that we can demand from others, he considers equality to be a right that particular others have claim to. We need to understand a person's right to equality in the context of her basic needs and interests.

Because he refers to the principle of equality in describing Weil's work, it would seem that Teuber should be providing us insight on the legal conception of equality. However, his conception of equality is at odds with our traditional conception of law. We think of courts as institutions that resolve disputes between people by considering, on some occasions, who has a *right* to act in a particular way. Weil's conception of compassion, like the Buddhist conception of compassion, is inconsistent with the idea that we should turn to an institution to resolve competing claims to rights. Rather, individuals should be able to work out their differences by better understanding the needs and interests of others. Hence, Teuber observes that Weil believes that "There is nothing built into this way of thinking about equality which says that the claims of any one person are better than or superior to the claims of anyone else."[33] When courts are used to resolve disputes, then we have necessarily failed to attain the aspiration of compassion. Weil, therefore, raises a very troubling issue for feminist jurisprudence—whether its use of the courts can ever meet the aspiration of compassion.

Catholics for a Free Choice, a pro-choice religious organization, has considered that issue and concluded that legal argumentation is not necessarily inconsistent with our aspirations. It observes that state abortion regulations, for example, often result in "legislative fiat,"[34] whereby the legislature is precluding the individual from acting in her own best interest. Thus, it argues that judicial intervention is often necessary to prevent the state from cutting off debate, decision, and reflection.

As long as women's lives are endangered through rape, battery, and unwanted pregnancy—acts that certainly don't reflect a respectful view of women's position in society—it seems appropriate to try to take steps to counteract that treatment. In some circumstances, litigation might be the appropriate tactic.

Rather than globally ruling out the possibility of using legal argumentation to protect women's well-being, the more appropriate question may be how to use the courts. Is there a way, for example, to engage in legal argumentation so that it is more dialogic and compassionate? Is it possible to frame arguments that maintain an openness to the other side, thereby demonstrating our respect and compassion for our opponent?

A compassionate perspective would seem to be at odds with the strong, forceful tone of legal argumentation. This difficulty is apparent in comparing Professor Martha Minow's academic and legal work. In an academic vein, Minow argues that, when we take a position, we must remain open to the possibility that on another occasion our opponents may convince us that they are right.[35] Her academic tone is cautious, apparently reflecting her belief that there is no objective truth and that we must maintain openness in articulating our viewpoint. On the other hand, Minow argued in a brief in *Webster* that the Missouri abortion statute was unconstitutional because it violated freedom of religion.[36] This criticism was not cautious; it was forceful and apparently confident of its accuracy. Her legal argumentation about abortion does not appear consistent with her academic perspective about how to represent a point of view. Is her inconsistency reflective of the fact that it is not possible to maintain openness and dialogue in the courtroom? I will try to show how we could speak in a more compassionate voice in the courtroom.

Some might say that an open voice is inappropriate for the courtroom, that there is no harm in speaking firmly in the courtroom and openly in an academic context. I reject that dichotomy. I believe that feminists can afford to speak in a more open voice in the courtroom, that their failure to do so threatens their feminist aspirations. Professor Lynne Henderson has made a similar observation. She argues that legal arguments should be couched in empathy or compassion:

> Empathy may enable the decisionmaker to see other "right" answers, or a con-
> tinuum of answers. Or it may simply make the decisionmaker aware that what
> once seemed like no choice or a clear choice is instead a tragic one. To mask the
> tragedy of choice by taking refuge in rules does not negate the tragedy.[37]

Thus, empathy or compassion can help one see one's own as well as the other's position more clearly.

Henderson's approach provides us with a framework through which we can argue that our opponent is wrong yet also recognize that our own position has tragic aspects. For example, I find it commonplace in personal discussions about abortion for feminists to acknowledge that abortion is a tragic choice. Nevertheless, I have never found compassion to be a part of any of the legal arguments constructed by feminists on the abortion issue.

As we shall see in part 3 of this book, the lack of compassion in feminist arguments against state regulation of abortion actually weakens the arguments. Feminists usually respond with silence to the emotional images of fetal life presented by pro-life advocates. They fail to address why we as a society regretfully must terminate that life to protect women's well-being, and they talk instead about women's well-being as if the reader is not struggling with the question of how to protect the value of prenatal life. However, if the courts and many Americans were *not* struggling with that question, then there would not be a legal controversy. In part 3 of this book, therefore, I will try to construct a legal argument that challenges most state regulations of abortion but do so in a framework that is respectful of the state's position.

C. Wisdom

There are at least two ways to think about the aspiration of *wisdom*. One way is to think that there are so-called right answers on difficult moral issues on which all reasonable people could agree. Another way is to think that there are answers for each of us that are consistent with our authentic self, yet those answers are not either necessarily the same for each of us or necessarily the same for any of us at all points in our lives. This latter approach is the one that I want to take in this essay. It is a Buddhist conception of wisdom.

The key elements to a Buddhist conception of wisdom are that our self-knowledge is under our control, ever changing, and subject to close examination. Our lives should be dedicated to close examination of our self. By understanding our self, we help move our self closer to our authentic self. Trying to attain wisdom through meditation is a process whereby we work to move closer to our authentic self.

Nancy Ross provides a good summary of the role of the aspiration of wisdom in Buddhism:

> In Buddhism it is ignorance, not sin, that gives man his difficulties, and ignorance can, by specific *teachable* techniques, be modified, even overcome. One has only to make the right effort! This is a key point worth repeating. Blame and guilt play no part in Buddhism; shame, however, over personal inadequacies can be a significant aspect of an individual's transformation.
>
> Self-knowledge is the one sure, indisputable path by which we can extricate ourselves from the branches of conditioned life. The Dhammapada states: "All that we are is made up of our thoughts." From this it would follow that since thoughts are subject to control, it is quite possible to alter one's attitude, an alteration that can drastically change an individual's life. This whole process is, however, much less simple than the mere exercise of mind over matter. . . . [38]

Meditation is the process that Buddhists use to attain wisdom. Although some people may mistakenly consider meditation to be a passive exercise, it is actually an active means whereby one can drastically change one's life.

The Buddhist practice of using meditation to attain wisdom is similar to the feminist practice of using consciousness-raising to improve women's consciousness of their existence. Feminist theory would benefit from some of the insights that Buddhists have attained through the practice of meditation. For example, feminist theory often seems embedded in the assumption that consciousness-raising is successful if women move from consciousness-raising to political work. Feminists do not sufficiently address the need to return again and again to consciousness-raising or other forms of meditative practice while they participate in political work. Buddhists, by contrast, emphasize the need to make meditation a way of life. Rather than move beyond meditative work, feminists need to find ways to embed meditative work in their everyday life and politics.

This discussion of wisdom may seem too passive for some feminists because, as MacKinnon warned, it suggests that we can change reality through our mind alone. But if we consider the Buddhist observation that there is no separation of self and other, we can see that self-knowledge relates to how we live our life and connect with others. It is not an isolated activity.

Considering the aspiration of wisdom, we would want to make it easier for women to come to an abortion decision that will move them toward their aspirations for their authentic selves. Feminists often seem reluctant to permit the state to impose any requirements on how women make abortion decisions because many of these requirements have been coercive and would not facilitate real dialogue. Yet, it is important to keep our aspirations in mind when analyzing these measures. We know that the abortion decision is very difficult for many women and that the wrong decision can create much emotional trauma.[39] Therefore, rather than being satisfied with any abortion decision made by a woman, we might want to consider how we can improve her qualitative judgment. Are there any ways that the state or private sources could facilitate increased dialogue or contemplation so that women can make the right abortion decision for themselves? I will consider that issue further in later chapters. For now, however, I would like to suggest that consideration of the aspiration of wisdom should leave us determined to facilitate the best possible abortion decision.

V. CONCLUSION

In this chapter, I have suggested three aspirations—love, compassion, and wisdom—that women should try to embed in their authentic selves. I have suggested that our consideration of political priorities would be strengthened by articulating our aspirations with more precision and openness. Finally, I have preliminarily shown how our consideration of the abortion issue would be affected by our consideration of these aspirations.

Notes

1. Adrienne Rich, *Integrity,* in A Wild Patience Has Taken Me This Far 8 (1981).
2. Catharine MacKinnon, Feminism Unmodified: Discourses on Life and Law 219 (1987).
3. Sonia Johnson, Going Out of Our Minds: The Metaphysics of Liberation 320–21 (1987).
4. See, e.g., Kate Bartlett, *MacKinnon's Feminism: Power on Whose Terms?* (Book Review), 75 Calif. L. Rev. 1559, 1565–70 (1987).
5. *See., e.g.,* Denise L. Carmody & John T. Carmody, Eastern Ways to the Center: An Introduction to Asian Religions 106–10 (1983).
6. Nancy Wilson Ross, Buddhism: A Way of Life and Thought 28 (1980).
7. Catharine MacKinnon, Toward a Feminist Theory of the State 94 (1989) (emphasis added).
8. *See, e.g.,* All the Women Are White, All the Blacks Are Men: But Some of Us Are Brave (Gloria Hull, Patricia Scott, & Barbara Smith eds. 1982); Home Girls: A Black Feminist Anthology (Barbara Smith ed. 1983); bell hooks, Feminist Theory: from margin to center (1984). *See also* Caroline Ramazanoglu, Feminism and the Contradictions of Oppression (1989); Elizabeth V. Spelman, Inessential Woman: Problems of Exclusion in Feminist Thought (1988).
9. Ruth Smith, *Feminism and the Moral Subject,* in Women's Consciousness, Women's Conscience: A Reader in Feminist Ethics 249–50 (Barbara Andolsen, Christine Gudorf, & Mary Pellauer eds. 1987) (footnote omitted).
10. Robert F. Kennedy, *quoted* by Roger Rosenblatt on the *MacNeil-Lehrer Newshour* (PBS television broadcast, July 4, 1988).
11. James Nelson, *Reuniting Sexuality and Spirituality,* The Christian Century, Feb. 25, 1987, at 189 (citing Anthony Kosnik, Human Sexuality: New Directions in American Catholic Thought (1977)).
12. John 13:34–35 (New Jerusalem Bible).
13. *See* Pinchas Lapide, The Sermon on the Mount: Utopia or Program for Action? (Arlene Swidler trans. 1986).
14. Audre Lorde, *Uses of the Erotic: The Erotic as Power,* in Sister Outsider 53, 55 (1984) (emphasis in original).
15. *Id.* at 58.
16. Adrienne Rich, Of Woman Born: Motherhood as Experience and Institution xxxiv–xxxv (1986) (emphasis in original).
17. *Id.* at xviii.
18. Etty Hillesum, An Interrupted Life: The Diaries of Etty Hillesum 1941–43 180, 183 (Arnold Pomerans trans. 1983).
19. Robert Coles, Dorothy Day: A Radical Devotion 24 (1987) (emphasis in original).
20. The Simone Weil Reader 51 (George Panichas ed. 1977) (emphasis in original) [hereafter The Reader].
21. Celia Kitzinger, The Social Construction of Lesbianism 117 (1987).
22. *Id.* at 118.
23. MacKinnon, *supra* note 2, at 218.
24. Rich, *supra* note 16, at xxxiv–xxxv.
25. *See* Hillesum, *supra* note 18, at 81.
26. *See* Nel Noddings, Caring: A Feminine Approach to Ethics and Moral Education (1984).
27. See Ross, *supra* note 6, at 89.
28. The Reader, *supra* note 20, at 51 (emphasis in original).
29. For example, Carol Gilligan's conception of responsibility has been criticized as being

insensitive to others across differences. *See* Carol Stack, *The Culture of Gender: Women and Men of Color*, 11 Signs: Journal of Women in Culture and Society 321, 321–24 (1986).

30. This argument is one of the most frequent arguments that I get from my students when I ask them why a woman does not have to consult with her sexual partner before having an abortion. Martha Minow generally describes (and rejects) this perspective: "A pessimistic view suggests that we can never glimpse another's world, because our self-absorption limits our own self-knowledge." Martha Minow, *Foreword: Justice Engendered*, 101 Harv. L. Rev. 10, 79 (1987).

31. *Id.* at 82 & 79.

32. Andreas Teuber, *Simone Weil: Equality as Compassion*, 43 Phil. & Phenomenological Res. 221, 235–36 (1982).

33. *Id.* at 228.

34. Brief for Catholics for a Free Choice, Chicago Catholic Women, National Coalition of American Nuns, Women in Spirit of Colorado Task Force, et al., as Amici Curiae in Support of Appellees, at 25–26, Webster v. Reproductive Health Services, 492 U.S. 490 (1989) (No. 88–605).

35. Minow, *supra* note 30, at 93.

36. *See* Brief Amicus for American Jewish Congress, Board of Homeland Ministries— United Church of Christ, National Jewish Community Relations Advisory Council, The Presbyterian Church (U.S.A.) by James E. Andrews as Stated Clerk of General Assembly, The Religious Coalition for Abortion Rights, St. Louis Catholics for Choice, and 30 other religious groups, Webster v. Reproductive Health Services, 492 U.S. 490 (1989) (No. 88–605).

37. Lynne Henderson, *Legality and Empathy*, 85 Mich. L. Rev. 1574, 1653 (1987).

38. *See* Ross. *supra* note 6, at 62.

39. *See* A. Spackhard, The Psycho-Social Aspects of Stress Following Abortion (1985) (unpublished doctoral dissertation) (available from University Microfilms International, Ann Arbor, Mich.).

CHAPTER TWO

The Critique

The Problems of Consciousness
and Sexual Objectification

> When we gather to share our lives, we are en-
> gaged in moral, not just therapeutic activity.
> Naming our own experience honestly, we as-
> sert our own worth and dignity as persons. For
> us to assert our dignity is, in itself, a morally
> courageous act in a world where women are
> too often defined as inferior.[1]

In this chapter, I will look at two aspects of the feminist critique: the problem of
consciousness and the problem of sexual objectification. I will first describe the
traditional feminist explanation of these problems and then describe how my understanding of those problems has been enhanced by consideration of the aspirations
of love, compassion, and wisdom. Similarly, I will discuss how theologians' understanding of these problems could be enhanced by considering the feminist critique
of women's condition.

I. THE PROBLEM OF CONSCIOUSNESS

A. A Description of the Problem

Because women are often unaware of their sex-based oppression, they sometimes
make decisions that they believe to be in their best interest but that actually detract
from their well-being. Simone de Beauvoir recognized this phenomenon and asked:

> Why is it that women do not dispute male sovereignty? No subject will readily
> volunteer to become the object, the inessential; it is not the Other who, in

defining himself as the Other, establishes the One. The Other is posed as such by the One in defining himself as the One. [2]

Similarly, Catharine MacKinnon has explained that the problem of consciousness has resulted in women believing that they have consented to sexual relations which result in their own subordination. Thus, MacKinnon has argued that the scope of the problem of consciousness "helps explain some of the otherwise more bewildering modes of female collaboration."[3]

The problem of consciousness results in women not authentically or truly consenting to some of the most basic and important decisions in their lives, such as decisions surrounding their sexual relations. Women may make decisions which detract from their well-being (or, in MacKinnon's term, contribute to their subordination) and yet believe that they made the decisions in their own best interest. But what does it mean to say that women do not always act in their own best interest or, more generally, have a problem of consciousness? Does it mean that they don't feel the conditions of their own existence? That they do feel their own existence fully but are afraid to describe it accurately or act upon their feelings authentically? How can we confidently know that a woman has not acted in her own best interest when a woman would evaluate her best interest differently than we would?

We can gather some preliminary answers to those questions from recent empirical studies of women's lives. Studies of battered women and victims of incest show that many women suppress their feelings of pain.[4] More generally, studies of sexual behavior show that women are not sure what they want, what gives them sexual pleasure.[5] Studies also show that women often have difficulty expressing their anger.[6] Studies of women who have come to regret their abortion decision reveal that these women sometimes did not have the societal support to act on their feelings.[7] Finally, the stories of women who regret an earlier abortion decision provide support for the observation that some women, themselves, recognize that certain so-called wrong decisions may have resulted from a troubled conscience. Thus, the problem of consciousness may be a combination of a problem of women not fully glimpsing their feelings—not being able to articulate fully the negative feelings that they do recognize, not necessarily being able to act on the feelings that they do recognize—and sometimes even making decisions that, with hindsight, they can evaluate as wrong. I consider this problem to be one of women not being able to glimpse and experience their authentic self. But I emphasize that it is not enough to be able to glimpse our authentic self. Women also have to be able to act upon that glimpsed reality.

Feminists often describe the problem of consciousness as only being relevant when explaining why all women are not feminists, why all women do not actively fight their subordination. Thus, they often seem to be trying to affirm certain decisions made by women and not others. In this book, I do not want to limit myself to that aspect of the problem of consciousness. The problem of consciousness arises each time a woman makes a difficult, fundamental life decision, irrespective of whether a clearly correct, pro-feminist decision exists.

It is possible that the problem of consciousness is actually a misnomer, that the real problem is a methodological one. How can women come to understand their authentic selves rather than the objectified image of themselves which society has created? Thus, feminists have increasingly turned to methodological areas, asking what would be a truly feminist methodology. *Consciousness-raising,* which was designed to overcome the problem of consciousness, was the first methodological inroad. The experience of consciousness-raising, as we shall see, has now been generalized to become *feminist methodology.* Feminist methodology, however, is a broader term than consciousness-raising. Consciousness-raising has greatly influenced and formed feminist methodology, giving women more tools to discover and experience their authentic selves.

B. Feminist Methodology

1. Consciousness-Raising

Feminists have tried to solve the problem of consciousness through a methodology called consciousness-raising. The mechanics or effectiveness of consciousness-raising, however, have rarely been discussed in feminist literature. Sonia Johnson, a feminist who is interested in spirituality, has described a technique of consciousness-raising which she calls "Hearing into Being."[8] Her technique involves each woman in a group having a certain amount of time to talk uninterrupted and without evaluation. It helps women break silence while also not being limited by others' views or judgments. The experience of "being seriously and completely listened to, being genuinely heard" was an extremely powerful experience for many women in Johnson's group. She reported that many of them cried, because the experience of being able to speak and be heard was so profound for them.

In sum, consciousness-raising is deeply feminist. It has helped women break the silence about their lives and question men's ability to have so-called right answers with universal application. Instrumentally, it has been a tool for overcoming subordination. The short-term benefits of consciousness-raising are obvious when women cry from the joy of hearing their experiences as women described, validated, and almost understood.

2. The Limitations of Consciousness-Raising

Although many women have reported that consciousness-raising has had a dramatic influence on their lives, it is also a technique that is open to criticism. In this section, I will explore some of the potential criticisms of consciousness-raising. In the next section, I will discuss how some theological insights could possibly assist women in overcoming the limitations of consciousness-raising.

a. Diverse Ways of Acquiring Knowledge

One recent book, *Women's Ways of Knowing*[9] has helped me think through some of the limitations of consciousness-raising for some women. The authors of this book trace the different ways that women acquire knowledge. They argue that women acquire knowledge in various stages of development, the most advanced and sophisticated being constructed knowledge. Although the authors correctly suggest that women have many different ways of acquiring knowledge, I have trouble with their suggestion that women have to go through stages of development in a linear fashion rather than picking and choosing among different methods at various points in their lives. In any case, their book should caution us in trying to reach women through one particular type of discourse since women will utilize different ways of acquiring knowledge throughout their lives. By relying exclusively on consciousness-raising, which is a type of experiential discourse, feminists may be stereotyping women as purely subjective seekers of knowledge rather than recognizing the diverse ways that women may acquire knowledge throughout their lifetime.

Although consciousness-raising may not be the perfect device for reaching all women throughout their lifetimes, it does offer some distinctive benefits. It provides women with a distinctive feminist methodology. Its experiential and subjective mode of discourse can provide women with a means to value their lives and identity, to insist upon looking intently at women's lives. It can be respectful and affirming of women's experiences while they live in a society that denigrates such experiences. Moreover, it can challenge feminists to reflect on the diversity of women's lives rather than to generalize from a small cross section of women. As a methodology, it can facilitate women's ability to survive in a society that devalues them and tries to make them invisible. Through feminist methodology, women can become fuller persons while they attempt to describe the fullness of their diverse lives. Indeed, they may find that such a methodology is especially valuable at certain stages of their personal journey. Feminists should affirm use of this methodology when it is most valuable in women's life journey, but they should not refrain from using other methodologies at other times along the way.

b. Problems of Partiality and Malleability

Even if we conclude that feminist methodology is the most appropriate tool to resolve difficult questions, we still need to be wary of how we use this tool. Women are attempting to use consciousness-raising to overcome influences in society that would lead them to unauthentic expressions of their selves. An assumption within consciousness-raising is that women are capable of being influenced in their self-expression. Consciousness-raising itself may influence women and possibly lead women away from, rather than toward, the discovery and expression of their authentic selves. This is a problem of both partiality and malleability. We can only engage in consciousness-raising with a limited number of people, so we can never fully be exposed to all the possibilities for ourselves. Who we are exposed to influences how we see ourselves. Thus, the fact that we have engaged in consciousness-raising should not leave us immune to questions about the authenticity of our choices.

Three coauthors who have studied the limitations of consciousness-raising and, in particular, the possibility for coercion within this methodology, have stated:

> We have some doubt that [consciousness-raising] can be utilised to articulate the entire individual experience. Some women have argued that the group itself can

be oppressive, in the sense that one orthodoxy, the orthodoxy of patriarchy, may well be replaced by another. This in its turn goes on to impose limits upon the revelation and authentication of experience. This suggests to us the problem we have already recognised in the process of transforming authorised normalities. The orthodoxy that emerges within the group may well be as much reflexive as reflective; that is to say, it may emerge equally in the guise of committed individualism as in the form of a considered "feminist morality."[10]

As should be clear from my discussion, the claim that consciousness-raising may reflect a feminist *morality* is no reason to dismiss the usefulness of consciousness-raising. The more important question is how feminism arrived at that ethic or morality. Is it a result of careful consideration or rash judgment? When consciousness-raising is coercive, then it would not facilitate an individual's coming closer to glimpsing her authentic self or formulating aspirations for her authentic self.

c. The Difficulty of Evaluating Insights Gained from Consciousness-Raising

Feminist theory also suffers from the problem of not having a mechanism to evaluate which perceptions derived from consciousness-raising should be credited as reflecting women's authentic sense of their well-being. Consciousness-raising is never a completed task, yet feminist theory necessarily draws conclusions about the reality of women's lives while consciousness-raising is ongoing. For example, feminist theory argues that male domination has been able to create sexuality on men's terms. It takes consciousness to draw any conclusions about what conditions facilitate women's well-being, yet feminist theory attempts to draw conclusions without explaining why it credits certain perceptions and not others.

The only way to evaluate feminist observations would be to have a theory of consciousness that could explain which perceptions women should believe and which they should distrust in creating their account of the world. Without an account of consciousness, feminist theory has difficulty in guiding women to experiences which would facilitate their well-being.

This problem becomes clearer in the context of MacKinnon's pornography analysis. MacKinnon argues that pornography is an act of sex discrimination; it perpetuates men's subordination of women.[11] She does engage in an experiential discourse to support this observation. She reports the story of Linda Lovelace, a woman who was enslaved and brutalized by the pornography industry. But MacKinnon's experiential discourse is highly selective. She discounts the stories of women within the industry who say that they have consented to working within the industry and find the work relatively satisfying. For example, MacKinnon says:

> You do it [participate in pornography] relatively convincingly. Linda's apparent enjoyment, which was a well-done charade, is the charade women learn in order to survive: to project sexual enjoyment whether we feel it or not. Underlying this is that out-of-it-ness, that same above-it-all equality, that not-really-into-it-ness of a lot of women under a lot of different conditions. This is what she conveyed, and the film was a success because it felt *real* to men. . . . Linda projected in *Deep Throat* what women learn in order to get by as women.[12]

In general, MacKinnon's epistemology is confusing. On the one hand, she embraces experiential discourse, suggesting that women need to turn to their own varying subjectivity to understand their experiences. On the other hand, her writing is full of broad generalizations about women's experiences that do not explicitly reflect an experiential discourse.

This is the structure of MacKinnon's argument. She says that women project their enjoyment whether they feel it or not. She implicitly recognizes that women may report that they do enjoy participating in pornography. Unlike Linda Lovelace, they are therefore projecting how they do feel. However, MacKinnon discounts the importance of their reports of satisfaction or enjoyment; their satisfaction appears unimportant because other women, like Linda Lovelace, participated in pornography under conditions of coercion. Obviously, MacKinnon is correct to argue that women should not be coerced to participate in pornography. But what about the women who report voluntariness and even satisfaction? MacKinnon does not explain whether we should insist that their consciousness is false or incomplete. Most importantly, she does not explain how eliminating the opportunity to work within the pornography industry, as her work would do, would change these women's consciousness of their existence. By suggesting external strategies to deal with the problem of pornography—legal restrictions on pornography—MacKinnon ignores the internal aspect of the problem of consciousness.

Other feminists argue that pornography is an act of political speech about women's sexuality that must be absolutely protected.[13] These feminists often discount the stories of degradation and subordination that come from some women within the industry. In addition, they point to stories by women who claim that participation in pornography has enhanced their lives. These feminists would not agree with MacKinnon's description of the problem of consciousness within the industry; therefore, they see no need to attack the problem. Similarly, they see no need to develop further external protections for these women because they do not agree that systematic abuse is occurring. Neither view meets the aspiration of compassion by trying to empower women to see for themselves the meaning of pornography in their lives. The problem of consciousness makes this task very difficult, because we do not know which versions of the pornography industry to believe. In order to tackle the problem of consciousness and choose legal-political strategies to improve the quality of women's lives, we need to know more about the process through which women can reach authentic decisions.

Robin West ties the selective validation of women's voices to methodological issues. She criticizes radical feminists, such as MacKinnon, who completely discount women's descriptions of pleasure under sexually submissive arrangements even when those statements of pleasure emerge from consciousness-raising:

> [T]o radical feminists, that women on occasion take pleasure in their own submissiveness, is simply a manifestation of their disempowered state, not a meaningful counter-example to the posited egalitarian ideal. As with radical legalists generally, the stated definitional ideal must trump the experiential counter-report.
>
> For feminists, this radical legalist methodology should raise serious warning signals. First, we should remember that the ideal and the description of "essential

human nature" on which it rests is itself drawn from a male, if "left" intellectual tradition, and is therefore *not* an ideal we should readily assume will be true of *women*. The ideal, in other words, against which we are judging our own and each others' consciousness to be "false" may be an ideal which is true of men, but not women. But second, and perhaps more fundamentally, it is feminism's most crucial insight that *our experience* must be primary—and not be trumped by posited ideals or definitions. As feminists, we should be wary of our attraction to a masculinist ideal, and we should be even more concerned when that ideal is then employed to run roughshod over [experiential] insights, painstakingly unearthed from our consciousness.[14]

West asserts that the reason MacKinnon discounts women's descriptions of pleasure, even those obtained through consciousness-raising, is that MacKinnon has an underlying but unjustified assumption about women's happiness: women cannot truly be happy under conditions of submission. Instead of assuming that subordination produces submission, which in turn produces women's unhappiness, West challenges radical feminists to explore more fully women's direct assertions of pain and pleasure.

West claims that women should try to avoid the evil of pain and move toward the ideal of pleasure.[15] She questions MacKinnon's assertion that the eroticization of controlled submission is closely tied to women's overall subordination. West asserts that MacKinnon has not connected her observations to pleasure and pain and, more specifically, has not used consciousness-raising to make that connection.

In order to evaluate both MacKinnon's and West's assertions, we need a framework within which we may learn about women's experiences. West turns to consciousness-raising for that data, but I am not entirely satisfied with that discussion because she has not been sufficiently critical of consciousness-raising. She seems to assume that so long as an expression of pleasure or pain is acknowledged through consciousness-raising, it is authentic, untainted by patriarchy or other forms of coercion.

Rather than talk globally about consciousness-raising, as if all women are engaged in consciousness-raising, it would seem that feminists need to be more open to discussions about the process that was used to reach various conclusions. We could then consider the ways in which women came to their conclusions in determining whether those conclusions are consistent with women's well-being. If we have evidence that their decisions were made as the result of listening to their inner voice and considering a variety of social messages, we would presumptively credit their observations as authentic. In contrast, if we have evidence that women have unreflectively accepted the dominant social message, we would be more skeptical that their observations are authentic.

C. Theological Insights on Consciousness: Dialogue and Meditation or Contemplation

Insights from theologians can contribute to our understanding of when consciousness-raising can work and what other steps may be taken to overcome the limitations of consciousness-raising. Because of the importance of the aspiration of wisdom, theologians have considered in much depth how wisdom can be attained. They often suggest dialogue and meditation or contemplation.

1. Dialogue

A theologian who emphasizes the importance of dialogue is Leonard Swidler. He offers the following definition of dialogue:

> Dialogue of course is conversation between two or more persons with differing views, the primary purpose of which is for each participant to learn from the other so that both can change and grow. Minimally, the very fact that I learn that my dialogue partner believes "this" rather than "that" changes my attitude toward that person; and a change in my attitude is significant change and growth, in me. We enter into dialogue, therefore so that *we* can learn, change, and grow, not so that we can force change on the *other*.
>
> . . . Dialogue is *not* debate. In dialogue each partner must listen to the other as openly and sympathetically as possible, in an attempt to understand the other's position as precisely and, as it were, as much from within, as possible.[16]

The key to dialogue, as defined by Swidler, is openness and empathy.

Dialogue can assist us in developing relational understandings of our role in society. According to Swidler:

> I learn by dialogue—that is, not only by being open to, receptive of, in a passive sense, extramental reality, but by having a dialogue with extramental reality. I not only "hear," receive, reality, but I also—and I think, first of all—"speak" to reality. That is, I ask it questions, I stimulate it to speak back to me, to answer my questions. Furthermore, I give reality the specific categories, language, with which, in which, to which it speaks, to respond to me. It can "speak" to me—really communicate to my mind—only in a language, in categories, that I understand. When the speaking, the responding, becomes more and more ununderstandable to me, I slowly begin to become aware that there is a new language being developed here and that I must learn it if I am to make sense out of what reality is saying to me. This is a *dialogic* view of truth, whose very name reflects its *relationality*.[17]

Feminists have also stressed the importance of dialogue. For example, bell hooks, relying in part on the work of the theologian Paulo Freire, has argued that leaders of the feminist movement "should have the ability to show love and compassion, show this love through their actions, and be able to engage in successful dialogue."[18] Whereas Swidler urges people to use dialogue to communicate across all of their differences, hooks urges feminists to use dialogue to communicate better across differences of race and class.

Although Swidler's dialogue is different from consciousness-raising because it involves active communication between speaker and listener, his observations about consciousness and openness mesh nicely with many feminist observations. First, he explains how the importance of consciousness is not simply a problem for women; it is a problem for all people. To the extent that artificial gender distinctions move women further away from consciousness, we can see how they move women further from their aspirations for their authentic self. Second, he affirms the importance of noncognitive and relational methodologies to achieving consciousness. Consciousness-raising is such a technique. Feminists often value intuition but have not been able to provide a full explanation of why intuition can be feminist (rather than simply feminine). Swidler provides us with a reason to value intuition independently of the fact that it is also labeled feminine. Finally, his emphasis on the importance of relational dialogue fits well with the connected aspect of our authentic self.

Swidler's description of dialogue can provide insight into how consciousness-raising could be more effective. He emphasizes that dialogue is a process of being open to others. Rather than entering dialogue to persuade others, we should enter dialogue to really hear and empathize with others. Through such openness, we can use dialogue to modify or reflect on our original perspective. If we each entered consciousness-raising with such openness, we might be able to be less fearful of others trying to indoctrinate us with so-called right answers. No one would enter the process thinking that she had the right answers; we each would enter the process intending to listen and consider the experiences and perspectives of others. Women might be less subject to problems of malleability if others were not so intent on persuading them to their point of view.

Nevertheless, Swidler's discussion of the benefits of dialogue may be too reflective of a male model of communication. To Swidler, the primary problem is a lack of openness which, he believes, can be overcome through dialogue. For women, however, a major problem is often a willingness to be too open to others and not sufficiently open to one's self. Because women are conditioned to accept others' perspectives, they may not need to struggle with techniques which emphasize openness. Instead, women may need to focus on techniques which help them break the silence. Too often the semblance of dialogue for those who have been located on the margin means being incorporated as a poor imitation of those who dominate them. In other words, dominant society may feel satisfied when women are included through participation on such activities as panels and workshops, but that participation may do little for women while making the dominant group feel self-satisfied that true conversation has occurred. These public conversations may serve some benefit, but they are not likely to help women decide for themselves what are their own views. Meditation or contemplation, which I will discuss next, may help achieve that end when coupled with consciousness-raising.

2. Meditation or Contemplation

It may be that dialogue could be combined with other methodologies to overcome the possibility of manipulation further. Another tool might be meditation or contemplation, which has been emphasized by Eastern theologians. Thomas Merton, a Catholic theologian who was very interested in Zen Buddhism, explained the importance of that methodology:

> [C]ontemplation is beyond aesthetic intuition, beyond art, beyond poetry. Indeed, it is also beyond philosophy, beyond speculative theology. It resumes, transcends and fulfills them all, and yet at the same time it seems, in a certain way, to

supersede and to deny them all. Contemplation is always beyond our own knowledge, beyond our own light, beyond systems, beyond explanations, beyond discourse, beyond dialogue, beyond our own self.[19]

One problem with meditation may be that it can be a vehicle for rationalization
rather than authenticization. Sometimes, I find myself reinforcing through meditation what I want to believe about myself rather than deeply probing parts of
myself that may be broken. Thus, meditation may suffer from some of the same
kinds of problems as consciousness-raising. It may be that we should share our
insights from meditation with others in order to obtain feedback as to whether we
are engaging in rationalization rather than insight. Interaction between meditation
and consciousness-raising may bring us closer to insights about our authenticity.

Consciousness-raising can expose us to questions from others; contemplation
or meditation can provide us with the space to resolve these questions removed
from others' expectations for us. Merton has described the nonjudgmental aspects
of meditation (or "Zen consciousness") that are important to our search for authenticity:

> Zen consciousness does not distinguish and categorize what it sees in terms of
> social and cultural standards. It does not try to fit things into artificially precon-
> ceived structures. It does not judge beauty and ugliness according to canons of
> taste—even though it may have its own taste. If it seems to judge and distinguish,
> it does so only enough to point beyond judgment to the pure void. It does not
> settle down in its judgment as final. It does not erect its judgment into a structure
> to be defended against all comers.[20]

By quoting this passage, I do not mean to suggest that we should aspire to a
completely nonjudgmental or nonnormative consciousness-raising. It is important
that others use their feminist norms and values to question us as we proceed along
our life journey. In fact, we may often need sharp questioning from others in order
to see ourselves more clearly and move forward. The problem lies in the process
of questioning. Is it done in a way that allows us the opportunity for private
reflection? Because we may not have control over how others make their judgments
known to us, the existence of contemplative space in our lives may provide us
with the necessary cushion against overly judgmental consciousness-raising. Further
exploration of that tradition may facilitate feminists in better understanding the
problem of consciousness. Contemplation or meditation is an even more internal
process than consciousness-raising as traditionally defined by feminists. It is probably
an even more individualistic enterprise than consciousness-raising because of the
lack of a group dynamic. It may, therefore, be even farther from feminist tradition.

The advantage of consciousness-raising over the kind of dialogue that Swidler
describes is that it focuses on the importance of women breaking their silence.
Swidler was concerned with the problem of openness, which may be more of a
problem for men than women. Women are conditioned to accept others' perspectives; they may not need to struggle with techniques that emphasize openness. But
women may need to develop techniques that help them break the silence.

3. Incompatibility of These Techniques with Feminist Theory and Practice

a. Critique of Rhetoric

Each of the techniques described above (consciousness-raising, dialogue, and meditation or contemplation) is open and empathetic. Feminists, especially feminist lawyers, do not always engage in such open and empathetic communication. Instead, they sometimes choose argumentation and rhetoric as tools of persuasion.

Some religious feminists disdain the use of argumentation or rhetoric, even as tools of persuasion. For example, Rita Gross, a Buddhist-feminist, has suggested that the rhetorical or hard edge of feminist theory "is a protective shell preserving one from immediate contact with situations."[21] She suggests that that kind of hard edge is bad for society because it prevents people from having a truly compassionate and open attitude to others and one's self. She suggests that meditation turns one away from rhetoric or dogma. She says that the gentleness that one learns through meditation may be much more effective than the anger of rhetoric:

> The point is *not* that if one is gentle rather than aggressive and angry suddenly everyone will automatically be won over. Many people are so entrenched that they are oblivious. But interactions based on anger will definitely not be very productive in any case. Gentleness may be more productive; but even when it is not, one's own well-being is enhanced more by gentleness than by aggressiveness.[22]

Some feminists may think that rhetoric is necessary to critique, that one is too accepting of the status quo without rhetoric. Gross suggests that feminists and others should attempt to attain a middle ground:

> some middle way between ideology and mindless acquiescence to anything whatever is in order. This non-dualistic, non-fixated allegiance to "neither this nor that" seems to be the hardest aspect of Indian spirituality to teach to Westerners in the classroom and it also seems to be the hardest actually to grasp. But it seems the only way to maneuver between the ideology of the radical and ideology of the conventional.[23]

Gross, therefore, challenges feminists not to be afraid to abandon some of their rhetoric, to be willing to live in the space of "neither this nor that." Feminism can afford to be less rhetorical while retaining a critique of society. Meditation may make feminists uncomfortable or ill at ease if it forces them to abandon some of their unexamined premises or be more open to others' views. Ultimately, however, feminism would benefit by truly embracing a dialogue with our self and others that is gentle rather than argumentative and rhetorical.

b. Defense of Rhetoric

The problem with Gross's critique of rhetoric is that it is too universal in its application to the world in which we live. Gross cautions us to be open and tentative in our views, yet she also asks us to throw away one communication tool—rhetoric. Even if it is true that argumentation has inherent limitations, we still may find ourselves needing to engage in argumentation because of the specific challenges of certain contexts. I would suggest that the key to determining when argumentation is appropriate is to be sensitive to context. This seems to be an especially important question for us, as women, because we are socialized to listen and not be heard; we live in a world in which men often seem ignorant of our lives while we know theirs all too well. If the purpose of dialogue is for us to learn from others rather than to impose our viewpoint on others, then it is easy to imagine how calls for dialogue could help perpetuate women's subordination.

There are also times when we are forced to choose silence over both dialogue and argumentation. For example, when I have been accosted or insulted by a man on the street, I have sometimes chosen silence out of fear. Engaging in dialogue, despite my religious-feminist sensibility, did not occur to me. On other occasions, when a man has yelled a derogatory expression at me, I have yelled a derogatory epithet back, despite my fear of his violence. I have chosen to speak angrily, not because I wanted to learn from him but because I wanted him to learn from me.

In sum, I am not willing to discard the possibility that dialogue, silence, and argumentation can be important to women's survival. The important point is to be aware of the shortcomings of each mode of discourse and to consider context carefully when deciding which mode to use. Consciousness-raising and meditation or contemplation may be very valuable tools to women at various times in their lives as they try to discover their authentic selves. In part 3 of this book, however, I will suggest that certain kinds of legal argumentation may also be valuable to women in order to help them survive in this state. I am trying to resist thinking of rhetoric and dialogue as bipolar entities. Instead, I will later explore how we might, as feminists, combine dialogue and argumentation. For now, I want the reader to grasp the value of consciousness-raising, dialogue, and meditation or contemplation, without necessarily throwing out rhetoric and argumentation.

II. THE PROBLEM OF SEXUAL OBJECTIFICATION OR NONMUTUAL LOVE

A. Description of the Problem

The problem of consciousness relates to the problem of sexual objectification or nonmutual love. Catharine MacKinnon argues that women have been socialized to believe that traditional heterosexuality is satisfying even though it has never been defined from a woman's perspective. For example, MacKinnon says:

> It may be worth considering that heterosexuality, the predominant social arrange-
> ment that fuses this sexuality of abuse and objectification with gender in inter-
> course, with attendant trauma, torture, and dehumanization, organizes women's
> pleasure so as to give us a stake in our own subordination.[24]

The fact that women report satisfaction within heterosexuality does not bring MacKinnon's thesis into question, because she would respond that the woman who reports satisfaction has been socialized to collaborate with her own oppression.

Feminists often refer to the problem of sexuality as a problem of *sexual objectification*. They define sexual objectification as men's treatment of women as an object rather than as full human beings with their own needs and desires.

Feminists are not the only theorists to consider the problem of objectification. Irving Singer, for example, uses that concept to explain Martin Buber's views on love. Singer says:

> When two people reciprocally communicate with one another as an I and a Thou, they respond as persons to the personhood in each. On the other hand, they enter into an I-It situation when they treat each other as objects or instrumentalities, things to be manipulated in the material world. Buber would seem to believe that virtually everything, whether or not it is a person, can be experienced as an It or a Thou. But only when we undergo an I-Thou relationship, Buber says, do we penetrate to the foundation of being.[25]

Feminists have contextualized this description of sexual objectification by explaining its implications in women's lives. Philosophers, like Martin Buber, have explored this problem more generally. As I will discuss later, however, theologians often do not focus enough attention on how this problem occurs in women's lives.

Sexual objectification takes many forms. An obvious example is when a man makes an obscene comment to a woman as she walks down the street. The woman's reaction is probably twofold: she may feel threatened by the possibility of physical violence, and she may feel that she was viewed one-dimensionally as an object for his pleasure.

It is hard to separate the problem of sexual objectification from the problem of violence against women. Because women fear sexual violence, they often respond with fear to casual comments about their appearance on the street during daylight hours. The problem of sexual objectification, however, is not only a reflection of a woman's fear of sexual violence. It is also a reflection of her distaste for being viewed as an object rather than as a subject (or, in Buber's language, as an It rather than a Thou).

Thus, the man who responds to a woman with an obscene comment has treated her as an object because he is unlikely to be taking any steps towards viewing her as a subject. He is responding to her with his own fantasy of who he thinks she is or should be.

B. Consent or Pleasure

One objection that is often offered to the feminist critique of sexual objectification is the issue of consent or pleasure. This problem becomes apparent if I change my example slightly. What if the man responds with a whistle rather than an obscene comment? I will assume for the purposes of this discussion that some women may enjoy a whistle from a man; it may make some women feel attractive or sexy. On the other hand, other women will feel abused by the whistle.

I argue that a man who whistles at a woman as she walks down the street has objectified her sexually *even if the woman takes pleasure from the whistle*. Formulating the example in this way makes it clear that it is not a single woman's desires that define what is sexually objectifying. A single woman may receive pleasure from the whistle and I would still describe it as sexually objectifying.

I have reached this conclusion by applying the aspiration of compassion. This aspiration suggests that the whistle is objectionable because a man who respected women would not whistle at any individual woman and take the risk of inflicting pain and fear on her. He would understand the life conditions which make it frightening and unpleasant for some women to be whistled at on a city street. If the man finds her attractive and wants to express those feelings, then he would find a more compassionate way to express those feelings. Thus, sexual responses do not need to be universally unwelcome in order to be problematic under an aspiration of compassion.

C. Emphasis on Male Domination

One final problem with the feminist description of the problem of sexual objectification is that it may put too much emphasis on the problem of male domination. For example, Catharine MacKinnon has argued that women have never experienced their own sexuality because it has been defined from the perspective of men's needs and desires. Because of the effectiveness of male dominance, women are also not aware of this lack of their own sexuality. By explaining this problem of sexuality from the perspective of male dominance, it would seem to imply that men have been able to define their sexuality from their own interests and needs, that men have experienced their sexuality in a way that facilitates their well-being.

Writings by men in feminist theory suggest that men have been gendered through socialization so as not to experience their sexuality in a way that facilitates their well-being.[26] Present sexual arrangements may keep some men in an economically superior position as compared with women, but present sexual arrangements do not bring men any closer to their authentic self than women. Male domination has certainly inhibited women from both achieving consciousness of their existence and experiencing their sexuality authentically, but gendered existence spreads further than male domination.

Rita Gross has explored that problem from a Buddhist-feminist perspective. She has concluded that feminist theory would benefit from considering the basic human problem of pain rather than limiting itself to pain caused by patriarchal, sexist values:

> Because feminism has no avenue of approach to basic pain, pain completely uncaused by the evil of patriarchy, much feminist theory and practice has some kind of frantic quality. That frantic quality actually compromises feminism's ef-

fectiveness and ability to communicate. What Buddhists see very clearly is that so long as one ignores the basic truth of suffering, one also expends a lot of painful energy maintaining that ignorance. That effort rebounds negatively to the cause of actually communicating and acting effectively with other people, to say nothing of the fact that it increases one's own misery at the same time. Therefore, understanding of suffering is extremely useful to feminists in two ways. First, it would afford individual feminists a quality of naive peacefulness and understanding that is not otherwise possible. Then, secondly, one actually knows what the problems are and how to work on them without alienating everyone in the process, which can further the cause of feminism significantly.[27]

Gross therefore challenges feminists to consider the human problems that cause our suffering irrespective of patriarchy.

A theologian who has done excellent work in enabling people to move towards their authentic self through sexuality is Dick Westley. Westley emphasizes that we have the power to bring meaning to sex, as we have the power to bring meaning to life.[28] The questions that Westley raises are deeply human questions, questions that all people need to face irrespective of their sex or sexual orientation.

Westley's analysis is compatible with the feminist observation that women should make choices in their lives to make their sexuality more meaningful. Some feminists suggest that women should seek lesbian existence to make their life more satisfying or meaningful. Irrespective of whether feminists accept that position, they generally agree that women should try to construct their sexuality so as to allow it to facilitate this movement towards their aspirations for their authentic self. By asking how we can add meaning to sexuality (rather than assume that the meaning of sexuality is a given), Westley is therefore making an observation that is compatible with the feminist critique of sexuality.

When Westley discusses homosexuals, he concludes that we should ask the same questions as we do for heterosexuals: have they properly brought meaning to the sexuality in their lives? For homosexuals who seem inherently homosexual, who could not experience satisfying sexual relations with someone of the opposite sex, Westley is relatively untroubled about their ability to engage in meaningful sexual activity.

His analysis, however, falls short when he gets to women who may choose lesbianism for political reasons. He tells the story of a woman who may have "chosen" to be a lesbian (when she was not "innately" homosexual) as the result of an abusive life experience with a man. In such a case, where a person may be in flux, not sure whether to choose homosexuality, he suggests that church officials should counsel the person about the "advantages and wider opportunities of heterosexual orientation" because the "track record for being able to retain a fulfilling lifestyle for the entire duration of a person's life is just not very good. The difficulties of being homosexual are not to be underestimated."[29]

Westley's analysis seems to be ignorant of the extensive lesbian literature on the political value of women *choosing* to be lesbians as an act of political resistance.

It is hard to imagine an action that could add more meaning to life than to embed one's sexuality in one's political movement towards fuller humanness. The lesbian lifestyle, as an act of political resistance, is meaningful because it is not innately determined, because it is an act of conscious choice.

Westley's seeming ignorance of lesbian existence is typical in literature about homosexuality. It is a problem that is not unique to theological literature. It is especially troubling, however, in Westley's case because his larger framework of asking how we can add meaning to sexual intimacy is compatible with feminist theory. As feminists can learn from insights from theology, theologians can obviously learn from insights from feminist theory.

Although Westley does not intend to raise the authenticity/political choice issue, his writing does raise it indirectly. If one starts with the assumption that all women are innately bisexual, a questionable but plausible assumption, then one might question any choice of exclusive sexuality as inauthentic. A woman who is innately bisexual but chooses lesbianism in response to a world which is hostile to women has, in a sense, acted inauthentically. Certainly, she has acted in a constrained way. Similarly, a woman who is innately bisexual but chooses heterosexuality in response to a world which is hostile to lesbians has acted inauthentically. In order to speak of the choice of exclusive lesbianism as inauthentic, then we must speak of the choice of exclusive heterosexuality as inauthentic. Both judgments rely on the assumption that we are innately bisexual.

In many ways, however, a political choice of lesbianism is very different than a political choice of heterosexuality. The choice of lesbianism is intended to further women's well-being by threatening the patriarchal power structure. The choice of heterosexuality gives into that power structure while also possibly making an individual woman's life easier. (We musn't forget, however, that the woman who chooses heterosexuality faces a higher risk of rape and battery.) I would therefore argue that the choice of lesbianism, even in an innately bisexual world, is more authentic than the choice of heterosexuality, because the choice is intended to transform the society in which we live toward our aspirations for our authentic selves. Political choices may therefore be constrained choices, but they can also assist us in moving toward our authentic selves.

D. Critique of Objectivity

Feminists often link a critique of sexual objectification to a critique of objectivity generally. That link is explicit within Catharine MacKinnon's work. She says:

> The male epistemological stance, which corresponds to the world it creates, is objectivity: the ostensibly noninvolved stance, the view from a distance and from no particular perspective, apparently transparent to its reality. . . . Woman through male eyes is sex object, that by which man knows himself at once as man and as subject.[30]

By noting that norms, values, and ways of being have often been constructed from a perspective that benefits men or speaks to men's needs, feminists such as MacKinnon have often criticized our ability ever to speak from an objective or universal perspective.

Although I generally agree with the feminist critique of the problem of sexual objectification, I do not agree that critique forces us to abandon our aspirations for objective or universal norms. Clearly, society's and the legal system's attempts to create objective norms have been a disaster. As Martha Minow has argued, when judges purport to speak from an objective perspective, they often rely on the norms of white, male, Christian, able-bodied society.[31] Minow responds to this observation by suggesting that we need to acknowledge our own partiality and "strive for the standpoint of someone who is committed to the moral relevance of contingent particulars." Concretely, she suggests that we "must acknowledge and struggle against [our] partiality by making an effort to understand [others'] reality and what it means for [our] own." Rather than "adopt and cling to some new standpoint" we ought to "strive to become and remain open to perspectives and claims that challenge our own."[32] Minow argues that this exercise and others would discourage judges from seeking "an illusory universality and objectivity."[33]

Minow seems to suggest in her concluding remarks that there is no such thing as nonillusory universality and objectivity. We are doomed to a partial, nonuniversal perspective. Yet, her own work would seem to be embedded in certain universal principles. One obvious principle is what she calls "equal respect" in the following passage:

> The plea for judges to engage with perspectives that challenge their own is not a call for sympathy or empathy, nor a hope that judges will be "good" people. Sympathy, the human emotion, must be distinguished from equal respect, the legal command.[34]

We should not find it surprising that Minow's work, like other feminist work, must be embedded in certain universal ethical principles. As I argued in a previous part of this book, feminist theory needs ethics to help us understand how to overcome human suffering. If we do not have a system of ethics, then we do not have aspirations to which we can turn to see if present society fails to meet our aspirations. In addition, we would have no basis for resolving competing claims because we would have no basis upon which we could ascribe content to the legal conception of justice.

The fact that we can aspire to ethical norms despite the feminist critique of objectivity does not mean that those norms can be numerous, wide-ranging or even constant over time. The feminist critique of the problem of consciousness should make us acutely aware of how difficult it is to generalize. The theological aspiration of wisdom through contemplation and dialogue should also lead us to be cautious in expecting ourselves to be able to attain universal principles easily.

Later in this book, therefore, I will explore how we can develop minimalist norms within law, norms that will recognize our limited capacity to speak in universalities.

Notes

1. Barbara Andolsen, Christine Gudorf & Mary D. Pellauer, *Introduction* in Women's Consciousness, Women's Conscience: A Reader in Feminist Ethics XV (Barbara Andolsen, Christine Gudorf & Mary D. Pellauer eds. 1985).

2. Simone de Beauvoir, The Second Sex xxi (H. M. Parshley trans. 1952).

3. Catharine MacKinnon, Feminism Unmodified: Discourses on Life and Law 7 (1987).

4. *See, e.g.*, Leonore Walker, The Battered Woman (1979).

5. *See, e.g.*, Barbara Ehrenreich, Elizabeth Hess & Gloria Jacobs, Re-Making Love: The Feminization of Sex (1987).

6. *See, e.g.*, Madonna Kolbenschlag, Kiss Sleeping Beauty Goodbye: Breaking the Spell of Feminine Myths and Models 181 (1979) ("Women's socialization tends to inhibit their ability to reveal their inner rage and bitterness.").

7. *See* David Reardon, Aborted Women: Silent No More (1987).

8. Sonia Johnson, Going Out of Our Minds: The Metaphysics of Liberation 130 (1987).

9. Mary F. Belenky et al., Women's Ways of Knowing: The Development of Self, Voice, and Mind (1986).

10. Anne Bottomley, Susie Gibson & Belinda Meteyard, *Dworkin: Which Dworkin? Taking Feminism Seriously*, 14 J. L. & Soc'y 47, 56 (1987).

11. *See e.g.*, MacKinnon, *supra* note 3, at 127–213.

12. *See* MacKinnon, *supra* note 3, at 128–29.

13. *See* Brief of Amici Curiae of Feminist Anti-Censorship Taskforce for the American Booksellers Ass'n, American Booksellers Ass'n v. Hudnut, No. 84–3147 (7th Cir. filed Apr. 8, 1985).

14. Robin L. West, *The Difference in Women's Hedonic Lives: A Phenomenological Critique of Feminist Legal Theory*, 3 Wis. Women's L. J. 81, 115–16 (1987) (emphasis in original) (footnotes omitted) (*Wisconsin Women's Law Journal* incorrectly substituted "experimental" for "experiential." Conversation with Robin West, March 9, 1988).

15. *Id.* at 142.

16. Leonard Swidler, *Interreligious and Interideological Dialogue: The Matrix for All Systematic Reflection Today*, in Toward a Universal Theology of Religion 6 (Leonard Swidler ed. 1987).

17. *Id.* at 10.

18. bell hooks, Feminist Theory: from margin to center 161 (1984).

19. Thomas Merton, New Seeds of Contemplation 2 (1961).

20. Thomas Merton, Zen and the Birds of Appetite 6 (1968).

21. Rita Gross, *Feminism From the Perspective of Buddhist Practice*, in Feminism and Buddhist Practice 78 (1981).

22. *Id.* at 78.

23. *Id.* at 78–79.

24. *See* MacKinnon, *supra* note 3, at 8.

25. Irving Singer, 3 The Nature of Love 332 (1987).

26. *See, e.g.*, Craig Owen, *Outlaws: Gay Men in Feminism*, in Men in Feminism 219 (Alice Jardine & Paul Smith eds. 1987); Beyond Patriarchy: Essays by Men on Pleasure, Power, and Change 81–194 (Michael Kaufman ed. 1987).

27. Rita Gross, *Feminism from the Perspective of Buddhist Practice* in Feminism and Buddhist Practice 75 (1981).

28. *See* Dick Westley, Morality and Its Beyond 182 (1984).

29. *Id.* at 227.

30. Catharine MacKinnon, *Feminism, Marxism, Method, and the State: An Agenda For Theory* in Feminist Theory: A Critique of Ideology 1, 23–24 (Nanner O. Keohane, Michelle Z. Rosaldo & Barbara C. Gelpi eds. 1982).

31. Martha Minow, *Foreword: Justice Engendered*, 101 Harv. L. Rev. 10, 38–45 (1987).

32. *Id.* at 76.

33. *Id.* at 95.

34. *Id.* at 77.

PART TWO

Women's Voices

CHAPTER THREE

Testimonials

The poverty of Love is when
the people are feeling hopeless
& their anger comes to live
like a bore worm in the apple of their eye.[1]

In chapters 1 and 2, I discussed the theological aspirations of love, compassion, and wisdom, and also the feminist critiques of the problems of consciousness and objectification. In this chapter, I will develop these critiques and aspirations more fully through literature about women's lives. I will explore testimonial or experiential literature that can give us more insight into how women make reproductive health decisions and what choices really exist in their lives. I will show that many women do not experience the preconditions in their lives for real dialogue and choice due to a coercive social environment. From this literature, I will try to suggest what steps we might take to make it more likely that women validate rather than regret their reproductive health decisions. If these steps would be successful, then we could be helping women better achieve the aspirations of love, compassion, and wisdom, which for too many women are not presently attainable.

I will provide testimonials of women making decisions concerning sexual activity, use of birth control, maintaining a pregnancy, and terminating a pregnancy. Two very inconsistent stories of women's experiences with abortion exist in the experiential literature. Most books usually discuss the so-called pro-life views or the so-called pro-choice views; rarely do authors discuss both literatures. Because of my interest in encouraging dialogue, as well as in helping us learn how to evaluate the authenticity of women's voices, I will include both voices in this chapter. In the next chapter, I will pursue these same subjects through empirical literature.

I. SEXUAL ACTIVITY

In order for women to be able to choose to use birth control or convince their male partner to use birth control, they must have control over the scope of their sexual activity. For teenagers especially, who may not have immediate access to birth control, it is paramount that they have the opportunity to say no to unwanted sexual activity. Unfortunately, the pressures for female adolescents to have sexual activity are enormous, with many people not always comprehending the sexual coercion in their lives. Although most of the testimonials that I will recite come from social-science interviews, legal cases can provide excellent testimonials. An excellent example of this invisible sexual coercion can be found in the Supreme Court case *Michael M. v. Superior Court of Sonoma County*, 450 U.S. 464 (1980).

The issue in the *Michael M.* case was the constitutionality of California's statutory rape law which automatically made it a crime for a male to have sex with a female under the age of 18 irrespective of whether the female consented to the sexual activity. The plaintiff, Michael M., an 18-year-old male had been convicted of having sexual intercourse with a female, Sharon, who was 17. Not surprisingly, the conservatives on the court overlooked the sexual coercion that was evident in the case. Unfortunately, even Justice Blackmun, the liberal on the Court who authored the *Roe v. Wade* decision and a person who prides himself on his sensitivity to women's issues, missed the sexual coercion that was evident in the case, even though he described it in his concurring opinion. He described the female victim, Sharon, as a willing participant who encouraged the sexual activity; thus, he concluded that it was an "unattractive" case to prosecute as a felony. At most, he suggested that the case should be prosecuted as a misdemeanor. In support of his contentions, he offered the following excerpt from the trial transcript:

Q. What happened at the railroad tracks?
A. We were drinking at the railroad tracks and we walked over to this bush and he started kissing me and stuff, and I was kissing him back, too, at first. Then, I was telling him to stop—
Q. Yes
A.—and I was telling him to slow down and stop. He said, 'Okay, okay.' But then he just kept doing it. He just kept doing it and then my sister and two other guys came over to where we were and my sister said—told me to get up and come home. And then I didn't—
Q. Yes
A.—and then my sister and—
Q. All right.
A.—David, one of the boys that were there, started walking home and we stayed there and then later—
Q. All right.
A.—Bruce left Michael, you know.
The Court: Michael being the defendant?
The Witness: Yeah. We was laying there and we were kissing each other, and then he asked me if I wanted to walk him over to the park; so we walked over to the park and we sat down on a bench and then he started kissing me again and we were laying on the bench. And he told me to take my pants off.

    I said, 'No,' and I was trying to get up and he hit me back down on the bench and then I just said to myself, 'Forget it,' and I let him do what he wanted to do and he took my pants off and he was telling me to put my legs around him and stuff—

Q. Did you have sexual intercourse with the defendant?

A. Yeah.

Q. He did put his penis into your vagina?

A. Yes.

Q. You said that he hit you?

A. Yeah.

Q. How did he hit you?

A. He slugged me in the face.

Q. With what did he slug you?

A. His fist.

Q. Where abouts in the face?

A. On my chin.

Q. As a result of that, did you have any bruises or any kind of an injury?

A. Yeah.

Q. What happened?

A. I had bruises.

The Court: Did he hit you one time or did he hit you more than once?

The Witness: He hit me about two or three times.[2]

The behavior and reaction that Sharon describes is strikingly similar to the behavior of other women, whom I will quote below, who were not able to persuade their partners to use condoms. (Of course, it is highly unlikely that Sharon was having protected or safe sex.) In the case of coerced sexual activity or choice of birth control, we see women try to communicate their desires but be unable to achieve any effective communication. Eventually, they often give up and relent to unwanted activity—unprotected sexual intercourse. They risk an unwanted pregnancy as well as HIV transmission.

The *Michael M.* case is a poignant reminder of how little control adolescent females often have of the conditions under which they engage in sexual activity. They are not legally entitled to have *any* sexual activity. Moreover, they lack the social power to effectuate their real desires. The California statutory rape statute, which was challenged by the male plaintiff, tried to coerce women into having no sexual activity while they were under the age of 18 irrespective of their desires or use of birth control. The Court's decision in upholding the statutory rape statute purported to "protect" female teenagers from pregnancy without inquiring into whether these women desire sexual activity or pregnancy. Justice Blackmun was the only member of the Court who purported to consider women's experiences, but he entirely misunderstood the experience that was put before him. Rather than observe the blatant coercion present in this case where Sharon did not have the power to make no mean no, Justice Blackmun blamed her for her participation in unwanted sexual activity. Unfortunately, the *Michael M.* case is typical of courts' and legislatures' response to teenage pregnancy; they assume that they know what teenagers need or want without really listening to them or trying to empower them.

It is an unavoidable fact that male and female teenagers will engage in sexual activity. The important question from a feminist perspective is how to make that sexual activity mutually chosen rather than coercive. Cases like *Michael M.* perpetuate women's lack of control over the conditions under which they have sexual activity without inquiring as to what women really want.

II. CONTRACEPTION DECISIONS

The abortion decision would rarely arise if women were able to control whether they had sex and whether birth control were used during sexual activity. Research concerning condom use, which has been instigated as a result of the AIDS crisis, provides excellent evidence of how little control women have over use of contraception, especially when contraception use requires dialogue with their male partner. Decisions about condom use determine not only whether women's lives will possibly be transformed by childbirth but also may determine whether women, their sexual partners, and their children have the opportunity to live at all.

Recent studies of women and condom use have demonstrated that dialogue (or a lack of dialogue) plays an extremely important role in contraceptive choices. Since women cannot directly use condoms, they can only facilitate the use of condoms by their male partner through dialogue. Recent studies, however, have consistently shown that dialogue is often not available to women due to society's views concerning sex as well as women's gendered roles in sexual relationships.

Women's lack of power to convince their male sexual partner to use condoms is exemplified in the following exchange by Dorothy, a woman who recently realized that her partner used IV drugs. Through public education efforts about HIV transmission, she had begun to take the HIV problem seriously but was, nonetheless, unable to convince her partner to use condoms. This is her explanation of her situation:

> I started two days hintin' upon it, you know. First I started playing around with it, you know. You know, little tricky questions, "How do you feel about this?" "Let's play a little game one night," you know, which I thought it was goin' to work with him, you know. I didn't want to just throw it at him, you know. You play around with it first, you know. . . . But he didn't go for that (laugh) . . . because, like I say, most men the first thing they think is that "you feel like I'm out here messing around." . . . He said, "Why should I be careful and you know you're the only person that I'm messing around with?"[3]

In fact, Dorothy knew that he was having sex with other women and maybe sharing needles with them. Yet, she did not push condom use, "because he knows that I don't trust him and it's like bringing back up the past, you know. Lashing out at it."[4] Dorothy's desire to maintain a relationship with her male partner was, in part, a desire to maintain a relationship with the father of her three children. Although she was not economically dependent on him, she wanted to maintain a relationship with him. If suggesting condom use did not have so many negative connotations for her male partner, she would not be faced with such a difficult choice.

In another interview, the negative connotations associated with condom use also prevented a woman from insisting that her male partner use condoms. This woman, Stella, was a sex worker who also had a regular male partner. She and her male partner also used a wide variety of drugs. She frequently used condoms in her *professional sex* but did not use them in her *personal sex*. She explains her choice in this way: "With tricks they are OK. I mean they are good. But for my man, no. He better not throw one on. . . . He ain't supposed to be screwing nobody but me."[5] Her interviewers concluded that she felt an emotional need to keep a domain for sexual intimacy that was marked by an absence of condom use. For her, the lack of use of condoms in her personal life was a way of being in control. It forced her male partner to trust her and for her to be sure that he was being faithful to her. Such a sexual tactic would be unnecessary in a relationship built on more trust. If real dialogue, respect, and trust existed in her relationship with her male partner, then a dangerous sexual tactic concerning lack of condom use would not be necessary.

An inability to communicate about condom use seems to be particularly a problem for adolescent women. One pregnant teenager, in a study of African-American women, described the inconsistency of her partners' condom use:

> You can't never put a man on a pedestal. I mean, some of 'em, they keep they stuff, they little dirty work down so deep, so good. And I can't, you know, I got a lot of faith in him but you know I'll be confused 'cause sometimes I'll ask him to wear one 'cause you know I'll just be goin' through the trip. . . . I'm kinda like torn between it like, 'cause I got [gonorrhea] now. But you know, sometimes I do it with and sometimes I don't. But the majority of the time I'll be havin' unprotected sex.[6]

Older women apparently reported more power to communicate sexually. For example, an older woman in the same study noted:

> I would say for most, almost exclusively, of the years that I was sexually active, I more or less would just go along. I always felt cheated. The last couple of years, the person I'm with now, I talk about up, down, in and out, everything. So, it's not a problem. And I have noticed a big change when you can do that. Especially when they respond and start satisfying you.[7]

Although that woman expressed an increased ability to communicate with her male partner about sex, other women in the study of African-American women reported that such communication was becoming increasingly difficult. For example, one woman reported:

> I think respect that used to exist for black women, to a large extent, does not exist anymore. I think that the fact that there are clearly more women than there are men and therefore they have more choices . . . the fact that black women

who are doing well educationally and professionally. I think that's hurt their relationships. It's just a reality and it hurts. And then you have whole element of black men who are cut out by alcohol, drugs and the jails. There's just so much.[8]

From these and other interviews with African-American women, the authors of the study concluded:

> [W]omen—and men—are acting/reacting in a context of community disintegration, in which men have been empowered to have greater sexual freedom, but women have lost ground in their ability to insist on protection from infection. . . . AIDS prevention [requires] . . . a means of communicating that will empower women to negotiate with men how, and under what circumstances, sexual activity (and relationships) will be conducted. . . . At the heart of such prevention is the development of explicit communication, free of jargon and ambivalence, set in a context in which black women are again restored to a position of respect.[9]

Interviews with these and other women have convinced AIDS educators that they need to train women to have negotiating skills so that they can protect themselves, their children, and their sexual partners. These training sessions are often built on techniques used in consciousness-raising groups. For women, dialogue is often synonymous with empowerment. Dialogue does not exist in a vacuum. It exists in a community environment in which women must be treated with sufficient respect such that their needs and desires are taken seriously. As one group of authors has noted, the challenge is not to develop the correct message; instead, the challenge is to use "social organization to intervene, to recreate human contact in the face of community disintegration."[10] Without the existence of the prerequisites of dialogue—love, compassion, and respect—no true dialogue concerning contraception will be possible to save the lives of women, their children, and their sexual partners.

Counselling, however, can only be effective in an environment where women have an interest in avoiding HIV infection or postponing pregnancy. Stella, quoted above, did not describe the environment in which she made contraceptive decisions. If she had done so, she probably would have described it as follows:

> In some urban poor communities . . . sexual activity begins as young as age 11 or 12 for girls and a few years older for boys. The role of sex in these children's lives is neither an erotic expression nor a response to romantic love, but rather a happening—a part of the "warm body syndrome" or the search for comfort. For many urban poor there is neither privacy nor time for loving sexual encounters and many of those which lead to pregnancy (and perhaps to HIV transmission) occur in hallways with both partners fully dressed. . . .
>
> . . . These conditions, in short, offer fertile ground for the spread of HIV infection. In such settings, women's risks—of abuse, violence, loss of housing,

illness, discrimination—are daily fare. To them, AIDS is just another, and less immediate, risk.[11]

With those social conditions in mind, it is easy to understand why some women who are HIV infected and have received counselling choose to bear children who risk being HIV infected. As two coauthors have noted:

> In their view, having babies may be not just a defensible moral choice; it may be the most reasonable and available choice, a natural outcome of all the forces in their lives, in which avenues for self-definition and expression other than mothering are largely absent. . . . In the reality of the 1990s, disease and deprivation frame the existence of many poor women.[12]

If we want poor women to make choices which might benefit the larger community then society needs to make choices which benefit poor communities. Society's failure to provide decent housing, nourishment, and healthcare to all of its citizens may seem as unreasonable to poor people as poor people's failure to use condoms may seem to middle-class people. Women need to be offered options for self-esteem and achievement that are not based on reproduction alone. Society needs to respect the lives of poor women by giving them real options to escape the cycle of poverty. When society offers poor women such respect then society can expect to receive respect in return.

Rather than respecting the lives and reproductive choices of poor women, society is presently moving in the opposite direction. The most recent evidence concerns the Norplant controversy. Poor women who are found guilty of child abuse or drug abuse are frequently being given the choice of a lengthy prison term or implantation of Norplant. These women need counselling and treatment. Rather than provide them with genuine assistance, we provide them with coercive contraception, which does not alleviate the basic, underlying problem, or we throw them in prison where they will receive no treatment at all (and might get pregnant). Middle-class white women and men, by contrast, rarely receive such coercive treatment. Unfortunately, however, middle-class white women and men are as likely to abuse children as are poor women. But it is unthinkable to treat middle-class people with the coercion that is basic to the lives of poor people.

Put somewhat differently, the values that poor women embrace are the values found in our society. Society tells them that their lives are not valuable, not worthy of respect, by failing to provide them with the basic prerequisites of humanity, such as food, clothing, and shelter. When poor people also act in ways consistent with those majoritarian values by not valuing the length of their lives, we should not be surprised or look to poor people to change. We need to change the social fabric in which we all live, in which we all fail to value life and choice for poor people.

When we talk about reproductive choices in the lives of poor, urban women, we are truly challenging our aspirations for ourselves and society. What would it mean for poor people's lives to be filled with love, compassion, and wisdom? How could their sexual activity be erotic rather than instrumental? How could their lives be filled with sufficient respect such that choices became meaningful? Rather than talk about reproductive health issues in a moral vacuum, it is crucial that we discuss these issues with the context of these women's lives clearly in mind.

III. MAINTAINING A PREGNANCY

In discussing reproductive health issues, it is important to remember that many women desire to carry their fetuses to term but are unable to do so due to coerciveness in their environment. Although the state frequently tries to coerce women to choose childbirth over abortion, it does little to facilitate the choice of childbirth for women who are not in an environment conducive to pregnancy or child rearing. A brief part of the interview with Stella captures this aspect of the coerciveness of our society. This is her story as reported by her interviewers:

> She got pregnant the first time she had sex, at the age of 12 or 13, and had an illegal abortion. She gave birth to her son, now 12, when she was 18. She got pregnant again at 26, but it was after she was raped and thus she was not sure of the father. She decided "it would be mine and I would love it period." But while she was pregnant, she tried to break up a fight between her son's father and his brother when the brother turned around and hit her in the stomach. "It was just a little bit too much." The baby was born stillborn at six months.[13]

Stella's story is a life filled with coercion. Her first pregnancy was apparently unwanted. Despite a coercive legal environment that made an abortion illegal, she procured an abortion. Her third pregnancy was the result of sexual coercion but nonetheless wanted. A hostile environment, however, caused her to have a nonviable, premature delivery. Until her life conditions make choices possible, it is difficult to conceive of her making authentic choices for herself. It is imperative that the kinds of reproductive choices that were absent from Stella's life be part of our reproductive health dialogue; the illegality of abortion was only a minor aspect of the lack of reproductive choice in her life. Chapter 8 will provide many more stories about the state's coercive treatment of women who wish to maintain their pregnancies.

IV. TERMINATING A PREGNANCY

When an unwanted pregnancy has occurred, women find themselves faced with an abortion decision. Writings by both pro-choice and pro-life advocates emphasize that dialogue is important to women making authentic abortion decisions. One modest way to assist women to engage in dialogue about their abortion decision would be to require all abortion providers to make available a free, nondirective counselling program, possibly modelled after consciousness-raising. It is impossible and fruitless to force anyone to engage in counselling; however, the availability of nondirective counselling may assist some women who are unsure of their decision or simply want someone with whom they can share their feelings. It would not be appropriate for the state to define the scope of such counselling, because the state might try to impose coercive counselling. Nevertheless, it would be reasonable for a state to insist that some free counselling be available at all licensed clinics.

Counselling is often available at abortion clinics; however, some critics claim that its focus is on crisis intervention rather than grief.[14] Idell Kesselman does an excellent job of describing the unmet need that she had for grief counselling following her abortions:

> I had an abortion when I was seventeen. It was illegal then, so my parents took me to Mexico. The memories were painful. But I never talked about them.
>
> When I was twenty-two I had an abortion, part of the ending of a marriage. It was still illegal in Arizona, so I went to California. . . .
>
> At age twenty-six a second marriage ended with my third abortion. It was now legal in Arizona, so I didn't have to run away. It was neat, clean, and fast. I woke from the anaesthetic sobbing. The nurse, trying to comfort me, repeated, "It's all right, dear. It's over. It's all over." I knew—that's why I cried. But I didn't talk about it.
>
> The American Psychological Association announced recently that "most women who have abortions experience a sense of relief," rather than "any lasting psychological trauma." I felt that relief—every time.
>
> I got on with my life, as everyone around me advised. . . .
>
> . . . That's how I did it—alone—for over twenty years. But my grief was so secret that I didn't even know it was there. Years passed; without my knowing it, little corners of pain melted and squirmed and squeezed out in my dreams. I didn't know what they meant, but I wrote them down for a short story I'd write someday.
>
> . . .
>
> . . . For so many years—I resisted—thinking about the abortions. It always hurt too much. After the first one, I would count years by their ages. I'd imagine how old each child would have been that year. After the second, after the third, it became too difficult to carry their ages. I knew it was a hurting thing to do. I accepted the abortions as done, as choices, awful choices, between fire and ice, between rocks and hard places. . . .
>
> . . .
>
> . . . I didn't have three abortions because I was a bad girl, but simply a hurting girl, alone and denying a part of myself I could not accept. No one told me that a woman, a girl, who chooses to end a pregnancy has the right to mourn. I thought that since I had *chosen* abortion, I had given up that right.[15]

Both pro-choice and pro-life advocates have also commented on the importance of women experiencing *inner peace* in order to make authentic abortion decisions. For example, David Reardon, a pro-life advocate, provides many stories of women who were at a very troubled period in their life when they had an abortion. It was only after their life became more stable and peaceful that they came to feel that they better understood what would have been the correct abortion decision for them. Reardon assumes that the only correct decision during a period of inner peace would be to bear the child rather than have an abortion. We can be skeptical of that conclusion yet learn from his observation that women feel best able to make authentic decisions when their lives are relatively peaceful.

Nancyjo Mann's story, which is excerpted in Reardon's book, particularly demonstrates how peacefulness can connect to authenticity:

> About nine months after leaving the hospital, I finally started to face the abortion I had tried so hard to bury. It was a very, very painful process. The wounds of abortion run deep, especially when they have been pushed down for so long. I nearly went through an emotional breakdown. I had to relive it all, to sort it all out. But this time the Lord was with me offering support and forgiveness. Step by step we went. But He was patient. It took three years, but finally I was able to forgive myself. That's the hardest part. God's forgiveness is ready and waiting. It's forgiving yourself that's hard.
>
> By 1981, I had not only found peace with my abortion experience but felt drawn to help other women to overcome their pain and hurt. I knew that if I had hurt so much, surely there must be at least one other woman who felt the same. In early 1982 I founded Women Exploited by Abortion (WEBA) to minister to the needs of aborted women, to help them heal their pains.[16]

Although Reardon predominantly describes women who came to regret their abortion decision, he does describe a small group of women who he perceives not to be troubled or harmed by the decision to have an abortion. He describes those women in quite unflattering terms (self-centered, aggressive, highly privileged) and dismisses the significance of the possibility that their lives might be enhanced by having an abortion.[17]

Thus, his evidence suggests that women may come to regret or *validate* their previous abortion decision when their lives become more peaceful. Nevertheless, he manages to disparage all the women who validate their decision to have an abortion. Interestingly, these women also seem to be the most feminist women who are described in the book in that they place value on their lives, as well as on the fetus. Hence, Reardon's book seems to suggest that feminism can never be an authentic political perspective—a troubling, although not surprising, implication. As Simone de Beauvoir pointed out, it is hard to explain why any women would be feminists. Reardon's subliminal message that women should not validate their own lives when making an abortion decision is part of the social consciousness that contributes to women not valuing their own lives. Reardon's critique of women who validate their abortion experiences is gratuitous in the larger context of his book. He could have made the point that many women come to regret their abortion experience without criticizing those women who do not come to regret their abortion experience. His critique, however, brings to surface his coercive message—that he wants women to make abortion decisions in a context in which they do not value their own lives.

Despite Reardon's claim that the women who regret their abortion decision ultimately found inner peace, I found myself skeptical of both decisions made by these women, because neither decision seemed very reflective. Their first decision (to have an abortion) was often made under conditions of coercion; their later decision (to regret having had an abortion) was often made after a religious conversion. In both cases, they appeared to turn to a dominating culture or an Other for an answer—a parent, boyfriend, social worker, or later, the church. I found myself wondering when these women would decide for themselves which decision would best contribute to their and society's well-being. They often changed their mind, because the dominant social message in their environment changed, not necessarily because their lives became more reflective. There is, therefore, no evidence that they moved toward their aspirations for their authentic self, despite Reardon's portrayal of their inner peace.

Pro-choice advocate Lynn Paltrow also agrees that women find inner peace when they make authentic abortion decisions. In her stories, women's increased peacefulness was able to validate their prior abortion decisions. These women, like the women described by Reardon, may have struggled with the abortion issue and only knew with hindsight, when their lives were more peaceful, that they had made the correct abortion decision. Rather than disparage these women's values, Paltrow affirms them. Here is one story from Paltrow's brief:

> Having an abortion seemed to be the most thoughtful and loving decision we could make, in fact, it seemed to be the only decision we could make which would still maintain our life goals and plans in helping serve others as we had hoped. I was a Christian then, as I am now, and constant prayer asking for guidance through peace is how I was able to feel that God guided me toward that decision, also. Since the abortion in 1977, I have helped hundreds of emotionally disturbed children, counseled twice as many parents about the loving ways of parenting, become known as the expert in the field of counseling children and families traumatized by sexual abuse, and in 1979 I married a Pediatrician who has been a wonderful husband and father to our four year old boy and our seven month old boy in utero (due in August). God has given me many blessings and much peace since 1977.[18]

Many of the women described in Reardon's book and Paltrow's brief were not able to reach an abortion decision in a reflective environment; they were coerced by a husband who did not want to help raise a child or a Catholic family that would not permit consideration of an abortion. Irrespective of what decision a woman ultimately comes to concerning abortion, it appears that she moves closer to the aspiration of wisdom if she can make the decision in a peaceful environment that facilitates reflection.

The issue then becomes what social conditions can facilitate a considered rather than coerced judgment. Paltrow suggests that women will make more authentic judgments in a social system in which there are few restrictions on abortion, because their lives will be subject to less coercion. Reardon suggests that women will make more authentic judgments in an environment in which physicians cannot be compensated for performing abortions, because the physician will not have an incentive to provide proabortion misinformation. They both agree that we need to think about solving the problem of consciousness in the context of political-social arrangements. We need to find ways to alleviate the coercion present in women's lives so that they can find the peacefulness to make authentic decisions.

Returning to my earlier suggestion that counselling be available at all abortion clinics, we can now see more potential problems with that requirement. The availability of that counselling might contribute to a coercive social message that women should be troubled by the decision to have an abortion but not be troubled by the decision to bear children.

A story may reinforce this point. When I was in law school, a classmate of mine decided to get sterilized. She was in her late 20s. She had been married and divorced, and she had chosen not to have children when she was married. She decided that she did not want to bear children or risk an unwanted pregnancy. Sterilization seemed the best alternative. The university physician refused to allow her to be sterilized unless she agreed to go to several sessions with a psychiatrist. She went to those sessions unwillingly and was eventually sterilized. By contrast, if she had gone to the same physician requesting that an IUD be removed (so that she could get pregnant), he would not have required her to see a psychiatrist. Nevertheless, a decision either to be sterilized or to bear a baby is essentially irreversible; it affects the woman for much of her lifetime. The actions of the physician and the psychiatrist reflected the dominant social message—that a healthy (white) woman should want to bear a child. I, therefore, do not want to contribute to the social message which suggests that only women who are considering whether to have an abortion should undergo group consciousness-raising.

Thus, it would seem to be necessary to require that free, nondirective pregnancy-counselling should be available at all health facilities that offer reproductive services. In addition, sex-education classes should provide the space for young women to discuss reproductive issues openly and freely. Rather than offer nondirective sex education, United States schools typically offer little or no information about reproductive health issues. In addition, current administration policy (which Congress is trying to overturn) refuses to permit publicly funded family-planning clinics from even *discussing* the possibility of terminating a pregnancy through abortion. Existing counselling is therefore quite directive rather than open.

As compared with other Western countries, the United States offers very ineffectual sex education. In 1978, Congress passed the Adolescent Health Services and Pregnancy Prevention and Care Act,[19] which promoted the distribution of contraceptives and abortion counseling or referral. In 1981, Congress folded the Adolescent Health Services and Pregnancy Prevention and Care Act into the Maternal and Child Health block grant to the states, and it enacted the AFLA (Adolescent Family Life Act). The AFLA is fundamentally different from the 1978 adolescent-pregnancy-prevention act in that it supports chastity and adoption, but not contraception or abortion. Although the 1978 act required grantees to offer counselling and referral about abortion, the 1981 act forbids such counselling or referral. Thus, rather than offer nondirective counselling, which might encourage dialogue, the 1981 act supports the unrealistic message of chastity and adoption.

The rationale behind this approach seems to be the assumption that sex education and the availability of contraceptives and abortions promotes sexual behavior and unintended pregnancies.[20] The message of abstinence is considered to be the most effective way to limit teenage sexual activity, and thus unintended pregnancies. However, empirical surveys suggest the opposite. Studies of teenage pregnancy in developed countries show that countries with more liberal attitudes about talking about sex have the lowest birthrates.[21] In addition, one study found that exposure to contraceptive education had no consistent effect on the probability that a woman, who had not previously experienced intercourse, would subsequently initiate intercourse.[22] A study of predominantly poor, inner-city African-American adolescents in Baltimore found that a program which combined sex education, counselling, and contraceptive services—with an emphasis on the development of personal responsibility, goal setting, and communication with parents—reduced pregnancy rates substantially and contributed to delaying the onset of sexual activity.[23] Thus, increased sex education may actually delay the onset of sexual activity as well as reduce the pregnancy rate. Most importantly, such sex education helps young women make responsible reproductive health decisions that they will later validate rather than regret.

Even when sex education does exist, it is often not adequate or effective. For example, one study found that of those adolescents who did have sex education, 34% could not correctly identify the time during the menstrual cycle when conception is most likely to occur. In addition, of the sex education that is provided in the schools, 90% of it occurs after ninth grade, despite evidence that adolescents initiate sexual activity in their early teens.[24] Thus, it is not sufficient for sex education to exist; it must be more comprehensive both in its intensive coverage of topics as well as in its audience.

United States policy on family planning, as compared to other developed countries, differs in one important respect. In the United States, policy analysts are not sure whether they should be preventing teenage sexual activity or unwanted teenage pregnancy. In other developed countries, national policy is squarely behind preventing unwanted teenage pregnancy irrespective of the prevalence of sexual activity among adolescents.[25] Thus, easily accessible and relatively free contraceptives, which are made available in most developed countries and which substantially help to lower the rate of unintended teenage pregnancy, is not part of the United States' national family-planning policy. Due to a lack of sex education or public discussion about contraception, adolescents are more likely to hear about abortion than about how to prevent pregnancy through contraception.[26] As one group of commentators has observed, United States adolescents "seem to have inherited the worst of all possible worlds regarding their exposure to messages about sex."[27] If we really respected the lives of adolescents, then we would want them to have access to an environment where they can discuss their reproductive lives openly and freely. Instead, we ineffectively try to coerce them by making available a limited range of reproductive options. As I will discuss in the next chapter, this coercion has devastating effects on their lives.

Even when decent sex education does exist, however, we have not done nearly enough to assist women to value their own lives. We need to create a society in which women like Dorothy or Stella have the incentive to care about their and their family's well-being. We need to change the conditions of their lives before education can be effective. A holistic approach that tries to improve the conditions of women's lives must be a part of any education or counselling program.

Notes

1. Judy Grahn, The Work of a Common Woman: The Collected Poetry of Judy Grahn 1964–1977, 150 (1978).

2. Michael M. v. Sonoma County Superior Court, 450 U.S. 464, 484–85* (Blackmun, J., concurring in judgment).

3. Stephanie Kane, AIDS, Addiction and Condom Use: Sources of Sexual Risk for Heterosexual Women, 27 J. of Sex Research 427, 440 (1990).

4. Id.

5. Id. at 437.

6. Mindy Thompson Fullilove, Robert E. Fullilove, Katherine Haynes & Shirley Gross, Black Women and AIDS Prevention: Understanding the Gender Rules, 27 J. of Sex Research 47, 57 (1990).

7. Id. at 58.

8. Id. at 60.

9. Id. at 62.

10. Id. at 63.

11. Carol Levine & Nancy Neveloff Dubler, Uncertain Risks and Bitter Realities: The Reproductive Choices of HIV-Infected Women, 68 The Millbank Quarterly 321, 330–31 (1990).

12. Id. at 323.

13. See Kane supra note 3, at 434–35.

14. Idell Kesselman, Grief and Loss: Issues for Abortion, 21 Omega: Journal of Death and Dying 241, 246 (1990).

15. Id. at 241–47.

16. David Reardon, Aborted Women: Silent No More xxii (1987).

17. Id. at 138–41.

18. Lynn Paltrow, Amicus Brief: Richard Thornburgh v. American College of Obstetricians and Gynecologists, 9 Women's Rts. L. Rep. 3, 22 (1986).

19. Patricia Donovan, The Adolescent Family Life Act and the Promotion of Religious Doctrine, 16 Family Planning Perspectives 222 (1984).

20. In the only legal argument that I have been able to find which defends this program, the author does not explain the rationale behind this policy choice. He simply repeatedly asserts that the government is entitled to choose childbirth over abortion, without explaining why that choice would be prudent for teenagers. Theodore C. Hirt, Commentaries: Why the Government is Not Required to Subsidize Abortion Counseling and Referral, 101 Harv. L. Rev.

1985 (1988) (author was the Assistant Branch Director in the Federal Programs Branch of the Civil Division of the Department of Justice).

21. Elise Jones, Jacqueline Darroch Forrest, Noreen Goldman, Stanley Henshaw, Richard Lincoln, Leannie Rosoff, Charles Westoff & Deirdre Wulf, *Teenage Pregnancy in Developed Countries: Determinants and Policy Implications*, 17 Family Planning Perspectives 53, 54 (1985) [hereafter *Teenage Pregnancy*].

22. James Trussell, *Teenage Pregnancy in the United States*, 20 Family Planning Perspectives 262, 267 (1988).

23. *Id.* at 267. However, Trussell cautions the reader that the delay in intercourse was mitigated by other factors, so that one needs to read that result with caution.

24. *See* Trussell, *supra* note 22, at 267.

25. *Teenage Pregnancy*, *supra* note 21, at 61.

26. *Id.* at 61.

27. *Id.* at 61.

CHAPTER FOUR

Empirical Data

> [N]o single individual scientist, scholar, or theo-
> rizer can produce the "whole truth" about a
> given phenomenon. . . . Together we illumi-
> nate many different facets, all varied aspects of
> the "truth." It is through this plurality of
> shared views and voices that we come to some
> understanding of nature, society, and ourselves.[1]

I. INTRODUCTION

In this chapter, I will explore empirical literature that can give us more insight into the scope of coercion that women face in their reproductive lives. This empirical literature will be drawn from the reproductive health literature on pregnant adolescents, because, in my opinion, adolescents face some of the most coercive conditions in our society with respect to reproductive health issues. From this literature, I will try to suggest what compassionate steps we might take to remove some of the coercion from women's lives, thereby helping them better achieve the aspiration of love. In later chapters, I will tie some of this discussion to our legal treatment of the abortion issue.

In the preceding chapter, I discussed how women might make authentic reproductive health decisions. Unfortunately, many women face unintended pregnancies. These pregnancies, which can be a result of coercive social conditions, have enormous consequences in their lives as well as the lives of their children. In this chapter, I will use empirical literature to describe the scope of the problem of unintended pregnancies and the consequences of these pregnancies for women and children.

Both experiential and empirical literatures serve important purposes. Experiential literature can describe the emotional impact of women's lives; empirical literature can give us a fuller picture of the factors that lead to certain social conditions. One problem with much of the experiential literature is that it may give the reader a false sense that race is an important variable predicting the coercion in women's lives. An examination of the empirical literature, however, demonstrates that class rather than race is often the more predictive variable. Middle-class African-American women are often situated more analogously to middle-class Caucasian women than to poor African-American women with respect to reproductive health issues. It is important to remember, however, that it is clearly women who are facing the dramatic consequences of our reproductive health policies. We must not lose sight of the gender issue as we come also to see the race and class issues presented by this data.

Before turning to the empirical literature, I need to describe the reproductive health and anti-essentialist perspectives that I will bring to this data. Gender essentialism is "the notion that a unitary, 'essential' women's experience can be isolated and described independently of race, class, sexual orientation, and other realities of experience."[2] It is exemplified in the work of many feminist academics,[3] who, when they are allegedly talking about an issue's impact on *women*, have, in fact, been talking about its impact on white, middle-class women.[4] Through footnotes or parentheticals, they have often noted the impact on poor, adolescent, women of color. An anti-essentialist perspective, however, points out that the parentheticals and footnotes only made it clear that women, unmodified, in fact, meant white, middle-class, able-bodied, heterosexual, adult women. As Angela Harris has noted, this tendency did not make all feminists who wrote from an essentialist perspective "racist."[5] Their awareness that they needed to observe the impact of policies specifically on women of color, for example, was based on an appropriate race-conscious sensitivity. Nevertheless, their general discussions of women with parentheticals concerning African-American or Hispanic women did not go far enough toward race-conscious sensitivity. An anti-essentialist perspective would encourage them to be more inclusive in their descriptions of women.

The anti-essentialism critique is not directed only at feminist academics. Many academic and political discussions of various issues suffer from the problem of essentialism. For example, the abortion debate, as reflected in both pro-choice and pro-life writings, has often been overly superficial and general in its description of how women are affected by various reproductive choices,[6] thereby suffering from a problem of essentialism. The variables of race, age, sexual orientation, handicap, religion, and social class affect how various reproductive decisions influence women's lives. Nevertheless, the abortion debate tends to focus on all women as if they are a monolithic category. Recently, it has become fashionable to discuss the *problem of teenage pregnancy*, but even this more focused discussion is unsatisfactory because it fails to reflect that pregnancy does not affect all teenagers in the same way. Finally, the popularity of the abortion debate is a reflection of the problem of essentialism because this debate chooses one issue for debate—abortion—and generally ignores the larger and more complex problems relating to reproductive health issues, of which abortion is only one part.

One source for helping us move beyond the problem of essentialism in the abortion debate is the empirical literature on reproductive health issues that concern adolescents ranging from contraception to postnatal care. Because of the rigorous nature of this literature and the broad scope of the range of its considerations, it can help us break down some of the universalist categories about women that are prevalent in abortion and pregnancy-related discussions. I will therefore now turn to explaining what I mean by a *reproductive health perspective* and how it can help us to understand better the phenomenon of adolescent pregnancy and abortion.[7]

A reproductive health perspective considers the full consequences of a woman's reproductive capacity and sexual behavior. "Reproductive health is a condition in which the reproductive process is accomplished in a state of complete physical, mental and social well-being and is not merely the absence of disease or disorders of the reproductive process."[8] In other words, a reproductive health perspective considers the nature of sexual activity (e.g., whether it is consensual), the use and availability of contraceptives, the availability of prenatal and postnatal care, the socioeconomic and physical consequences of motherhood, the socioeconomic status and physical health of the child that is born, and the availability of adoption, as well as the availability and consequences of abortion, in discussing women's reproductive lives.

The abortion debate has not represented a reproductive health perspective. In the cases and literature, it often sounds like women find themselves pregnant without ever having engaged in sexual behavior or used contraceptives.[9] Moreover, the consequences of carrying a fetus to term or aborting it seem largely absent from the debate.[10] This ignorance of the larger socioeconomic circumstances is a problem with both the pro-choice and anti-abortion scholarship. For example, in *Hodgson v. Minnesota*,[11] a case involving the constitutionality of a two-parent notification requirement for adolescents, both the Justices in the majority and those in the dissent ignore the socioeconomic conditions under which adolescents find themselves pregnant including, for example, coercive sexual experiences and inaccessible contraceptives. The primary focus of all of the opinions is how a parental notification requirement affects the existing family unit—parents and pregnant teenager—and largely fails to consider how such a requirement affects the pregnant teenager's life, as well as the lives of her future offspring and family unit.[12]

In addition, the Court's decision in *Hodgson* is fundamentally flawed because it ignores the empirical literature concerning the impact of parental notification statutes in the lives of female adolescents. By relying on vague legal precedent rather than empirical facts, the Court was able to base its judgment on an inaccurate picture of family life and teenage pregnancy. It is appalling that Supreme Court decisions can be based on imagined fantasies of family life rather than on cold, empirical facts about coercion and battery and on lives destroyed by teenage pregnancy.

Nonetheless, I do not want to suggest that the reproductive health literature is unproblematic. The empirical, reproductive health literature is accustomed to placing people into categories—Hispanic, African-American, poor, female, and so forth. These categories themselves are riddled with assumptions. How do we define who is "African-American"? How poor is "poor"? In addition, this literature selects only *certain* categories to examine. For example, I was able to find substantial amounts of literature on African-American women, some literature on Hispanic women, and virtually no literature on other racial subgroups. Very little literature discusses the special problems faced by adolescent women who are handicapped, lesbian, or victims of incest. These categories then become even more important as they are used in later research, such as mine, which builds on those primary sources.

II. SCOPE OF THE PROBLEM
OF UNINTENDED PREGNANCIES

One out of every ten women 15 to 19 years old becomes pregnant each year in the United States, a proportion that has changed little in the last fifteen years.[13] It was estimated in 1981 that more than five million women 15 to 19 years old were at risk of unintended pregnancy.[14] Although half of all women who face unintended pregnancies use contraceptives, three-fourths of all unintended adolescent pregnancies occur to those who do not practice contraception.[15]

The United States teenage birthrate is much higher than that of other developed countries, with the maximum relative difference occurring for adolescents under the age of 15. Moreover, this disparity is growing.[16] Since 1973, although the proportion of wanted births has risen for women aged 25 to 39, the proportion of births that were considered "mistimed" for never-married adolescents increased by 37%.[17] Unintended childbearing is more common among unmarried African-Americans than among comparable whites (30% versus 18%) but varies little among unmarried African-American women by the mother's current age. By contrast, unwanted childbearing among single white women is almost cut in half after the age of 24. In other words, we are much more successful in preventing unwanted childbirth for adolescent white women than for adolescent African-American women. White and African-American women appear to be similarly situated after age 33 with respect to unwanted childbirth but quite dissimilarly situated under age 24.[18]

Statistics for Hispanics are often not reported separately. However, one study indicated that in 1985, about 39,000 Hispanics aged 15 to 19 obtained an abortion, for an abortion rate of 50 per 1,000 births. The abortion rate was about 32% higher than the abortion rate for whites of the same age, but almost 30% lower than that of nonwhites.[19] Hispanics aged 15 to 19 had approximately 65,000 births in 1985 for a birthrate of 85 per 1,000, which was close to the nonwhite rate of 90.[20] In other words, Hispanic women, aged 15 to 19, are about as likely as nonwhite women to give birth but less likely to have an abortion.

In 1979, 47% of white metropolitan women aged 15 to 19 were sexually active, as were 66% of comparable African-Americans.[21] Although African-American adolescents are more likely to be sexually active than white adolescents, they are also less likely to use contraceptives. Forty percent of African-American adolescents, as contrasted with 24% of whites, reported never using a contraceptive during intercourse. These statistics yield the not-surprising result that in 1979,

30% of African-American teenage women in metropolitan areas had a premarital pregnancy as compared to 14% for whites.

In understanding these statistics, however, it is important to control for social class. Within the group of African-American teenage women, for example, dramatic differences in contraceptive use exist depending upon social class. One study found that 44% of African-American teenage women who were of high social class, had intact families, and resided in a nonghetto neighborhood used a contraceptive at first intercourse, as compared with only 12% of those who were of low social class, did not have intact families, and resided in a ghetto neighborhood.[22] The statistics for these "higher class" African-American women appears to be similar to a comparable group of white women, thus demonstrating the importance of considering social class in understanding the problem of adolescent pregnancy. This finding about contraceptive use at first intercourse is very important because other studies demonstrate that those who use contraceptives at first intercourse are more consistent users thereafter.[23]

Thus, the problem of unintended pregnancies is dramatic for all groups of adolescents. Thirty percent of unmarried, African-American adolescents living in metropolitan areas face an unintended pregnancy, and 14% of similarly situated white adolescents face an unintended pregnancy. Each year, more than five million sexually active female adolescents face a possible unintended pregnancy, which is compounded by the fact that three-fourths of them are not practicing contraception. One million of them do become pregnant each year, with 470,000 giving birth to a child.[24] These statistics demonstrate that the phenomenon of large numbers of unwanted births is primarily a class-based phenomenon. In other words, poor adolescent women do not have the opportunity to choose the conditions under which they become pregnant to the same extent as middle-class women. Because the problem of unwanted pregnancies is a class-based problem, which disproportionately affects female adolescents, the expenditure of public funds targeted at adolescents could make a real difference in the lives of women. Nevertheless, as I will discuss, we have an entirely ineffective public program for limiting unwanted adolescent pregnancies. In fact, our public policy encourages childbirth over contraception or abortion, meaning that we facilitate the problem rather than solve it.

III. CONSEQUENCES OF EARLY CHILDBIRTH FOR THE MOTHER

In order to understand the magnitude of the problem of unintended pregnancies for adolescents, we need to understand the impact on the physical health of the mother, as well as the socioeconomic consequences stemming from early childbirth. Female adolescents face substantial negative consequences from early childbirth although the source of these problems may often be socioeconomic rather than age-related. Early childbirth, in itself, need not cause negative physical and socioeconomic consequences. It does, however, because the adolescents who undergo early childbirth are disproportionately poor and do not receive effective assistance from the state and others for their pregnancies and childbirth responsibilities.

A. Physical Health

Adolescent mothers between the ages of 15 and 19 are twice as likely to die from hemorrhage and miscarriage than mothers over the age of 20.[25] The maternal mortality and morbidity rate is 60% higher than for older women.[26] Adolescent mothers are 23% more likely to experience a premature birth with complications such as anemia, prolonged labor, and nutritional deficiency, and 92% more likely to experience anemia than older mothers. The risk of health problems and medical complications is even higher for African-American adolescents because of the inequitable distribution of resources in society.[27]

Socioeconomic factors, rather than age, seem to contribute substantially to adverse health consequences from teenage pregnancy.[28] In countries where adverse health consequences were not found for adolescents, they had an excellent prenatal care system.[29] Recent research in the United States has shown that many of the adverse health consequences of adolescent childbearing that were documented in earlier studies were overstated because of a lack of adequate controls for socioeconomic status.[30] Several studies suggest that pregnancy outcomes among adolescents who receive good prenatal care are no different from, or are better than, those of older women.[31] Thus, the underlying problem is one of poverty. As we shall see, our Medicaid policies do little to assist women and their children during pregnancy.

B. Education

Education is a very important variable because it correlates strongly with socioeconomic status. Since no literature that I have been able to find actually traces the relative earning power of pregnant and nonpregnant adolescents, the literature on educational attainment comes as close as possible to predicting the earning power of pregnant adolescents versus nonpregnant adolescents.

High-school graduation rates are affected markedly for women aged 21 to 29, by age at first birth. As of 1986, African-American women who delay their first birth until age 20 have a better than 92% chance of graduating from high school. By contrast, African-American women who have their first child under the age of 17 have only a 60% chance of high-school graduation, and African-American women who have their first birth at the age of 18 or 19 have only a 75% chance of high-school graduation. For white women, the statistics are comparable except that white women who have their first child under the age of 17 have only a 54% chance of high-school graduation.[32] Thus, both African-American and white women who bear children while they are under the age of 20 have a significantly greater chance of not graduating from high school than women who delay childbirth until after age 20.

Another study found that in 1983, 95% of white women, 93% of African-American women, and 87% of Hispanic women who had not borne children had received a high-school diploma or GED certificate. For African-American and white women, roughly 60% of them completed high school if they had a child within seven months after leaving school. Hispanic women, however, had only a 33% chance of completing school if they conceived a child while in high school but gave birth after leaving school, and they had a 59% chance of completing high school if they both conceived and gave birth before leaving school. The latter statistic is about ten percentage points lower than the comparable group of African-American and white women; however, the former statistic is more than twenty percentage points lower than the comparable group of African-American and white women. Thus, early childbearing has an especially dramatic influence in the educational lives of Hispanic women.

Although the impact of early childbearing may be more significant for Hispanic women than African-American or white women, it is interesting to note that Hispanic women are much less likely to bear children before leaving school than are African-American women. Nineteen percent of African-American women gave birth before leaving school in 1983, whereas only 7% of Hispanic women gave birth before leaving school. (The figure for white women was 4%.) Thus, if we decide to target African-American and Hispanic women to utilize contraception during high school so that their pregnancies will be more likely to be intentional rather than unwanted or mistimed, we are targeting them for somewhat different reasons. African-American women are at a greater risk of giving birth before leaving school whereas Hispanic women, although not as likely to give birth before leaving school, are more likely to face serious consequences when they do give birth before leaving school.

More adolescent mothers are now graduating from high school than ever before; however, graduation rates did not increase equally for all racial and socioeconomic groups, and the increases did not occur in the same periods for all groups.[33] Ironically, African-American adolescents made the greatest progress in graduating from high school, despite their pregnancy, *before* federal law made it illegal for schools receiving federal funds to expel students because of pregnancy or childbirth.[34] The statistics also make clear that race, rather than socioeconomic status, is an important predictor of high-school graduation among pregnant adolescents. For example, the increase in the graduation rate from 1975 to 1986 among white mothers from disadvantaged backgrounds was over 200%, as compared with 87% for similar African-American mothers.[35]

This evidence suggests that we need to modify our strategy for assisting adolescents to stay in school during and after their pregnancies. Federal law prohibiting pregnancy-related discrimination in education does not appear to be reaching African-American adolescents.

IV. CONSEQUENCES OF EARLY CHILDBIRTH ON THE CHILD

Children born to adolescents do not fare well. Despite the media's focus on race and age of mother affecting the child's health, socioeconomic factors seem to be the most important determinant of both prematurity and low birthweight, rather than the age of the mother itself.[36] Inadequate prenatal care has been singled out as an important determinant to health problems for the child.[37] The age of the mother seems to affect the long-term future consequences for the child more than the immediate consequences for the child. Although studies show association of socioeconomic status with neonatal, postnatal, and sudden infant death, they show association of age with the cognitive, social, and economic development of the child.[38]

The gap between the rates for African-American and white low birthweight and very low birthweight infants has been increasing in recent years. The relative risk for African-American infants, as compared with white infants, of being low birthweight increased from 2.1 times the white rate in 1975 to 2.2 times the white rate in 1985 where it has remained. The relative risk of very low birthweight babies born to African-American mothers also increased (from 2.6 times the white rate in 1975 to 2.9 times the white rate in 1987).[39] Within each high-risk subgroup (unmarried, under 20 years of age, less than 12 years of education, inadequate prenatal care) African-American mothers are generally twice as likely to have low birthweight infants and two to three times as likely to have very low birthweight infants as white women.[40] Because low birthweight is considered to be an important indicator of infant morbidity and mortality, these statistics are very disappointing. In quantitative terms, one author concluded that almost 20,000 African-American infants who died during the first year of life over the last five years would not have died had their chances for healthcare been equal to that of white infants.[41]

It is important, however, not to focus entirely on low birthweight as a problem contributing to infant mortality. Recent studies have found that normal and optimal birthweight babies born to African-American mothers have a poorer survival rate than normal and optimal birthweight babies born to white mothers.[42] Thus, even if we succeed in creating social policies which will raise the birthweight of African-American babies, we need also to create social policies that will assist these babies, after birth, when they have achieved normal or optimal birthweights.

Some studies have shown that inadequate or no prenatal care is an important factor in predicting infant mortality. For both African-American and white infants, the risk of mortality is approximately double if there is no prenatal care or if care is not obtained until the third trimester.[43] Among Hispanic infants, however, the odds of infant mortality remain quite low, regardless of when prenatal care is obtained.[44] This result is puzzling since Hispanics tend to be of low socioeconomic status; it deserves further attention.

Children born to adolescents are more likely to be involved in accidents during the first five years of life, and more likely to be admitted to a hospital because of accidents and gastrointestinal infections, than are children born to older women.[45] This relationship exists after adjustment for the effects of socioeconomic and biological factors.

One needs to be careful not to overgeneralize concerning the relationship between maternal age and the well-being of children. In one study, conducted entirely on African-American and Hispanic women who had given birth to their first children on the wards of a New York City hospital in 1975, it was found that there was no relationship between maternal age and the well-being of children.[46] This study suggests that previous studies may not have appropriately controlled for socioeconomic and racial status. If one controlled for socioeconomic and racial status, age would not be a significant factor, at least for poor Hispanic and African-American women.[47] Programs to improve reproductive health services for all poor Hispanic and African-American women might improve the well-being of children; however, there is no reason to believe that it will disproportionately improve the well-being of children born to teenage mothers.

Finally, one cannot leave the topic of children born to adolescent mothers without discussing the impact on the child of being an unwanted pregnancy. Although not all children born to adolescent mothers are unwanted, some of them clearly are. Since contraception and abortion have not been a real option for most adolescent mothers, a fair percentage of their children must result from unwanted pregnancies.

Before discussing the consequences of being the result of an unwanted pregnancy, I need to distinguish between an unintended pregnancy and an unwanted pregnancy. Not all unintended pregnancies result in unwanted pregnancies. In addition, a pregnancy that is initially unwanted may become wanted before birth. And, of course, the converse is true. An initially intended pregnancy may become unwanted as a woman's life conditions change during her pregnancy. Moreover, it is difficult to determine which pregnancies are unwanted. Even women who seek and are refused an abortion may often later deny that their pregnancy was unwanted or that they ever sought an abortion. Thus, any data on "wantedness" needs to be viewed with some degree of caution given the difficulty of the subject.

Despite the inherent problems with studying children who are the product of an unwanted pregnancy, some excellent data does exist from countries which have abortion-approval committees.[48] One of the most carefully performed studies occurred in Prague, Czechoslovakia, where the government liberalized abortion in 1957 while also creating abortion commissions to review applications. Using a paired double-blind sampling method, women who applied for and were denied an abortion both at the commission level and on appeal were compared with similarly situated women who reported not to apply for an abortion. The physical health of the children did not differ significantly at birth.[49] The children were then studied at age 9 and at ages 14 to 16, 16 to 18, and 21 to 23. The study found that significant differences existed between the children born as a result of an unwanted pregnancy and that those differences widened over time. These differences concerned factors such as criminal propensity, personal qualities, psychological development, and maladaption. Interestingly, those results carried over into the next generation. A husband or a wife who was originally born as the result of an unplanned pregnancy also seemed to be a worse parent than his or her matched cohort. Thus, the consequences to society of coercing a woman to bear an unwanted pregnancy may be with us for generations.

In sum, the consequences to children of being born to adolescent mothers, especially when the pregnancy was unwanted, seem to be quite significant. Once again, poverty seems to be a key factor in predicting the health and well-being of children. By not having effective welfare programs which help these children achieve basic food, education, and housing, we are helping perpetuate a gruesome cycle of poverty.

V. CONTRACEPTION

An important aspect of an effective contraceptive policy would be to have a wide range of inexpensive contraceptive services available to adolescents. American adolescents, however, do not have many services readily available to them. Most adolescents obtain contraceptives, if they obtain them at all, at family planning clinics rather than from private physicians.[50] Only seven out of ten clinics, and five out of ten private physicians, accept Medicaid payment for contraceptive services. Thus, poor adolescents may have no affordable way to obtain the contraceptive pill, which is generally considered to be the most appropriate birth-control option for adolescent females. In addition, many private physicians will not serve an unmarried minor on the basis of her own consent so that contraceptives become unavailable if she cannot obtain parental consent.[51] We know the difficulties of parental consent and notification statutes from the abortion cases. If a pregnant teenager feels uncomfortable telling her parents that she is pregnant in order to be able to obtain an abortion, then she would likely feel uncomfortable in telling her parents that she is sexually active in order to get their Medicaid card to see a doctor to obtain the contraceptive pill.

The only good news in the family-planning area is that the United States Congress has modified Medicaid so that women who do not meet the income and family-structure criteria for cash assistance are eligible for Medicaid as long as they meet certain income criteria. By July 1990, states had to extend Medicaid coverage to infants and pregnant women with incomes up to the federal poverty level and had the option of covering infants and pregnant women with incomes up to 185% of the poverty level. As of July 1988, forty states have opted to expand their Medicaid programs to cover infants and pregnant women with incomes of 100% of the poverty level.[52] It is too soon to assess whether that money is actually reaching poor, pregnant adolescents.

It is important to recognize that an effective sex-education program will not prevent unintended pregnancies so long as women and men only have available the current contraceptive technology. Fifty-one percent of all abortion patients in 1987, for example, reported that they were practicing contraception during the month in which they conceived.[53] Of those not practicing contraception, about 15% had ceased using the pill within one month of becoming pregnant, 44% had ceased using the pill within three months of becoming pregnant.[54] These former pill-users were probably not using contraceptives because they mistakenly believed that after a woman stops using the pill that she has a several month grace period during which she will not become pregnant.[55] Only 9% of women obtaining abortions had no prior contraceptive experience.[56] It is simply not true, therefore, that women who have abortions are ignorant of the importance of practicing contraception or unwilling to make an effort to avoid pregnancy. The evidence strongly suggests that women experience problems in successfully using even the most effective methods of contraception.[57] Rather than place all the blame on women, it is important to recognize that contraceptive technology, itself, has inherent limitations which result in many unintended pregnancies.[58]

We also need to remember that contraceptives are never likely to solve the problem of unintended pregnancies even if we achieved universal use of contraception. This is because of the inherent failure rate associated with many contraceptives. The following table summarizes these failure rates:

Lowest Expected and Typical Reported Failure Rates During the First Year of Use of a Contraceptive Method in the United States[59]

	Lowest Expected % of Women to Get Pregnant in First Year of Use	Typical % of Women to Get Pregnant in First Year of Use
Cap	5	18
Diaphragm	3	18
Condom	2	12
IUD		6
Medicated	1	
Nonmedicated	2	
Pill		3
Combined	0.1	
Progestogen	0.5	
Only		

The lowest expected failure rates represent the authors' best estimate of the percentage of users expected to experience an unintended pregnancy during the first year of use even when they have used the method consistently and correctly. The typical figures, which are much higher, are based on reported results from actual studies. The typical figures for contraceptive failure rates reflect that people, not perfect machines, make use of contraceptives; human failure, as well as medical failure, is unavoidable. But even ignoring user failure, we see that some failure from contraceptive use can always be expected.

In addition, it is important to note that unintended pregnancies cannot be prevented without also preventing coercive sexual activity. A woman who has not chosen to engage in sexual intercourse is not likely to have the opportunity to choose to use contraception (and certainly will not be able to persuade her partner to use contraception). Although it is impossible to quantify the extent to which female adolescents experience unwanted intercourse, the pervasiveness of rape and sexual harassment in our society should make us aware of the frequency of this problem. Studies on female adolescents and HIV transmission have indicated that female adolescents find it virtually impossible to persuade their male partners to use condoms or abstain from sexual activity to protect both of their lives.[60] If these women cannot get their partners to act responsibly to avoid HIV transmission, then it is unrealistic to expect that these women currently have the power to choose the conditions under which they engage in sexual activity. No amount of research on contraceptive technology will assist the female adolescent who does not have the power to say no to sexual activity.

Finally, given the high rates of coercive sexual activity, misinformation about contraception, and contraceptive failure rates, we will always need to have abortion available as an option to women. Unfortunately, United States family-planning policy refuses to recognize that reality. Thus, it currently forbids family-planning services from providing any abortion information. Congress may possibly change that result although the courts have been unreceptive to understanding the relationship between abortion services and family planning in a highly imperfect world.[61]

In sum, United States contraception and sex-education policy is entirely ineffective in preventing unintended teenage pregnancy. Our policies send a confused and ineffectual message to adolescents and cause the United States to have the least effective contraception and sex-education program in the Western world. We assume that female adolescents have the power to say no when sexual activity is unwanted. In addition, we have failed to devote adequate resources to developing safe, cheap, and effective contraceptives. Legislative policy is inept, with poor, pregnant adolescents disproportionately paying the heavy price for this incompetence.

VI. PRENATAL CARE

Another way to avoid some of the negative consequences of early childbirth, especially for the child, is to have available an excellent system of prenatal care. The importance of adequate prenatal care cannot be overstated. Six in ten women, in general, are treated for some pregnancy-related medical problems.[62] Three in ten women are reported to have had major complications from pregnancy.[63] Women who do not obtain adequate prenatal care are much more likely to have a low birthweight baby, a premature birth, and to gain too little weight during pregnancy.[64] Since nearly half of women under the age of twenty receive less than adequate or no prenatal care,[65] these women are at high risk of having pregnancy-related complications. By not preventing these complications early in the pregnancy, we raise the ultimate cost of the medical complications associated with the pregnancy and place the mother's and child's health at risk.

Despite the importance of effective and accessible prenatal care, it is no more available to poor adolescents than were contraceptives and sex education. Although much controversy exists concerning appropriate contraceptive policy, no controversy exists concerning the importance of adequate prenatal care for pregnant women. In 1980, the United States Surgeon General called for an increase to at least 90% by 1990 in the proportion of women in each racial and ethnic group who receive care in the first trimester of pregnancy.[66] The United States has made progress in reaching this goal for married, white, adult, nonpoor women, but has made no progress in reaching this goal for adolescents of all racial subgroups. In fact, the proportion of them that received first-trimester care between 1980 and 1982 actually declined.[67] Some commentators attribute this decline to tightened eligibility for Medicaid coverage and cutbacks in funding of maternal health services for the poor.[68] The unavailability of publicly funded prenatal care becomes especially troubling when one realizes that 32.1% of the babies born are born into families at 150% or less of the poverty line.[69] Not surprisingly, only 65.6% of this group receives first-trimester prenatal care as contrasted with about 83% for the rest of the population.[70] Females under the age of 18, however, receive the least amount of prenatal care; 48.5% receive first-trimester prenatal care, and 12.7% receive third-trimester care only, or no care.[71] In addition, the percentage of female adolescents who receive third-trimester only or no care is about 50% higher for African-American and Hispanic adolescents than for white adolescents.[72]

The structure of the federal Medicaid program explains the unavailability of prenatal care for certain groups in society. Eligibility for Medicaid is based on poverty and family structure. As of 1985, only one state, Vermont, had an eligibility level that exceeded the federal poverty level and twenty-three states had income limits that were less than half of the federal poverty level.[73] If the new Medicaid rules attain their desired effect,[74] then these figures should start to improve. In addition, prenatal, delivery, and postpartum care are not mandated under the Medicaid program. Two states do not cover prescription drugs; five states do not cover clinics, which are a major source of health care for poor women; twenty-seven states do not cover diagnostic services; thirty-one states do not cover screening services such as amniocentesis or ultrasound; and ten states limit the number of outpatient visits below the number recommended for an uncomplicated pregnancy.[75] Only twelve states provide all of the services under Medicaid which are considered part of an "adequate" prenatal health care system.[76] Pregnant adolescents can have special problems receiving Medicaid coverage because they often need to present their parent's Medicaid card at the doctor's office to receive treatment.[77] Finally, it can be difficult to find a doctor who will accept Medicaid payment; a 1983 study indicated that only 46% of obstetrician-gynecologists in private practice accept Medicaid for a delivery.[78] In sum, our prenatal-care policies are substantially harming the health and well-being of fetuses and of poor, pregnant, teenage women.

VII. ABORTION

Another way to avoid early childbirth stemming from unintended pregnancies that are also unwanted is to have abortion accessible, especially at the early stages of pregnancy when it is the safest. But the Supreme Court has long supported restrictions on abortions for adolescents. Moreover, the restrictions approved in *Webster v. Reproductive Health Services*, 492 U.S. 490 (1989), which increase the costs of second-trimester abortion and which make abortions unavailable in hospitals on public property, will have a dramatic effect on adolescents, because they are disproportionately affected by these measures. Although adolescents manage to have abortions in relatively large numbers, they do so by overcoming substantial burdens that are placed in their way. The consequence is that they disproportionately have late-term abortions, thereby increasing the health risks of the procedure and raising its cost.[79]

Despite parental consent laws and the unavailability of Medicaid for abortions, about 6% of females 18 to 19 years old had abortions in 1981, the highest rate of any age group.[80] Female adolescents are the second most likely group to face a pregnancy and the most likely group to terminate it by abortion, despite the relative difficulty for them of obtaining an abortion.[81] Except for women over the age of 40, females under 15 have the highest abortion ratio (defined as the number of abortions per 100 live births and abortions).

The rate of abortions per 1,000 women was much higher in 1981 for nonwhite adolescents as compared to white adolescents (59.7 compared with 33.5). However, the ratio of abortions per 100 abortions plus live births was higher for white adolescents than nonwhite adolescents (41.8 compared with 39.6). These statistics reflect a much higher pregnancy rate in the nonwhite community than the white community. Thus, in absolute terms, nonwhite adolescents experienced many more abortions *and* births than white adolescents, and were, overall, less likely to terminate a pregnancy through abortion. Nonwhite adolescents are therefore in much greater need of all family planning services than white adolescents.

Adolescent females are disproportionately likely to have abortions in the second trimester. For women over the age of 25, between 6% and 8% of the abortions performed are performed at thirteen or more weeks' gestation.[82] For women under the age of 20, between 10% and 23% of the abortions performed are performed at thirteen or more weeks' gestation, with the highest statistic being for women under the age of 14.[83] There appears to be an inverse, geometric relationship between age and second-trimester abortions for women under the age of 20. Thus, when adolescent females do face unintended pregnancies and do decide to have an abortion, they disproportionately face the high health risks of second-trimester abortions.[84] Our silence about contraception and abortion, plus parental consent rules, may cause them to risk their lives and health in order to incur an abortion.

Abortion mortality statistics show a steady decline since abortion was legalized. In 1972, ninety women died as a result of abortion, with 43% of those deaths (thirty-nine women) dying as a result of an illegal abortion. By contrast, in 1984, eighteen women died as a result of an abortion, eleven were associated with a legally induced abortion, and six with a spontaneous abortion.[85] Abortion has therefore become a relatively safe procedure. Unfortunately, recent attempts to make abortion illegal in certain states will increase the abortion mortality rate as women, once again, are forced to seek illegal abortions from unskilled practitioners in inadequate facilities.

Although a lot of information exists concerning the health consequences of abortion, few studies trace the socioeconomic effects of the decision to have an abortion. Only one study that I have found analyzes the short-term and long-term consequences for adolescents who procure abortions as compared with pregnant adolescents who bear the child and care for it or relinquish it for adoption. A study of 360 African-American teenage women of similar socioeconomic background who sought pregnancy tests from two Baltimore family-planning providers sought to determine if the young women who terminated their pregnancies fared differently than the women who carried their pregnancies to term.[86] In terms of educational status, the study found that the women who carried their pregnancies to term attained significantly less education. Interestingly, the difference became more significant over the two-year period of the study.[87] This negative change in their educational experience was not consistent with their educational expectations, as expressed during interviews. As for economic well-being, the abortion group's economic status improved over the two-year period while the child bearer's economic well-being deteriorated over this time period. Even when the effect of the presence of the baby was removed from the calculation of household income, the abortion group fared significantly better than the child bearing group.[88] Finally, no significant results were found in contraception use or subsequent pregnancy based on whether the women aborted or carried their pregnancies to term. A somewhat higher percentage of the women who had an abortion (76.9% as compared with 68.2%) reported using contraceptives always or most of the time, but a somewhat higher percentage of the women who had an abortion (57.5% as compared with 54.5%) had a subsequent pregnancy within two years of the first pregnancy.[89] In interpreting these statistics, however, one has to remember that the women who carried the pregnancy to term were at risk of pregnancy for a much smaller portion of the two years of the study than the women who had abortions.

This study confirms my initial thesis, which is that pregnancy, in itself, need not be a problem for adolescents. The pregnancy becomes problematic due to the socially created, negative life consequences of carrying the pregnancy to term and the high possibility of another unintended pregnancy, which may also be carried to term. Adolescent women who procure an abortion will, on average, fare better than their peers who bear the child. However, both sets of adolescents remain at high risk of undergoing another unintended pregnancy with subsequent childcare responsibilities. By putting substantial obstacles in the path of adolescents who want abortions, we cause them to delay their abortion and thereby undergo significant health risks. By contrast, by facilitating their ability to procure an abortion, we may be improving the quality of their lives as well as the lives of the children that they will bear later in life.

VIII. ADOPTION

Another way to avoid the consequences of early childbirth is to have adoption be an easily available option. Adoption, however, is not considered to be an acceptable alternative by most pregnant women and especially by pregnant, African-American or Hispanic women. The federal government does virtually nothing to facilitate adoption. In addition, state governments probably deter rather than promote adoption. State regulations that make it difficult for couples to adopt children by subjecting them to many layers of screening and which permit adopted children to learn who was their biological mother deter adoptions. They make pregnant women unwilling to relinquish their child for adoption and make prospective parents unwilling to undergo the cost and time of adoption.

One of the biggest flaws in the adoption system is that it is based on a heterosexual, middle-class, nuclear-family model. Although we increasingly live in a world where children have diverse and extended families and parental relations, adoption is modelled on the assumption of one male and one female parent per child.[90] Thus, in *Quilloin v. Walcott*, 434 U.S. 246 (1978), the United States Supreme Court approved the adoption of an 11-year-old boy by his mother's new husband. The result terminated all visitation rights of his biological father with whom the boy had had an ongoing relationship. The adoption by the mother's new husband was not problematic; it was the desired result from the perspective of the mother and 11-year-old boy. However, the complete termination of the relationship with the biological father was not desirable or beneficial to the boy. Our custody laws might have acted more expansively by recognizing the constellation of parents in the boy's life; however, our adoption laws insist upon reflecting a rigid, nuclear-family structure. Forcing parents and children to make such rigid choices does not facilitate adoption.

Another context in which the rigidity of our adoption system deters adoption is in the lesbian and gay context. Several states absolutely forbid lesbian and gay people from adopting children. This result has been especially unfortunate when gay couples have been forbidden to adopt even a hard-to-place child, leaving the child in institutionalized care rather than in a family environment. Many states require the parents of adoptive children to be male and female, forbidding, for example, a lesbian who has been artificially inseminated from an anonymous donor from choosing her female lover to be the second parent. In that scenario (which is increasingly occurring), the child is left without the legal and financial protections of having a second parent. Thus, our adoption rules forbid some children from having two adoptive parents and never permit a child to have a constellation of several parents.

As with rigid rules regarding nuclear families, rules about confidentiality are also quite rigid. Unless a mother who wants to relinquish her child for adoption participates in an independent or private adoption, she must comply with the confidentiality rules of the particular state in which she lives. Her state may require that identifying information about birth be made available to an adult adoptee. Alternatively, her state may permanently seal adoption records, giving her no opportunity to learn about the well-being of her child. Either or both results may be unacceptable to a pregnant woman causing her to choose an abortion or keep an unwanted child. The state-sponsored adoption system assumes that a particular confidentiality result is desired by or best for all adoptive mothers, not permitting flexible bargaining other than in an independent or private adoption.[91]

A. Frequency of Adoption by Race

Information on adoption is limited and the statistics are difficult to understand. The federal government stopped compiling national adoption statistics in 1975.[92] Statistics from the 1980s suggest that despite the public emphasis on the adoptability of all children, adoptions may have declined during the mid-1980s.[93] Most of the decline in adoption appears to have taken place among white women. For adoptions of unrelated children, the white rate fell from 1.9 % in 1982 to 1.4 % in 1987; the rate for African-American women fell from 0.9 % in 1982 to 0.8 % in 1987; the rate for Hispanic women increased from 0.2 % in 1982 to 0.4 % in 1987.[94] Although the rate of adoption among Hispanic women is not declining and the African-American level is relatively constant, the absolute numbers of African-American and Hispanic women who adopt unrelated children is much lower than the rate for white women. Because interracial adoptions constitute only about 8% of all adoptions and those adoptions consist primarily of the adoption of children of races other than African-American or white by white adoptive mothers,[95] African-American and Hispanic children have a much lower likelihood of being adopted than do white children. Eighty-seven percent of the mothers who adopt are white; 7% are African-American; about 2% are Hispanic.[96] The adoptive mother and child are of the same race 92.4% of the time. Given the higher pregnancy rate among African-American and Hispanic women than white women, one would therefore suspect that adoption is not seen as a real option, other than with relatives, in the African-American and Hispanic communities. Unfortunately, there are no statistics on the number of unadoptable African-American and Hispanic children.

The women who place their children for adoption are not the most disadvantaged women in society. Babies born to single white women were much more likely to have been placed for adoption (12%) than were those born to single African-American women (less than 1%) in 1982.[97] Of the white women who did place their child for adoption, they were three times more likely to have had fathers who had some college education than women who kept their babies.[98] Single women who had placed their children for adoption were less likely to be receiving public assistance, less likely to be poor, and more likely to have completed high school than were single women who kept their babies.[99] Thus, adoption is not seen as a real option for the most disadvantaged, pregnant, single women.[100]

B. Consequences of Adoption

Adoption is often considered to be the panacea for the need for abortion. Few studies, however, compare the consequences for adolescents based on whether they abort, raise the child themselves, or relinquish the child for adoption. One study has compared these latter two alternatives, but it has not compared either of these two groups to women who abort an unintended pregnancy.[101] Despite the fact that women who relinquish their children for adoption would seem to face fewer financial, emotional and childcare demands than those who raise their children, previous studies had suggested that there are significant negative, psychological consequences stemming from the relinquishment decision.[102] Nevertheless, one recent study found that relinquishers are generally more successful than child rearers in terms of completing vocational training, delaying marriage, avoiding a rapid subsequent pregnancy, working following the birth of the child, and living in a higher income household.[103] As compared with adolescents who do not bear a child, however, both relinquishers and child rearers attain lower socioeconomic status.[104]

IX. CONCLUSION

Early childbirth has substantial negative health effects on adolescent mothers, including a higher mortality and morbidity rate than for older women. The cause of these adverse health effects appears to be inadequate prenatal care since there is no physical reason why women between the ages of 15 and 19 should face more difficult pregnancies than older women. Countries which have instituted a successful state-funded prenatal care system have been able to avoid many of these adverse health consequences.

Early childbirth also impacts substantially on a woman's educational opportunities. African-American and Hispanic women are generally less likely to graduate from high school than white women; early childbirth compounds this problem. Federal policy appears to have helped assist white pregnant women stay in school; however, it appears to have been rather ineffectual in assisting African-American and Hispanic women stay in school. In monitoring our progress in this area, it is not sufficient to look at the overall statistics for adolescents and be satisfied. We need to target each subgroup and see that virtually no progress has occurred for African-American and Hispanic adolescents even if the general statistics have improved due to the numerosity of white women.

In addition, early childbirth impacts dramatically on the well-being of the child born. Inadequate prenatal care, again, is a major factor causing both prematurity and low birthweight. Race, however, does appear to be an important variable in low birthweight, because the relative risk of low birthweight for African-American children is more than twice as high as for a comparable group of white children, with the difference increasing over time. African-American children, unfortunately, appear to have a disproportionately higher mortality rate even when they have normal birthweights, meaning that we really need to target the healthcare needs of African-American children. In quantitative terms, nearly 20,000 African-American infants died in the first year of life over the last five years who would not have died had their chances for healthcare been equal to that of white infants. It also appears to be the case that avoiding teenage pregnancies is not going to solve the health problems for African-American children. It appears that the problems of low birthweight and high mortality exist among all African-American children irrespective of the age of their mothers.

Despite the clear need for effective sex education, contraception, availability of abortion, prenatal care, and adoption services, Congress and many of the states do very little to achieve these goals. They continue to promote childbirth by curtailing contraception, sex education, and abortion services for adolescents and by not improving the quality of prenatal care. They speak in the negative—limiting access to certain family-planning services—but do not take any effective affirmative steps to encourage real family planning among adolescents. The results are the high rates of unintended teenage pregnancies, which I have described above. In the following chapters, I will discuss legal strategies to make Congress and the states act more responsibly with respect to family planning and to reproductive health issues.

One of the important lessons that comes from this and the previous chapter is that the lack of effective reproductive health strategies severely impair the lives of women and their children. Because nearly all women in society bear children, the availability of effective reproductive health services is important for most women. In addition, because women have been socialized to bear nearly all of the burdens of childcare, reproductive decisions have a very long-term impact on women's lives. Thus, if we are to protect women's basic civil rights, we must have a long-term holistic approach to reproductive health. Unfortunately, our entire reproductive health strategy has become moderated as we focus nearly exclusively on the legality of abortion. Abortion needs to be legal and widely accessible to all groups in society. However, abortion also must be discussed in the larger context of reproductive health. Only then shall we begin to have a meaningful dialogue about all of the lives implicated by reproductive health decisions.

Notes

1. Ruth Bleier, Science and Gender: A Critique of Biology and Its Theories on Women 203 (1984).

2. Angela Harris, *Race and Essentialism in Feminist Legal Theory*, 42 Stan. L. Rev. 581, 585 (1990).

3. The feminists who are often cited as fitting into this category include Catharine MacKinnon and Robin West. *See infra* note 4 (authors criticizing West and MacKinnon for being essentialist). However, I would include some of my own work in this category. *See, e.g.*, Ruth Colker, *Anti-Subordination Above All: Sex, Race, and Equal Protection*, 61 N.Y.U. L. Rev. 1003 (1986) (attempting to describe women's subordination in universal terms).

4. *See generally* Angela Harris, *Race and Essentialism in Feminist Legal Theory*, 42 Stan. L. Rev. 581 (1990) (referring to "post-essentialism"); Elizabeth Spelman, Inessential Woman: Problems of Exclusion in Feminist Thought (1988); Nitya Duclos, *Lessons of Difference: Feminist Theory on Cultural Diversity*, 38 Buff. L. Rev. 325, 374 (1990) (referring to "renegotiated feminism"); Nitya Duclos, *Same Sex Marriage: Complicating the Question*, 1 L. & Sexuality: Rev. of Lesbian and Gay Legal Issues 31, 34 (1991) (referring to the "anti-essentialist" stance); Maria C. Lugones & Elizabeth V. Spelman, *Have We Got a Theory for You! Feminist Theory, Cultural Imperialism and the Demand for 'The Woman's Voice'*, 6 Women's Studies Int. Forum 573 (1983).

5. *See* Harris, *supra* note 2, at 585.

6. *See, e.g.*, John Hart Ely, *The Wages of Crying Wolf: A Comment on Roe v. Wade*, 82 Yale L.J. 920 (1973) (disagreeing with Roe decision); Christine Overall, Ethics and Human

Reproduction (1987) (pro-choice); Mary Ann Glendon, Abortion and Divorce in Western Law (1987) (disagreeing with *Roe* decision). A somewhat more sensitive account of the abortion issue is provided by Rosalind Petchesky. *See* Rosalind Pollack Petchesky, Abortion and Woman's Choice: The State, Sexuality, and Reproductive Freedom (1984). However, Petchesky does not discuss adolescents until page 200 and does so in universal terms, describing teenagers as if they are a monolithic group.

7. The group most responsible for articulating a reproductive health perspective is the Alan Guttmacher Institute with its publication, Family Planning Perspectives. Fortunately, this organization's scholarship has received increased attention by Justices Marshall, Brennan, and Blackmun in *Hodgson. See* Hodgson v. Minnesota, 110 S.Ct. 2926, 2951–60 (1990) (Marshall, J., dissenting) (opinion joined by Justices Brennan and Blackmun).

8. Mahmoud Fathalla, Reproductive Health: A Global Overview (forthcoming).

9. Fifty-one percent of women using contraceptives become pregnant unintentionally. *See infra* note 13.

10. For an especially insensitive account of the impact of reproductive decisions on women's lives, see Robert Araujo, *Fetal Jurisprudence—A Debate in the Abstract*, 33 Catholic Lawyer 203 (1990). When I saw the title of this article, I thought it was a spoof because I couldn't imagine anyone *deliberately* creating an entirely abstract argument which considers fetuses but not pregnant women. However, as far as I can tell, the author is quite serious in trying to hide himself behind a veil of ignorance.

11. 110 S. Ct. 2926 (1990).

12. *See Hodgson*, 110 S. Ct. at 2941–44.

13. James Trussell, *Teenage Pregnancy in the United States*, 20 Family Planning Perspectives 262 (1988).

14. Margaret Terry Orr, *Private Physicians and the Provision of Contraceptives to Adolescents*, 16 Family Planning Perspectives 83 (1984).

15. *See* Trussell, *supra* note 13, at 262.

16. Elise Jones, Jacqueline Darroch Forrest, Noreen Goldman, Stanley Henshaw, Richard Lincoln, Leannie Rosoff, Charles Westoff and Deirdre Wulf, *Teenage Pregnancy in Developed Countries: Determinants and Policy Implications*, 17 Family Planning Perspectives 53, 55 (1985).

17. *Unwanted Childbearing in United States Declines, But Levels Still High Among Blacks, Singles*, 17 Family Planning Perspectives 274 (1985) (Digest section, reporting William F. Pratt and Marjorie Horn, Wanted and Unwanted Childbearing United States, 1973–1982, 108 Advance Data from Vital and Health Statistics 1 (May 9, 1985)).

18. *Id.*

19. Stanley Henshaw & Jennifer Van Vort, *Teenage Abortion, Birth and Pregnancy Statistics: An Update*, 2 Family Planning Perspectives 85, 86 (1989).

20. *Id.* at 86.

21. Dennis Hogan, Nan Marie Astone & Evelyn Kitagawa, *Social and Environmental Factors Influencing Contraceptive Use Among Black Adolescents*, 17 Family Planning Perspectives 165 (1985).

22. *Id.* at 168.

23. *Id.* at 169.

24. Comment, *Risking the Future: A Symposium on the National Academy of Sciences Report on Teenage Pregnancy*, 19 Family Planning Perspectives 119 (1987).

25. Alva Barnett, *Factors that Adversely Affect the Health and Well-Being of African-American Adolescent Mothers and Their Infants* in Teenage Pregnancy: Developing Strategies for Change in the Twenty-First Century 101, 105 (Dionne Jones & Stanley Battle eds. 1990).

26. *Id.*

27. *See* Barnett, *supra* note 25, at 106.

28. Carolyn Makinson, *The Health Consequences of Teenage Fertility*, 17 Family Planning Perspectives 132 (1985). For example, one United States study found that African-American teenagers in urban clinics had a high rate of pregnancy-induced hypertension, anemia,

prematurity and perinatal mortality but that teenagers from more economically advantaged backgrounds did not have more health complications than older women. *Id.* at 133.

29. *Id.* at 133 (reporting Swedish experience).

30. *See* Trussell, *supra* note 13, at 268.

31. *See* Trussell, *supra* note 13, at 268.

32. Dawn Upchurch & James McCarthy, *Adolescent Childbearing and High School Completion in the 1980's: Have Things Changed?*, 21 Family Planning Perspectives 199 (1989).

33. *Id.* at 199.

34. *Id.* at 199 (reporting that African-American teenagers made the greatest progress between 1958 and 1975; whereas, Title IX of the Education Amendments of 1972 did not become effective until 1975). The author of this study is not exactly accurate in her description of Title IX of the Education Amendments of 1972, 28 U.S.C. 1681 *et seq.* That law prohibited sex-based discrimination in educational programs or activities receiving federal financial assistance. The regulations accompanying the statute interpreted the law to forbid pregnancy-based discrimination. The Supreme Court's subsequent conclusion in General Electric v. Gilbert, 429 U.S. 125 (1976) that sex-based discrimination under Title VII, 42 U.S.C. 2000e *et seq.*, does not include pregnancy-based discrimination would also seem to apply to Title IX. Thus, the regulations to Title IX may have applied to pregnancy-based distinctions; however it is questionable whether those regulations were valid.

35. *Id.* at 202 (also reporting that one needs to view statistics about improvements in gaining high school diplomas with caution because other studies indicate that adolescents who become mothers are less likely to continue their education in college, which is not discussed in studies of high school completion).

36. *See* Makinson, *supra* note 28, at 135.

37. *Id.* at 135.

38. *Id.* at 137 & 138.

39. 39 MMWR 150 (March 9, 1990).

40. *Id.*

41. *See* Barnett, *supra* note 25, at 107.

42. *Way to Lower Black Neonatal Mortality Not Simple, Study Finds*, 17 Family Planning Perspectives 129 (1985) (Digest Section, reporting Nancy J. Binkin, Ronald L. Williams, Carol J. R. Hogue & Peter M. Chen, *Reducing Black Neonatal Mortality: Will Improvement in Birth Weight be Enough?*, 253 J.A.M.A. 372 (1985)).

43. Jeannette Johnson, *U.S. Differentials in Infant Mortality: Why Do They Persist?*, 19 Family Planning Perspectives 227, 231–32 (1987).

44. *Id.* at 232.

45. *Children Born to Teens More Likely to Be Injured or Hospitalized by Age 5*, 16 Family Planning Perspectives 238 (1984) (Digest Section, reporting B. Taylor, J. Wadsworth, *Teenage Mothering, Admission to Hospital, and Accidents During the First 5 Years*, 58 Archives of Disease in Childhood 6 (1973)).

46. Katherine Darabi, Elizabeth Graham, Pearila Namerow, Susan Philliber, Phyllis Varga, *The Effect of Maternal Age on the Well-Being of Children*, 46 J. of Marriage and the Family 933 (1984).

47. *Id.*

48. *See* Henry P. David, Zdenek Dytrych, Zdenek Matejcek, Vratislav Schüller, Born Unwanted: Developmental Effects of Denied Abortion (1988).

49. *Id.* at 67.

50. Orr, *supra* note 14, at 86. *See also* William Mosher, *Use of Family Planning Services in the United States: 1982 and 1988*, 184 Advance Data 1 (April 11, 1990) (reporting that black women, poor women, and teenagers were more likely to rely on clinics for their family planning services than white, higher-income, and older women).

51. *Id.*

52. Rachel Benson Gold & Sandra Guardado, *Public Funding of Family Planning, Sterilization and Abortion Services, 1987*, 20 Family Planning Perspectives 228 (1988).

53. Stanley Henshaw & Jane Silverman, *The Characteristics and Prior Contraceptive Use of U.S. Abortion Patients*, 20 Family Planning Perspectives 158, 165 (1988).

54. *Id.* at 165.

55. *Id.* at 165.

56. *Id.* at 167.

57. *Id.* at 168.

58. I have not even discussed the lack of contraceptive research in the United States, as compared with Europe. Although only a minority of people who oppose abortion also oppose contraception, that small fringe of the pro-life movement has managed to curtail contraception research in the United States. Although RU 486 is not, in most cases, a contraceptive, the total stalemate in the United States concerning this drug reflects the lack of progress being made in the United States with regard to contraceptives.

59. Robert A. Hatcher, Felicia Guest, Felicia Stewart, Gary Stewart, James Trussell, Sylvia Cerel Bowen & Willard Cates, Contraceptive Technology: 1988–89, 151 (1988).

60. *See* Nan Hunter, *Marriage, Law and Gender*, 1 L. & Sexuality: Rev. of Lesbian and Gay Legal Issues 9 (1991).

61. Rust v. Sullivan, 111 S. Ct. 1759 (1991).

62. Rachel Benson Gold, Asta M. Kenney & Susheela Singh, *Paying for Maternity Care in the United States*, 19 Family Planning Perspectives 190, 192 (1987).

63. *Id.* at 192.

64. *Id.* at 193.

65. *Id.* at 192.

66. Susheela Singh, Aida Torres & Jacqueline Darroch Forrest, *The Need for Prenatal Care in the United States: Evidence from the 1980* National Natality Survey, 17 Family Planning Perspectives 118 (1985).

67. *Id.* at 119.

68. *Id.* at 119.

69. *Id.* at 120.

70. *Id.* at 120.

71. *Id.* at 120.

72. *Id.* at 121.

73. Rachel Benson Gold, *Paying for Maternity Care*, 17 Family Planning Perspectives 103, 107 (1985).

74. *See supra* text accompanying note 52.

75. *See* Gold, *supra* 73, at 108–09.

76. *Id.* at 108–09.

77. *Id.* at 109.

78. *Id.* at 109. *See also* Margaret Terry Orr & Jacqueline Darroch Forrest, *The Availability of Reproductive Health Services from U.S. Private Physicians*, 17 Family Planning Perspectives 63, 67–68 (1985).

79. *See* Hodgson, 110 S.Ct. at 2951 (Marshall, J. concurring and dissenting).

80. Stanley Henshaw, Nancy Binkin, Ellen Blaine & Jack Smith, *A Portrait of American Women Who Obtain Abortions*, 17 Family Planning Perspectives 90 (1985).

81. *Id.* at 90.

82. David Grimes, *Second-Trimester Abortions in the United States*, 16 Family Planning Perspectives 260 (1984).

83. *Id.* at 262.

84. *Id.* at 262–63.

85. 38 MMWR at 13 & 14.

86. Laurie Schwab Zabin, Marilyn Hirsch & Mark Emerson, *When Urban Adolescents Choose Abortion: Effects on Education, Psychological Status and Subsequent Pregnancy*, 21 Family Planning Perspectives 248 (1989).

87. *Id.* at 250.

88. *Id.* at 251.

89. *Id.* at 253.

90. For further discussion, see Linda Smith, *Adoption—The Case for More Options,* 1986 Utah L. Rev. 495 (1986).

91. For further discussion, see John Stoxen, *The Best of Both "Open" and "Closed" Adoption Worlds: A Call for the Reform of State Statutes,* 13 J. of Legislation 292 (1986).

92. *Unmarried White Women Are Those Most Likely to Place Children for Adoption, NSFG Data Show,* 19 Family Planning Perspectives 29 (1987) [hereafter *Unmarried White Women*] (Digest section, reporting Christine Bachrach, *Adoption Plans, Adopted Children, and Adoptive Mothers,* 48 J. of Marriage and the Family 243 (1986)).

93. Bachrach et al. at 2 (declining from 2.2 percent of all ever-married women 20 to 44 years of age in 1982 to 1.7 percent in 1987; declining for adopting an unrelated child from 1.7 percent in 1982 to 1.3 percent in 1987).

94. *Id.* at 3.

95. *Id.* at 1–2.

96. *Id.* at 5.

97. *Unmarried White Women, supra* note 92, at 29.

98. *Id.*

99. *Id.*

100. Eleanor Smeal, President of the Feminist Majority, has suggested to me that society deliberately limits abortions for adolescents so that some white adolescents will "choose" to relinquish their children for adoption rather than obtain an abortion. The fact that both abortion and adoption are relatively unavailable for nonwhite women is of little concern to people who profit from adoptions.

101. Steven McLaughlin, Diane Manninen & Linda Winges, *Do Adolescents Who Relinquish Their Children Fare Better or Worse Than Those Who Raise Them?,* 20 Family Planning Perspectives 25 (1988).

102. *Id.* at 25.

103. *Id.* at 32.

104. *Id.* at 32.

PART THREE

Reproductive Health Cases

An Equality Perspective

Anti-Subordination Above All

> The inequality [or anti-subordination] approach . . . sees women's situation as a structural problem of enforced inferiority that needs to be radically altered.[1]

Chapters 3 and 4 have demonstrated that state restrictions on abortion act coercively in the lives of women in a way that is detrimental to their health and well-being as well as to the health and well-being of their fetuses and future children. Chapter 4 provided a fuller picture of this coercion in the lives of female adolescents. Throughout all of these chapters, I have insisted that an equality rather than a privacy perspective would provide a superior framework to consider abortion restrictions. In this chapter, I will develop that equality perspective by arguing for a group-based anti-subordination approach to reproductive health issues.

I. INTRODUCTION

Traditionally, the courts have used a privacy framework to resolve abortion cases. An equality (or equal protection) approach has rarely been utilized. In *Roe v. Wade*,[2] the Supreme Court found that the right of privacy was "broad enough to encompass a woman's decision whether or not to terminate her pregnancy."[3] The Court did not find an absolute right of privacy; rather, it held that the right of privacy should be "considered against important state interests in regulation."[4] In the fifteen years that followed, the Court applied this framework to invalidate nearly all restrictions against abortion except: (1) congressional and state limitations on Medicaid that made it very difficult for poor people to obtain government-funded abortions,[5] and (2) parental consent and notification statutes that made it difficult for adolescents to preserve their privacy and obtain expeditious abortions.[6] Many feminists criticized the Court's privacy approach because it could not protect the most disadvantaged women from coercive antiabortion regulations. Concurrently, they credited the privacy framework as being more rigorous than the intermediate scrutiny standard applied to sex-based equal protection claims and thereby achieving important victories.[7]

In addition, feminist pro-choice litigators have used the privacy approach rather than the equality approach because of doctrinal problems with the equality approach. The Supreme Court rejected the view that discrimination against pregnant women constitutes per se sex-based intentional discrimination in *Geduldig v. Aiello*.[8] Thus, one could not argue that abortion restraints constitute per se sex discrimination. An argument that a pregnancy-related distinction constituted intentional sex-based discrimination would therefore have to meet the difficult standard of proof for indirect discrimination as set forth in *Personnel Administrator v. Feeney*.[9] In *Feeney*, the Supreme Court required that a plaintiff in an indirect discrimination case prove that the institution "selected or reaffirmed a particular course of action at least in part 'because of,' not merely 'in spite of,' its adverse effects upon an identifiable group."[10] This test has proved almost impossible to meet, because a "smoking gun" demonstrating a desire to cause harm is rarely discoverable. Attempts to meet this standard in cases involving abortion-related restrictions have failed.[11]

The privacy approach, however, has its share of doctrinal problems. Although the Supreme Court denies that it has modified the *Roe* framework, it has watered down the privacy standard by suggesting that the state need assert only a "legitimate" interest to sustain an abortion-related restriction.[12] This lenient standard has allowed the state to increase the costs of second-trimester abortions and make abortions unavailable at public facilities which are disproportionately used by poor women. This watered down privacy standard is less rigorous than the "important" state-interest standard required under intermediate scrutiny for sex-based equal protection cases. The weak justifications that are presently surviving privacy scrutiny might therefore not survive equality scrutiny.

II. THEORETICAL OBSERVATIONS

Both the privacy and equality approaches are therefore troubled doctrinally. Neither approach offers an easy solution to the abortion controversy from a pro-choice perspective. My decision to explore an equality perspective is, therefore, based on theoretical rather than doctrinal grounds. I believe that a particular version of equality doctrine, which I will call an *anti-subordination* perspective, is most compatible with the description of our selves and society that I have tried to present in this book.

In the first several chapters of this book, I argued that we should think of ourselves as connected selves. Even our own self is actually a connection of selves. When we think of our aspirations of love, compassion, and wisdom, we need to think about those aspirations in terms of how we live in a community of connected selves.

Privacy doctrine, as it has been applied to the abortion context, does not reflect this view of the self. Feminist pro-choice litigators attempt to argue that we should consider the women's right to autonomy in isolation from the state's interest in protecting life. Instead of seeing pregnant women as having an implicit connectedness to the fetus, and thus a responsibility to the well-being of that fetus, pregnant women are described in isolation from that fetus. Pro-life advocates do no better. As Rosalind Petchevsky has pointed out, they try to remove fetuses from women's bodies and pretend that we can protect fetal life without controlling women's lives. [13] Their concern for the autonomy or well-being of fetuses causes them to disregard women's lives.

Both views of the abortion decision are troubling because they each rely on the assumption of an autonomous sphere—women and fetuses. Although some people have suggested to me that privacy doctrine need not be so dependent on the autonomy of spheres, I think that result is highly unlikely. By its very terminology—privacy—the doctrine suggests at its core that it is plausible to divide the world into two spheres: the public and the private. The presupposition is that privacy should be protected because private acts do not affect public life.

My analysis of the self and our interconnectedness as selves, however, resists that assumption. The decisions that women make about how to use their reproductive capacities profoundly affect our society. Similarly, the decisions that the state makes with regard to reproductive health policies profoundly affect the lives of women. The public and private are deeply interconnected spheres generally, and certainly so in the context of reproductive health decisions. Thus, it does not make sense to frame an abortion analysis on the argument that women should be left alone in their privacy. Such an argument yields the decision in *Harris v. McRae*, 448 U.S. 297 (1980), that the state can leave women alone, even when doing so jeopardizes the health and well-being of themselves and their family.

An equality perspective, by contrast, does not rely on such assumptions about lack of connectedness. Equality doctrine, at its core, requires that people be treated with equal respect, irrespective of their group status. Thus, equality doctrine doesn't demand that women be allowed to choose to have abortions because women are entitled to be treated with autonomy. Instead, it insists that women be allowed to choose to have abortions because of women's position in society—the roles and responsibilities of women in society in relation to others. In other words, we would inquire about how society's regulation of abortion is a part of society's general treatment of and respect for women. It is because women are saddled with virtually all of the expenses of pregnancy and childbirth, as well as the costs of childcare, that we must insist that women be allowed to choose the conditions under which they become pregnant. The need for women to control their reproductive decisions is a response to a larger problem—a fundamental disrespect for the lives of women in society. We have seen in the previous chapter that nearly all women become pregnant during their lifetime yet the state provides coercive and inadequate reproductive health services which jeopardize the lives of women and their fetuses. Those practices are basic to the subordination of women in society. It is because of society's disrespect for women's well-being and reproductive health that women must be permitted to take control of their lives and well-being by making reproductive decisions.

Arguing that women are entitled to be treated with respect does not negate a state's interest in valuing life. Life, however, must be considered in all of its interconnected forms. The state may not value the life of the fetus while ignoring the value of the life of the pregnant woman. It is also important not to view the pregnant woman and fetus as having oppositional interests. As chapter 4 indicated, fetuses do benefit from respectful treatment of pregnant women. By providing prenatal and postnatal care, as well as childcare and abortion, the state assists both women and fetuses. A connected view of all reproductive health policies gives a much more accurate picture of women's treatment than a narrow view of abortion regulations.

I do not want to pretend that all women act wisely at all moments while pregnant. Certainly, women sometimes act in ways that are not in the best interest of the fetus that they are bearing. Nevertheless, I believe that a privacy perspective often inaccurately portrays women and fetuses as being distinct entities with inconsistent interests. By using a connected, equality approach, we can see that fetuses are dependent upon women who, in turn, generally do try to act in ways that are consistent with both the fetuses' well-being and their own. In a later chapter, I will examine cases from an equality perspective that purport to contain conflict between pregnant women and fetuses. I will show how a connected, equality perspective can expose the elements of commonality rather than opposition. The state, I will show, is often the entity that acts in opposition to the interests of women and fetuses, not pregnant women. Coercive treatment against pregnant women usually acts to the detriment of women and fetuses by discouraging women from seeking reproductive health services.

Finally, an equality perspective emphasizes that women's basic ability to exercise their right to be full participants in our society is predicated on their ability to control their reproductive lives. Nearly all women in society get pregnant at some point in their lives. For young women, especially, the timing and numerosity of their pregnancies can have lifetime consequences both for themselves and their offspring. A woman who is saddled with compulsory pregnancy throughout her lifetime cannot begin to exercise any meaningful options in her life—from work to housing to education to basic sustenance. Thus, women's equality with men must, at a bare minimum, contain the opportunity to exercise meaningful choice in reproductive health decisions. An equality perspective emphasizes the public consequences to women of a regime of compulsory pregnancy.

Theoretically, then, equality doctrine would seem to offer much more promise than privacy doctrine. This is not to say, however, that the courts are incapable of diluting or destroying equality doctrine. As I will soon show, the courts have constructed a rather bizarre equality doctrine that relies on the concept of autonomy of spheres and is therefore insufficiently protective of women's lives and well-being. It is an equality doctrine that looks more like privacy doctrine than like equality doctrine. I will expose those inconsistencies and suggest what doctrinal changes are necessary in order for equality doctrine to represent the interconnected view that I have described above.

III. ANTI-SUBORDINATION VERSUS ANTI-DIFFERENTIATION PERSPECTIVES

Although I have argued above that equal protection doctrine is inherently more group-based and systemic than privacy doctrine, the legal development of the doctrine has not always reflected that potential. In fact, what we have seen is that equal protection doctrine has become increasingly atomistic. Rather than view society's treatment of reproductive health issues as reflecting its systemic treatment of women, the Supreme Court has consistently tried to portray pregnant women as atomistic individuals whose treatment when pregnant is not reflective of society's subordinate view toward women's status.

Before describing and categorizing the case law in detail, I would like to offer some theoretical distinctions that might clarify the case law. Two general views of equality doctrine exist, which I will call the *anti-subordination* and the *anti-differentiation* perspectives. Under the anti-subordination perspective, it is inappropriate for certain groups in society to have a subordinated status because of their lack of power in society as a whole. This approach seeks to eliminate the power disparities between men and women, and between whites and nonwhites, through the development of laws and policies that directly redress those disparities. From an anti-subordination perspective, policies are invidious when they perpetuate racial or sexual hierarchy.

For example, a policy excluding persons who have primary childcare responsibilities from consideration for employment, although phrased in sex-neutral terms, would have a disparate impact on women. It would also perpetuate a history of sexual hierarchy by penalizing women for their societally imposed childcare responsibilities. Subordination opponents would seek to eliminate such a policy because of its role in perpetuating women's class-based oppression.

Under the anti-differentiation perspective, it is inappropriate to treat individuals differently on the basis of race or sex because of a stereotyped view of their race or sex-based abilities. The anti-differentiation perspective is an individual rights perspective in two respects. First, it focuses on the motivation of the individual institution that has allegedly discriminated, without attention to the larger societal context in which the institution operates. Second, it focuses on the specific effect of the alleged discrimination on discrete individuals rather than on groups. Race- and sex-specific policies or actions are invalid under this perspective because they reflect invidious motivation and result in dissimilar treatment for similarly situated individuals. It is equally invidious for white men to be treated differently from black women as for black women to be treated differently from white men under this perspective, because both situations violate the preeminent norm of equal treatment. Anti-differentiation advocates therefore argue for color-blindness or sex-blindness in the development and analysis of legislation and institutional policies, and they frequently criticize affirmative action as violating that principle.

For example, a policy excluding persons who have primary childcare responsibilities from consideration for employment would not necessarily be considered to violate sex equality under the anti-differentiation approach. Under the anti-differentiation perspective, the plaintiff would have to show that such a policy was created for the purpose of harming women. Evidence of disparate impact against women would not be sufficient, because this perspective only considers inequality on an individual rather than group level. By contrast, if the employment policy had specifically excluded women but not men who had childcare responsibilities, then an anti-differentiation perspective would have no difficulty concluding that sex-based inequality existed.

In contrast to the anti-differentiation approach, the anti-subordination perspective is a group-based perspective in two ways: First, it focuses on society's role in creating subordination. Second, it focuses on the way in which this subordination affects, or has affected, groups of people. It is more invidious for women or blacks to be treated worse than white men than for men or whites to be treated worse than black women under this perspective, because of the differing histories and contexts of subordination faced by these groups. Anti-subordination proponents therefore advocate the use of race- or sex-specific policies, such as affirmative action, when those policies redress the subordination of racial minorities or women.

The courts have struggled with the choice between the anti-differentiation and anti-subordination perspectives. The most obvious sources of this tension have been the affirmative action cases; however, this tension actually exists in nearly all race or sex discrimination cases. The very structure of the requirements of proof reflect choices between these principles. And, unfortunately, the atomistic anti-differentiation principle has increasingly gained ground. I will now trace the evolution of these principles in some leading cases.

IV. THE EVOLUTION OF THE PERSPECTIVES

Since the beginning of the 1950s, many black plaintiffs have brought cases alleging violations of state policies which were invalid from both anti-differentiation and anti-subordination perspectives because they explicitly differentiated on the basis of race and subordinated blacks.

As the case law developed, the Supreme Court had to confront two crucial issues: First, they had to determine what constituted a prima facie case of discrimination. Second, when a plaintiff succeeded in establishing a prima facie case of discrimination, the Court was faced with the question of what types of arguments by the defendant should be permitted to justify such discrimination. Each critical issue will be treated in turn.

A. The Prima Facie Case

Two separate issues confronted the Court in defining the prima facie case: First, should only race- or sex-specific policies violate the equal protection clause or should race- or sex-neutral policies that also produced a disparate impact on the basis of race or sex also violate the equal protection clause? Second, what constitutes race- or sex-specific discrimination? In the race area, the second issue was not too difficult. In the sex area, however, the Court has had great difficulty resolving cases involving women's physical differences from men, particularly in the area of reproductive health.

1. Disparate Impact Controversy

The Supreme Court ultimately determined that only race- or sex-specific policies should be considered per se violations of the Constitution. Disparate impact, alone, was not considered to be sufficient to establish a prima facie case of discrimination. The Court resolved the different treatment/disparate impact controversy through an analysis of the pragmatic implications of each choice. It decided that it would be too disruptive to the government if all of its policies could be readily challenged on the basis of impact alone. The Court explained its decision as follows:

> A rule that a statute designed to serve neutral ends is nevertheless invalid, absent compelling justification, if in practice it benefits or burdens one race more than another would be far-reaching and would raise serious questions about, and perhaps invalidate, a whole range of tax, welfare, public service, regulatory, and licensing statutes that may be more burdensome to the poor and the average black than to the more affluent white.[14]

Let us assume that the state decides not to fund abortions under Medicaid. Under an anti-subordination perspective, one might argue that the state cannot exclude abortions from Medicaid, because such an exclusion would have a disparate impact on poor pregnant people, who are female and disproportionately black. Under the anti-differentiation view, which the Supreme Court adopted in the above quotation, such an argument is not readily available under equality doctrine. It is not sufficient for the plaintiff to show that the government's policy has a disparate impact on the basis of sex. In *Personnel Administrator v. Feeney*,[15] the Court held that a plaintiff must prove that a specific action, which has a disparate impact against women, occurred "because of" rather than "despite of" the legislature's desire to harm women. Proof of invidious intent must be quite specific. It is not sufficient to show a general disrespect for women that is reflected in the particular challenged legislation; instead, the plaintiff must produce evidence of a discrete statement which showed the legislature's invidious state of mind. Thus, in the above example, a female plaintiff must also show that the government acted with an invidious race- or sex-conscious motive. She must show that abortions were excluded from Medicaid in order to harm women or blacks, not despite that harm. As we will see, such proof is virtually impossible to mount.

The *Feeney* decision is subject to attack from a systemic, anti-subordination perspective, because the standard of proof articulated in *Feeney* is inappropriately narrow. The facts in *Feeney* exemplify the unsatisfactory nature of the "but for" causation requirement. The *Feeney* case involved the constitutionality of a lifetime veteran's-preference statute. Because the statute was written in terms of veterans and nonveterans, the Court considered it to be gender neutral. Nevertheless, the facially neutral statute produced a disparate gender-based impact. The policy excluded 98% of women from consideration for employment. Thus, the Court inquired as to whether the impact was "intentional." The veteran's preference was enacted before women were eligible for most civil-service jobs.[16] The Massachusetts legislature did not enact the veteran's-preference statute to harm women, since its original enactment had little to do with women. Thus, showing a discriminatory intent was impossible. The original enactment gave one group of men preference over another group of men, because job classifications were generally sex-segregated. The preference, however, was maintained after civil-service jobs were no longer officially sex-segregated in the early 1970s.[17] Since 98% of veterans were men, the preference served to exclude women from nearly all jobs open to the preference on a lifetime basis, even after the sex-segregation rules were lifted.[18]

The fact that the legislature never consciously thought about how the classification would affect women, once women became eligible to compete against men for most civil-service employment, should not be an acceptable defense. We should insist that legislatures wrestle with a statute's impact on women. Thus, the appropriate doctrinal question should be whether a legislature would have been willing to impose these kinds of burdens on women if it fully considered their well-being. Would it be willing to exclude all men from civil service jobs to benefit a subcategory of women?[19]

By formulating a narrow intent test, the Court failed to ask the questions that are likely to go to the core of women's equal protection problems. Legislatures are more likely to act on the basis of patronizing stereotypes about white, middle-class, adult women's best interests than on the basis of an intention to discriminate against women.[20] Alternatively, legislatures are likely to ignore all women's interests altogether and thereby act to preserve the status quo of unequal opportunity between men and women.[21] An *unthinking* attitude can be as harmful to women as direct animus, because it serves to keep women's interests in society invisible. The "but for" causation requirement of *Feeney* gives a legislature the incentive to say nothing about women's interests when enacting legislation, making it all but impossible to prove discriminatory intent. Such silence, however, should not be the goal of the equal protection clause. A full and considered legislative debate about the impact of a policy on women's well-being should be the goal of the equal protection clause. The intent test encourages legislatures to be *unthinking* with reference to women's equality interests.

In addition, the intent test requires the plaintiff to come forward with a discrete "smoking gun" showing that the legislature consciously tried to harm women. The legislature's actions, however, when viewed systemically should speak louder than their words. How could a legislature not be aware that its policies had excluded

98% of women from civil-service jobs? How could we say that a legislature is governing fairly or effectively when it insists on being so ignorant of the consequences of its actions?

Thus, I am suggesting that the Court could continue to insist that discriminatory intent be established when a state develops a facially neutral statute which impacts disproportionately against women. However, the definition of *intent* does not have to be the narrow definition utilized in *Feeney*. A legislature, for example, could be considered to have an unconstitutional state of mind (or intent) when it entirely ignores a statute's impact on women and imposes burdens on women that it would not be willing to impose on men. If equal protection doctrine is truly designed to protect women and men equally, then the Court should not tolerate conscious blindness to women's needs, interests, and well-being. Permitting legislatures to burden women through legislative oversight should not be tolerated, yet that kind of oversight is exactly what *Feeney* encourages.

Returning to the example of female adolescents, I believe that it should be sufficient to present the following two-step analysis in order to show a gender-based violation of equal protection: First, using the empirical evidence that I have described above, we would show that our current reproductive health policies have a disparate impact against female adolescents. Because all of the individuals in that category are female, we would argue that we have shown that a facially neutral policy produced a gender-based disparate impact. Second, using my modified *Feeney* test, we would argue that a legislature which respected the well-being of female adolescents would not have passed the legislation in question. A legislature that had considered, rather than ignored, the well-being of female adolescents, we would argue, would not have passed the legislation in question. Because pregnant, female adolescents are often poor and do not necessarily even have the right to vote, they are especially deserving of the Court's protection.[22] It is difficult to imagine that legislatures would deliberately want to harm female adolescents; however, if their blindness to the effects of their policies on this group is causing enormous disadvantages for this group, then I would argue that the equal protection clause mandates that the Court intercede.[23]

2. Definition of Sex-Specific

The Supreme Court held in *Geduldig v. Aiello*[24] that state policies with respect to pregnancy, which only are capable of affecting women, are nevertheless not gender-based actions. Feminists have criticized *Geduldig* by focusing on the absurdity of the Court's saying that pregnancy is not a sex-based condition.[25] They have argued that it is ridiculous to suggest that a legislature is unaware that pregnancy-related restrictions adversely affect women and not men, since everyone knows that only women can become pregnant.

These critiques of *Geduldig* have been unsuccessful, in part, because they misunderstand the Court's reluctance to extend heightened scrutiny to pregnancy-related distinctions. I understand the Court to be saying that pregnancy-related restrictions are not first-order sex-based equal protection problems, because they are based on a real physical difference between men and women. Consistent with that view, the Court has been reluctant to use heightened scrutiny in cases relating to women's "rapability" or ability to become pregnant during teenage sex.[26] In the Court's view, these kinds of distinctions are less problematic than nonbiological restrictions on women and therefore deserve lower scrutiny. The Court's persistent use of a low level of scrutiny in biologically-based equal protection claims is consistent with its movement toward a low level of scrutiny in pregnancy-related privacy cases. The Court simply does not see those biologically based restrictions as, in Justice O'Connor's words, "unduly burdening" women's lives.[27]

The fundamental mistake in the Court's analysis is that pregnancy is not actually entirely a physical condition. The issue in *Geduldig* was the applicability of a state disability-policy to leave required for a normal pregnancy. The female plaintiff was seeking modest compensation for the work that she would miss due to her pregnancy. The fundamental issue, then, was who bears the costs of pregnancy. Do we expect pregnant women to bear all of those costs or do we insist that the state demonstrate its concern for women and children by bearing some of those costs? By not covering those costs, the state exacerbates the poverty of women in society, a poverty that is related to the financial burdens of childcare that women disproportionately face.

In other words, pregnancy and motherhood are deeply gendered roles in our society. The experience of being pregnant and raising children is one of the strongest gender-based roles in our society. Despite the feminist revolution, studies continue to show that women do nearly all of the household chores and nearly all of the childcare work. In single parent households, women are disproportionately the single parent. The state of California's disability plan was part of this system of placing all of the burdens of pregnancy and childcare on women and thereby perpetuating women's poverty.

Returning to the example of female adolescents, we saw that many of the physical, social, and economic burdens that they faced due to their pregnancies were not inevitable. These burdens could have been alleviated had the state offered proper contraception, abortion services, prenatal care, postnatal care, and adoption services. A biological view of pregnancy sees these results as inevitable, whereas a social view sees the many steps that the state could take to alleviate the disparate burdens that women face.

Geduldig was fundamentally about who pays—women or the state. The state's decision not to pay is, in my opinion, reflective of its assumption that women should bear all of the burdens of pregnancy, childbirth, and childcare. By seeing *Geduldig* narrowly as a case about women's *physical* condition and not looking at it as a part of women's gender-socialization in society, the Court failed to see the basic gender element of the case.

B. The Justificatory Stage

The second critical issue confronting the Court arose in the next phase of analysis, the stage of justification. This stage occurs if the plaintiff has met the burden of stage one, if she has demonstrated that the defendants' policies do constitute intentional race or sex discrimination. At stage two, the defendant gets to try to justify its racial or sexual policies. Thus, at stage two, the Court had to determine what arguments by the defendant could be permitted to justify race- or sex-specific policies or actions once the plaintiff had shown a prima facie case of discrimination. This issue first arose in the constitutional challenges to race-specific policies in higher education that allegedly subordinated blacks.

In the late 1940s, there were two practical routes to expansion of blacks' educational opportunities in higher education: to press for the opening of all-white universities to blacks or to insist that the southern states build separate and truly equal facilities. In 1948, the Supreme Court held in *Sipuel v. Board of Regents*, 332 U.S. 631 (1948) that states could determine for themselves the best way to create these opportunities. Although the Court recognized that blacks were entitled to receive quality higher education, it permitted the state of Oklahoma to create a separate law school for blacks rather than to admit a black plaintiff to a white law school.

Other states responded by opening institutions of higher education for blacks to avoid desegregating white institutions. The NAACP Legal Defense Fund (LDF) challenged that response because of the message of inferiority it sent to blacks and whites about blacks' intellectual capabilities. They brought the case of *Sweatt v. Painter*, 339 U.S. 629 (1950) to argue more strongly than they had argued in *Sipuel* that the Supreme Court should overrule *Plessy v. Ferguson*, 163 U.S. 537 (1886) and rule that separate can never be equal.

The Court's opinion in *Sweatt* acknowledged the link between separate education and subordination. For the first time, the Court recognized the subjective factors that caused the black institution to be inferior to the white institution and ordered a black student admitted to a school previously restricted to whites. However, the Court refrained from overruling *Plessy*, leaving plaintiffs to argue in individual cases that individual schools for blacks were unequal to their corresponding white schools.

Faced with the prospect of arguing cases of unequal educational facilities one by one for the next half century, the LDF pushed for a stronger statement from the Court about the harm to blacks caused by segregation. Finally, in 1954, the Supreme Court held in *Brown v. Board of Education*, 347 U.S. 483 (1954) that racially separate education cannot be equal education.

A superficial examination of *Brown* suggests that the Court was emphasizing the principle of anti-differentiation over the principle of anti-subordination in its ruling that separate can never be equal. However, closer examination shows that the anti-subordination principle dominated the Court's analysis. For example, the Court adopted the following finding from one of the lower courts:

> Segregation of white and colored children in public schools has a detrimental effect upon the colored children. . . . A sense of inferiority affects the motivation of a child to learn. Segregation with the sanction of law, therefore, has a tendency

to [retard] the education and mental development of Negro children and to deprive them of some of the benefits that they would receive in a racial[ly] integrated school system.[28]

The *Brown* decision viewed integration as beneficial to black students because it would help them overcome subordination. The Court seemed to contemplate the desegregation only of white institutions; the desegregation of black institutions was left an open question. These observations support the conclusion that the Court was using an anti-subordination approach.

The justificatory rule that evolved from the *Brown* decision is what is termed *strict scrutiny*. Under this level of scrutiny, racially differentiating rules are deemed to be unconstitutional unless the defendant can establish that they serve a compelling state purpose. Other than affirmative action, virtually no argument has been deemed to pass this test.

Let me recast this justificatory rule in anti-subordination and anti-differentiation language. If the Court would adopt a pure anti-differentiation approach then *no* justification for an explicitly race-specific policy would be acceptable, because race-specific policies are always invidious. Under an anti-subordination perspective, however, the justification that the race-specific policy was attempting to *remedy* a history of subordination would be deemed acceptable. Discrimination against a group with power would be acceptable if the discrimination served to remedy the subordination of a less powerful group.

Thus, by adopting a strict rule against race-specific policies which also permitted some of those policies to pass muster when the justification was remedial, the Court appeared to choose an anti-subordination perspective in the mid-twentieth-century race cases. Irrespective, however, of whether one characterizes the Court's framework as anti-differentiation or anti-subordination, there is no question that the Court's justificatory requirements for the defendant were quite strict. No justification other than affirmative action would pass muster. (However, not all affirmative action would pass muster; the affirmative action would have to remedy past discrimination rather than create additional problems such as racial stereotyping.)

The strict standard of scrutiny did not survive importation to other, non-race-based claims of equal protection violation, such as claims of sex discrimination. In the early sex discrimination cases, male plaintiffs brought constitutional challenges to preferential policies for women, and women challenged subordinating sex-specific policies. After exploring various levels of scrutiny, the Court settled on approaching these cases with an "intermediate" level of scrutiny under which some sex-specific policies or actions were invalidated while others survived. Justifications that were not purely remedial were able to pass muster.

Intermediate scrutiny has developed gradually in the sex discrimination context. Before the advent of modern equal protection doctrine on sex-based classifications, courts were relatively unconcerned about the subordination of women. The courts easily accepted justifications for sex-specific policies or actions that served to perpetuate, rather than eliminate, the subordination of women to men. For example, in 1873, in *Bradwell v. Illinois*, 83 U.S. 130 (1873), the Court upheld a rule against women practicing law. Justice Bradley, in his famous concurrence, justified this rule on the basis that "civil law, as well as nature herself, has always recognized a wide difference in the respective spheres and destinies of man and woman. Man is, or should be, woman's protector and defender."[29] Indeed, until the 1940s, virtually all of the cases challenging sex-specific classifications involved such subordinating views of women.

In these early cases, the Court did not even apply an equal protection framework. Hence, it upheld sex-based distinctions without inquiry into the problems of differentiation or subordination. It was not until the 1970s that the Court began to move toward intermediate scrutiny as a means to redress the subordination of women. In *Reed v. Reed*, 404 U.S. 71 (1971), the Court purported to use rational basis scrutiny in striking down an Idaho statute that provided a mandatory preference for males over females in the selection of the administrators of estates, but the Court actually applied a heightened level of scrutiny. Two years later, in *Frontiero v. Richardson*, 411 U.S. 677 (1973), a plurality of the Court used heightened scrutiny to invalidate a statute that presumed that servicemen but not servicewomen were the major providers in households. The plurality stated:

> There can be no doubt that our Nation has had a long and unfortunate history of sex discrimination. Traditionally, such discrimination was rationalized by an attitude of "romantic paternalism" which, in practical effect, put women, not on a pedestal, but in a cage. . . . As a result of notions such as these, our statute books gradually became laden with gross, stereotyped distinctions between the sexes and, indeed, throughout much of the 19th century the position of women in our society was, in many respects, comparable to that of blacks under the pre-Civil War slave codes. Neither slaves nor women could hold office, serve on juries, or bring suit in their own names, and married women traditionally were denied the legal capacity to hold or convey property or to serve as legal guardians of their own children. . . . And although blacks were guaranteed the right to vote in 1870, women were denied even that right—which is itself "preservative of other basic civil and political rights"—until adoption of the Nineteenth Amendment half a century later.[30]

The *Frontiero* Court used this history to justify the application of what it termed "strict judicial scrutiny." After justifying the use of heightened scrutiny, the Court considered justifications for the sex-specific policy, noting that the statutes in question were "not in any sense designed to rectify the effects of past discrimination against women."[31] The Court thus suggested that it was appropriate to consider the principle of anti-subordination in ruling on the constitutionality of a sex-specific rule.

Unfortunately, it soon became clear that anti-subordination was not the only justification for sex-specific policies that the Court was willing to accept. Later cases revealed that other justifications were also to be considered which reflected a weak anti-differentiation model without an anti-subordination foundation.

A year after *Frontiero*, the range of justifications for sex-specific policies or actions emerged more clearly in *Kahn v. Shevin*, 416 U.S. 351 (1974), in which the Court used an explicitly lower level of scrutiny than it had purported to employ in *Frontiero*. In *Kahn*, a widower challenged a state property-tax exemption that was available only to widows, blind persons, or totally and permanently disabled persons. The Supreme Court upheld the statute using the *Reed* heightened-rational-basis test. Its analysis provided the state with wide discretion in justifying sex-specific policies.

The real weakness of the Court's sex discrimination analysis became evident in *Michael M. v. Superior Court*, 450 U.S. 464 (1981). The petitioner in *Michael M.* challenged the constitutionality of California's statutory rape law under which it was illegal to have sexual intercourse with a female under the age of eighteen but not illegal to have sexual intercourse with a male under the age of eighteen. The seventeen-and-a-half-year-old male plaintiff, Michael M., had been convicted of statutory rape when he had sexual relations with a sixteen-and-a-half-year-old female, Sharon.

Justice Rehnquist, writing for a plurality, assumed that the state statute discriminated against men because it made "men alone criminally liable for the act of sexual intercourse."[32] Relying on the prior cases, Justice Rehnquist applied intermediate scrutiny, asking whether the gender-based classification had a fair and substantial relationship to legitimate state ends or important government objectives. He concluded that the statute served the strong state interest in preventing illegitimate pregnancy. In addition, he concluded that because all of the significant harmful and inescapable consequences of teenage pregnancy fall on the young female, the legislature had acted within its authority in electing only to punish the participant who, by nature, suffers few of the consequences of his conduct.

Although the Court purported to ask how this legislation affected women, it did not do so from an anti-subordination perspective. For example, Justice Rehnquist did not consider whether Sharon desired state protection or found the sexual intercourse objectionable. He recognized that "this is not a case where a statute is being challenged on the grounds that it 'invidiously discriminated' against females."[33] But he never examined the statute's significance to women. From an anti-subordination perspective, that issue should have been the heart of the inquiry.

Justice Rehnquist avoided that issue by asserting that the statute was "an attempt by a legislature to prevent illegitimate teenage pregnancy."[34] The paucity of evidence before the Court, however, strongly suggested that the desire to control pregnancy was, at best, a post hoc rationalization. Moreover, that rationalization did not even fit with the provisions of the statute because the statute made intercourse unlawful irrespective of the use of birth control or whether the female had reached physical maturity. The interest in limiting teenage pregnancy seemed to be a reflection of the state's interests in protecting its financial resources and in protecting an outmoded view of women.

The use of intermediate scrutiny enabled Justice Rehnquist to bring in considerations unrelated to the elimination of women's subordination in order to uphold a sex-based statute. Under the sloppy framework of intermediate scrutiny, he was able to allow such a statute to pass muster, although it is doubtful that an analogous race-based statute could have passed muster under strict scrutiny.

When a plaintiff establishes a prima facie case of sex-based discrimination, the inquiry should be: Does this statute further or remedy the subordination of women? To answer this question, one would have to listen to voices of adolescent females. Ironically, the Court had the voice of Sharon available in this case. I quoted it in chapter 3. She was the adolescent female whom the Court described as consenting to intercourse despite evidence that she had been hit several times by Michael M. and then "gave up" resisting.

One problem with statutory rape laws is that they don't require the female to testify about any coercion; the state simply needs to establish that sexual activity took place. The court is then free to act paternalistically and protect the female from activities from which she may not need protection. On the other hand, we know that female adolescents, such as Sharon, often do need protection from coercive males. The solution is to require the courts really to listen to the voices of the females in these cases and, on that individualized basis, determine whether a rape has occurred. The low level of scrutiny that Rehnquist applied in *Michael M.* permitted him to avoid taking on the responsibility of really listening to Sharon's voice. It was important for the Court to determine whether the prosecution of Michael M. was yet another coercive event in Sharon's life, or, in fact, a protection that she desired from coercive male actions. Unfortunately, the Court's opinion does not deal with that question.

V. CONCLUSION

An examination of equality doctrine certainly does not leave one with the conclusion that it can eliminate all reproduction-related coercion of women in society. Although equality doctrine, under an anti-subordination perspective, can reflect a connected, group-based perspective on society, the Court has increasingly moved away from such a perspective. Doctrinal hurdles such as *Geduldig, Feeney,* and intermediate scrutiny stand in the way of easy use of this doctrine. Nevertheless, I believe that the advantages of moving in that direction are enormous. Had black plaintiffs given up after *Plessy v. Ferguson,* they never would have obtained *Brown v. Board of Education.* Feminist jurisprudence awaits its *Brown v. Board of Education.*

Notes

1. Catharine MacKinnon, Sexual Harassment of Working Women: A Case of Sex Discrimination 5 (1979).
2. 410 U.S. 113 (1973).
3. *Id.* at 153.
4. *Id.* at 154. In other cases, the Court has required the state to present "compelling"

reasons for abortion restrictions. *See* Akron v. Akron Center for Reproductive Health, 462 U.S. 416, 427 (1983).

5. *See* Harris v. McRae, 448 U.S. 297 (1980).

6. *See* Bellotti v. Baird, 443 U.S. 622 (1979).

7. *See, e.g.*, Sarah Burns, *Notes From the Field: A Reply to Professor Colker*, 13 Harv. Women's L.J. 189, 201 (1990).

8. *See* Geduldig v. Aiello, 417 U.S. 484 (1974).

9. 442 U.S. 256 (1979).

10. *Id.* at 279.

11. *See, e.g.*, Harris v. McRae, 448 U.S. 297 (1980) (failed attempt to prove a violation of equal protection rights of poor women). For an excellent critique of the *Feeney* standard, see Note, *Discriminatory Purpose and Disproportionate Impact: An Assessment After Feeney*, 79 Colum. L. Rev. 1376 (1979) (authored by Bruce Rosenblum).

12. Webster v. Reproductive Health Services, 109 S. Ct. 3040, 3058 (1989).

13. *See, e.g.*, Rosalind Petchesky, *Fetal Images: The Power of Visual Culture in the Politics of Reproduction*, 13 Feminist Stud. 263 (1987).

14. Washington v. Davis, 426 U.S. 246, 247–48 (1976).

15. Personnel Administrator v. Feeney, 442 U.S. 256 (1979).

16. *See Feeney*, 442 U.S. at 270 n.22 (noting that single-sex hiring was explicitly authorized under the 1884 Civil Service statute, which predated the Veteran's Preference statute). This practice was apparently not officially eliminated until 1971 when Massachusetts required that single-sex examinations receive the prior approval of the Massachusetts Commission Against Discrimination. *See Feeney*, 442 U.S. at 266 n.14.

17. *See supra* note 16.

18. *See Feeney*, 442 U.S. at 270 (noting that only 1.8% of women who were hired by Civil Service were veterans).

19. I find it ironic that the Court can uphold a life-time veteran's preference for men in *Feeney* while overturning limited preferences for African-Americans and women in other cases. The fact that the Court will rarely approve affirmative action for women, and then only when it is of a limited duration, suggests that society is not willing to place the kinds of burdens on men that it is willing to place on women. Women are asked to give up all hopes of procuring decent civil service jobs while men are not asked to step aside for even a brief period of time to help women advance in the workplace. *See generally* City of Richmond v. J. A. Croson, 488 U.S. 469 (1989) (creating very rigid rules for affirmative action plans).

20. I say "white, middle-class, adult women" because I think that this is the group of women considered by legislators, if they consider women at all. Legislators have rarely had positive or patronizing stereotypes of African-American or poor women.

21. Feminists provide a twofold description of women's subordinate status. First, feminists argue that women's needs and burdens are not fully understood; women are often silent, not heard, or not considered. *See generally* Adrienne Rich, On Lies Secrets and Silence: Selected Prose 1966–1978 (1979); Tillie Olsen, Silences (1978). Second, feminists argue that when men do observe women, they often do not see women as whole persons; they do not respect women. This is often called a problem of "sexual objectification." *See generally* Catharine MacKinnon, Feminism Unmodified: Discourses on Life and Law (1987). Men may love women yet may treat women as sexual objects for their sexual pleasure. Men may value women's ability to bear children yet may use that biological ability as a reason to preclude women from a range of work outside the home. As Justice Brennan once commented, the pedestal can be a cage. Frontiero v. Richardson, 411 U.S. 677, 684 (1973). Brennan was probably thinking of white, middle-class women since, for poor women, there is only a cage. For all women, however, to varying degrees, it is a cage of limited opportunity where women's needs are not fully understood and women are not given the opportunity to achieve their full potential.

22. Teenagers under the age of eighteen do not have the right to vote. Although 46% of the population eligible to vote did so in 1986, only 18.6% of teenagers aged eighteen to twenty did vote. Regional Differences in America: A Statistical Sourcebook 189 (Alfred Garwood ed. 1988).

23. This view is similar to the general perspective articulated by John Hart Ely. *See* John Hart Ely, Democracy and Distrust: A Theory of Judicial Review (1980). Unfortunately, even if I could persuade the courts to modify the *Feeney* test, as I have suggested, one major doctrinal problem might remain. In equal protection analysis, we are accustomed to talking about the impact of a policy on one particular subgroup that receives close scrutiny by the courts such as African-Americans or women. The Supreme Court has refused to use close scrutiny in analyzing the impact of restrictive abortion policies on a subgroup of women— poor, minority women. *See* Harris v. McRae, 448 U.S. 297 (1980) (rejecting equal protection claim by poor, minority women). In the Title VII context, some courts have recognized that it is unlawful to have combined categories, such as African-American women, face different treatment; nevertheless, the courts have never defined a subclass on the basis of *class*, race, and sex terms. *See, e.g.*, Jeffries v. Harris Co. Community Action Ass'n, 615 F.2d 1025, 1032 (5th Cir. 1980) (recognizing that Title VII forbids race or sex discrimination, which includes combinations of those categories). Moreover, the recognition that African-American women constitute a protected class has not been broadly utilized under Title VII; nor has it been introduced into equal protection doctrine. It is important for this concept of combined categories to be introduced into equal protection doctrine in order for legal doctrine to be sensitive to the essentialism critique. For further discussion of the importance of recognizing combined categories, see Note, *Invisible Man: Black and Male Under Title VII*, 104 Harv. L. Rev. 749 (1991).

24. Geduldig v. Aiello, 417 U.S. 484 (1974).

25. *See generally* Sylvia Law, *Rethinking Sex and the Constitution*, 132 U. Penn. L. Rev. 955, 983 (1984) (describing the numerous criticisms of *Geduldig* as a "cottage industry").

26. *See* Dothard v. Rawlinson, 433 U.S. 321 (1977); Michael M. v. Superior Court, 450 U.S. 464 (1981).

27. Akron v. Akron Center for Reproductive Health, Inc., 462 U.S. 416, 453 (1983) (O'Connor, J., dissenting).

28. 347 U.S. at 494.

29. 83 U.S. at 141.

30. 411 U.S. at 684.

31. Id. at 698 n.22.

32. 450 U.S. at 466.

33. Id. at 475.

34. Id.

R_oe_ $v.$ W_ade_

Reproductive freedom means the ability to
choose whether, when, how, and with whom
one will have children.[1]

In the next several chapters, I will apply the previous discussion to the legal debate
concerning abortion. My purpose in these chapters is twofold: First, I would like
to apply an equality framework to the abortion issue. Second, I would like to
suggest to feminists how they should approach the legal, abortion controversy.
These two purposes converge, because my central thesis will be that the abortion
issue should be primarily approached from an equality rather than a privacy perspective. My equality framework will value women's well-being while not denying
that the state may legitimately try to protect our valuation of life in all of its
various forms. Neither the courts nor feminists have relied on an equality perspective. My comments will, therefore, be critical both of feminist legal strategies as
well as the Court's abortion decisions ranging from _Roe v. Wade_, 410 U.S. 113
(1973) to _Webster v. Reproductive Health Services_, 492 U.S. 490 (1989).

I. GOOD-FAITH DIALOGUE

One central question that I will be asking throughout this chapter is whether any
of the arguments or frameworks that have been suggested to resolve the abortion
issue are truly _feminist_. Although I realize that there is not one definition of
feminism, I will try to suggest one criterion for consideration that should be acceptable to most feminists as well as nonfeminists. This criterion is _good-faith
dialogue_. A good-faith dialogue is one embedded in respect for the people affected
by the issue under discussion as well as the arguments made on each side of the
issue. Let us assume that two people disagree about the morality of women having
abortions. Their discussion might not be a good-faith dialogue if, for example, the
pro-life advocate did not respect the well-being of women. Alternatively, the

discussion might not be in good faith if the pro-choice advocate did not respect the value of prenatal life. On the other hand, that discussion could be a good-faith dialogue. Why? Because people who respect the well-being of women can consider abortion to be immoral. In addition, people who consider abortion to be moral can respect the value of prenatal life. Of course, not all people who take a pro-life position respect the well-being of women and not all people who take a pro-choice position respect the value of prenatal life.

This criterion of good-faith argumentation emerges from my consideration of both feminism and theology. Feminism instructs us that women need to try to protect their well-being in society; that protection does not naturally exist under patriarchy. But theology instructs us that we are not likely to transform society through hard-edged rhetoric; instead, we need to try to engage in dialogue. Dialogue, however, is not possible unless respect and openness exist. Thus, my definition of good-faith argumentation defends the possibility of feminists using argumentation yet also reminds us that we should try to structure that argumentation so as to be able to transform society. When we engage in argumentation, we should try to do so in a way that (1) maintains respect and openness to other perspectives and (2) does not corrupt our substantive position.

By applying this criteria to the *Roe* and *Webster* cases, I will show that neither the plaintiff nor the state's arguments were particularly feminist. The plaintiff's privacy approach refused to acknowledge the legitimacy of the state's interest in protecting our valuation of life. The state's approach refused to acknowledge the legitimacy of women's interest in protecting their health and well-being by avoiding coerced childbirth. I will suggest that we can consider both of these cases under an equality framework that respects both women and the value of life and move to a discussion of abortion restrictions that is based on dialogue rather than on rhetoric.

II. ROE V. WADE

A. Background

Roe v. Wade is the Supreme Court's most famous and important abortion decision. In that case, the Court held that a Texas statute was unconstitutional which provided for criminal sanctions for a woman procuring an abortion unless her life would be jeopardized by her pregnancy. In a landmark decision, the Supreme Court concluded that the Texas statute violated a woman's "right to privacy" and broadly stated the parameters of a constitutional abortion statute. Not only could a state not criminalize abortions, but it could not regulate abortions in the first trimester, could only regulate them in the second trimester for the purpose of protecting the pregnant woman's health, and could regulate them in the third trimester (post-viability) for the purpose of preserving fetal life only so long as those regulations also protected the pregnant woman's health.

Roe v. Wade is a very important decision for two reasons: First, it set the framework for how the courts would resolve abortion cases. That framework, as I will discuss, was based on the liberty–due process clause of the Fourteenth Amendment[2] rather than the equal protection clause. It is characterized as *privacy* doctrine rather than *equality* doctrine. Second, it set the tone for how activist the Court would be in our lives. Rather than simply rule for the plaintiff in *Roe v. Wade*, thereby invalidating the challenged Texas abortion statute, the Court outlined the parameters of a constitutional abortion statute. In other words, the Court drafted a model statute rather than simply striking down the Texas statute. Such judicial involvement in legislative activity is considered to be highly *activist* because the Court, in a sense, is displacing the legislature's role in society. Such activism is often criticized for interfering with legislative dialogue, because the judiciary, an undemocratic institution, has substituted its judgment for that of the legislature. I will therefore discuss whether the Court's activism has been beneficial to the kind of dialogue in society that we would desire on an important issue such as abortion.

B. Abortion Framework

The Texas legislation at issue in *Roe* made it a crime to procure or to attempt an abortion unless the abortion was for the purpose of saving the life of the pregnant woman. The penalty for violating the statute was two to five years imprisonment. The state provided no alternative mechanism for lawfully procuring an abortion in cases in which a pregnancy did not threaten the woman's life. The plaintiff in the case had allegedly become pregnant as the result of a rape.[3] She had already lost custody of one child because she was not able to take care of her. She was poor and unable to take care of another child. Under the Texas statute, she could not lawfully obtain an abortion, because her life was not endangered by her pregnancy.

In order to determine whether the Texas legislation was constitutional, the Court properly considered it necessary to undertake a two-step analysis: First, it had to determine whether the state had infringed a constitutional right of the plaintiff. Second, because it concluded that a fundamental constitutional right had been infringed, it had to determine whether the state was justified in infringing that constitutional right. Because the right that was infringed was fundamental, the Court properly required the state to offer a compelling justification for the infringement and to use only necessary means to achieve that compelling state interest. Nevertheless, as I will show, that analysis was insufficiently respectful of both women's lives and the state's interest in protecting the potential life of the fetus. It therefore has not contributed to good-faith dialogue about abortion.

1. Infringement of a Constitutional Right

At the first step, the Court had the obligation to understand how the statute burdened the plaintiff to determine if a constitutional right had been infringed. This is how the Court described the burden of the Texas legislation at issue in *Roe* on the plaintiff under privacy doctrine, which it found embedded in the Constitution's protection of liberty:

> The detriment that the State would impose upon the pregnant woman by denying this choice altogether is apparent. Specific and direct harm medically diagnosable even in early pregnancy may be involved. Maternity, or additional offspring, may force upon the woman a distressful life and future. Psychological harm may be imminent. Mental and physical health may be taxed by child care. There is also the distress, for all concerned, associated with the unwanted child, and there is the problem of bringing a child into a family already unable, psychologically and otherwise, to care for it. In other cases, as in this one, the additional difficulties and continuing stigma of unwed motherhood may be involved. All these are factors the woman and her responsible physician necessarily will consider in consultation.[4]

I find this description of the burdens of the legislation inadequate because they are not sufficiently attentive to the life of the plaintiff, especially the gender-based aspects of her life. It is an abstract discussion of the abortion issue removed from the reality of the plaintiff's actual life, except for a passing reference to her status as an unwed mother. It is hard to imagine how our judicial system can fully respect women's well-being through such abstract discourse, discourse which ignores that the plaintiff claimed to have become pregnant as the result of a rape and that she was a poor woman who had already lost custody of one child. If we want to ask judges to consider the plaintiff's liberty interests from the perspective of the plaintiff's life (rather than from some imagined sense of the plaintiff's life), then those kinds of facts need to be in front of the courts and society.

The *Roe v. Wade* decision is not unique in having an inadequate description of the plaintiff's injury from the challenged legislation. In another major case in the liberty or privacy area, *Bowers v. Hardwick*, 478 U.S. 186 (1986), the same problem emerged. In that case, Michael Hardwick was arrested under Georgia's sodomy statute after a police officer, who came by his home to harass him about an already-paid ticket, happened to witness him having oral sex with another man in the privacy of his own bedroom. Hardwick unsuccessfully challenged the constitutionality of the state statute under which he could have been imprisoned for five years for engaging in consensual sexual activity with another man. The Court tried to determine whether the plaintiff had a privacy right to engage in "homosexual sodomy" without understanding how it was the case that a policeman could have found himself outside the plaintiff's door to watch the plaintiff engage in sexual activity, what were the full consequences of the state's sodomy statute in the plaintiff's life, and what were the implications to the plaintiff of being unable to engage lawfully in sexual expressiveness. By framing his complaint in privacy terms, Hardwick implicitly suggested that the private facts of his life were irrelevant to the legal analysis because all the Court needed to do was protect him in his privacy. I would suggest, by contrast, that pregnant women and lesbian and gay people need to "come out of the closet" about the gender-based inequalities that are part of their lives. When these gender-based inequalities are out in the open, it will be more apparent why pregnant women should not be coerced to continue their pregnancies or lesbian and gay people should not be coerced to abstain from sexual activity with persons of the same sex.

Although the plaintiff in Roe was successful under privacy doctrine (and the plaintiff in Bowers was not), the Roe Court did not provide a very convincing record to persuade others of the correctness of its decision. It did not explain the implications of coercing women to carry fetuses to term in strong enough terms to convince commentators that abortion restrictions do impinge women's constitutional rights. Thus, liberal commentators have often criticized the Court's privacy rationale.[5] In fact, the Court could have done a stronger job with liberty-privacy doctrine without even describing the case in equality terms. The Texas legislation gave a woman absolutely no opportunity to procure an abortion lawfully if her very life were not endangered. The plaintiff had allegedly become pregnant as the result of a gang rape and did not have the economic resources to support another child. Thus, her pregnancy was the result of a highly coercive experience in her life. To require a poor woman who has been forcefully raped to serve a prison sentence because she does not feel capable of carrying her fetus to term would result in a very serious infringement on her liberty for conditions that were not in her control.

An even stronger argument, however, that the Texas statute constituted an unconstitutional infringement of the plaintiff's rights, can be seen from an equality perspective that would focus on the gender-based implications of the case. This case was about women's powerlessness within society with respect to reproductive issues. It is only women who become pregnant as a result of a rape. It is women, not men, who are socialized to bear and raise children. Bearing an unwanted child puts women into a deeply gendered role in our society. The conditions surrounding a woman's decision to have an abortion often reflect that she will have virtually no support for that deeply gendered role. She will not be provided with prenatal care, postnatal care, pregnancy leave, or childcare. If we are committed to women moving toward their aspirations for their authentic self, then we need to avoid coercing women to enter a deeply gendered role. Few roles are more gendered in our society than motherhood. Roe was about women's right to say no to a fundamental, gendered change in their lives. Had the Court fully described the plaintiff's injury in equality terms, then liberal commentators would have had more trouble dismissing the constitutional significance of the plaintiff's injury.

One might excuse the Roe Court's superficial discussion of the plaintiff's case by noting that the plaintiff did not allege many facts that gave the Court a complete sense of her injury. However, the Court decided Roe on the same day that it decided another case, Doe v. Bolton, 410 U.S. 179 (1973), which was rich with facts about the individual plaintiff. Nevertheless, the Court did not utilize the facts in Doe either.

In Doe v. Bolton, the challenged Georgia statute made abortion a crime and provided that a person convicted of that crime shall be punished by imprisonment for not less than one nor more than ten years. The statute contained three exceptions, when a physician's best medical judgment determines that an abortion is necessary because

(1) A continuation of the pregnancy would endanger the life of the pregnant woman or would seriously and permanently injure her health; or (2) The fetus would very likely be born with a grave, permanent, and irremediable mental or physical defect; or (3) The pregnancy resulted from forcible or statutory rape.[6]

In addition, the woman had to obtain a written concurrence by at least two other Georgia-licensed physicians indicating that she met the above criteria.

The plaintiff, Mary Doe, had not been able to obtain an abortion under the Georgia statute. This is her story as contained in her complaint:

(1) She was a 22-year old Georgia citizen, married, and nine weeks pregnant. She had three living children. The two older ones had been placed in a foster home because of Doe's poverty and inability to care for them. The youngest, born July 19, 1969, had been placed for adoption. Her husband had recently abandoned her and she was forced to live with her indigent parents and their eight children. She and her husband, however, had become reconciled. He was a construction worker employed only sporadically. She had been a mental patient at the State Hospital. She had been advised that an abortion could be performed on her with less danger to her health than if she gave birth to the child she was carrying. She would be unable to care for or support the new child.

(2) On March 25, 1970, she applied to the Abortion Committee of Grady Memorial Hospital, Atlanta for a therapeutic abortion under [the Georgia statute]. Her application was denied 16 days later, on April 10, when she was eight weeks pregnant, on the ground that her situation was not one described in [the Georgia statute].[7]

The Supreme Court concluded that the hospital's abortion-committee and two-doctor concurrence requirements were not constitutionally justifiable. Nevertheless, the Court was not troubled by the criteria stated in the statute for permitting an abortion. The Court concluded that the stated medical factors "allows the attending physician the room he needs to make his best medical judgment."[8] It did not discuss the inequity to Doe of not being able to convince a hospital board that she satisfied these criteria. It considered the case entirely in privacy terms that were insensitive to Doe's life rather than in equality terms that would have fully understood the scope of the injury to her life and well-being.

I suggest, however, that the record in Doe's case amply demonstrated that the narrow range of exceptions in the Georgia statute resulted in not giving sufficient weight to her well-being. It is easy to see how Doe's well-being was substantially impacted by her inability to procure an abortion—her marriage would be strained, her already precarious financial condition would be worsened, she might face the social stigma of giving up another child for adoption, her already weak emotional health might be further harmed. In addition, Doe had been sufficiently responsible to seek an abortion immediately upon learning that she was pregnant. She applied for an abortion during her fifth week of pregnancy when the fetus was at a very early stage of development (and not even yet properly characterized as a fetus). Nevertheless, the Georgia statute valued the life of a five-week-old fetus over the health and well-being of an adult woman and her family.[9] None of these significant aspects of her well-being were recognized by the Georgia statute, thereby leaving her unable to protect her own well-being by choosing an abortion. The problem in a case like this is the extreme absoluteness of the state's statute. If she does not fit into the three areas of exceptions, she has no opportunity to demonstrate how her well-being is being affected by not being able to procure an abortion; moreover, she must face the minimum sanction of one year in prison. Such restrictions should violate the liberty–due process clause. We should expect the due process clause to entitle a woman to demonstrate the significant impact that a reproductive decision would have in her life. By not permitting her to have that due process, the Georgia legislature discounted the importance of her well-being.

In addition, under the equal protection clause, a potential prison sentence seems inappropriately harsh in gender terms. Her husband was able to abandon her and provide no support for the existing children and face no criminal sanctions; nevertheless, she faced potential criminal sanctions for life conditions that were, in part, created by him. If one major purpose of criminal abortion laws is to deter women from choosing abortions, then it would seem that we would want to deter both women and men from engaging in unprotected sexual activity which results in an unwanted pregnancy. Texas and Georgia, like most other states, have sought only to criminalize the woman's and physician's actions, not the man with whom the woman engaged in sexual activity. Women already have strong biological and social deterrences to becoming pregnant unintentionally: If they choose an abortion, then they must experience an unwanted pregnancy for at least a month, experience the surgery necessary to perform the abortion, deal with the emotional consequences of having an abortion, and face potential medical complications resulting from the abortion. If they choose not to have an abortion, then they are very likely to face all of the costs of raising the child or relinquishing the child for adoption. It is hard to imagine that a potential prison sentence adds much more incentive for a woman not to engage in unprotected sexual activity when she does not desire to become pregnant. But the man faces few deterrents from engaging in unprotected sexual activity. Thus, in using the criminal laws to penalize women who make abortion decisions, our laws seem to be reaching the wrong person in the sexual relationship. It would seem that effective deterrents are needed to encourage men not to engage in unprotected sexual activity when a pregnancy is unwanted.

To reinforce that point, it may be helpful to remember that women do not engage in sexual activity because they want to experience an abortion. An abortion is always the unintended consequence of the sexual activity. The most effective way to prevent the need for abortions is to prevent unprotected sexual activity when a pregnancy is not desired. If we could achieve that result, then abortions would only be needed when birth control failed. At present, our legal system and society do little to encourage men to act responsibly when engaging in sexual behavior. By imposing all of the burdens of unprotected sexual activity on women,

I am therefore suggesting that states violate women's right to equal protection of the laws.

Thus, it is difficult to see how the criminal law would ever be an appropriate response to the abortion issue. I suspect that an examination of the harshness of criminal solutions to the abortion issue would cause even some pro-life advocates to agree that criminalizing abortion is not an appropriate means to engender love and compassion. Pro-life advocates, however, seldom seem to consider this aspect of the abortion debate. Indeed, the impact on women's lives of statutes criminalizing abortion is so little discussed in the pro-life movement that a question about it caught George Bush off guard during the 1988 presidential campaign.[10]

Although I am arguing that the criminalization of abortion is inappropriate under the aspirations of love and compassion, my defense of women's ability to choose to have an abortion is not absolute. It is contingent upon existing social circumstances of inequality; it is *not* embedded in the argument that a woman has the right to control her body under any circumstances. From the perspective of love and compassion, I accept the argument that women have responsibilities in this world to nurture love and life. Since we are connected selves, we have no claim to act in ways to protect our bodily autonomy in isolation from society. However, society must allocate the responsibilities of its members compassionately and respectfully. A woman, in my view, has the right to seek an abortion to protect the value of her life in a society that disproportionately imposes the burdens of pregnancy and childcare on women and does not sufficiently sponsor the development and use of safe, effective contraceptives.

As a final note, I should observe that *Doe v. Bolton* was actually an abortion *funding* case. The reason that Doe wanted to get an abortion at Grady Memorial Hospital was that Grady would have given her a free abortion. Apparently, a private hospital did approve her for an abortion but would have made her pay for it. This inequity shows an additional problem with statutes like the Georgia statute. It ends up giving nonindigent women more legal rights, because nonindigent women are more likely to be able to find a physician who will liberally interpret the statute to permit an abortion in her case. We should find that result troubling. If we value women's liberty and equal protection interests then we should value those interests irrespective of their economic status.

Thus, if we are concerned about women's liberty or equality interests, we can conclude that the Texas statute, as well as the Georgia statute, infringed those interests. By having a completely closed mind to the possibility that any woman would have a good-faith argument for an abortion when very limited preconditions existed, the Texas and Georgia legislatures infringed her liberty-privacy interest. In addition, by imposing substantial criminal sanctions on a woman who is the victim of an unwanted pregnancy, the states infringed women's equal protection interests.

2. Fetal Life/Viability Distinction as Justification

The fact that the states of Texas and Georgia infringed the plaintiff's liberty interest does not end the analysis. The next question is whether the state had a compelling justification for the infringement and used only necessary means to achieve that compelling state interest.

In *Roe*, the state argued that it was justified in infringing the woman's liberty interest because it wanted to protect life from and after conception. The Court, by contrast, concluded that the state may not adopt "one theory of life" to "override the rights of the pregnant woman that are at stake."[11] The *Roe* Court did not accept the state's articulation of its compelling interest. Rather than conclude that protecting fetal life is a compelling state interest, the Court ruled that protecting life is only a compelling state interest when the fetus is viable. I will suggest that the state of Texas was correct in its articulation of a compelling state interest; its statute should have been struck down under the necessary means test rather than the compelling state interest test. I will argue that criminalizing abortion does not increase our valuation of life; instead, criminalizing abortion in the absence of any societal support for pregnant women and children demonstrates our devaluation of the lives of women and children. I will first discuss whether viability should be the appropriate criterion in determining whether the state had a compelling interest. I will suggest that protecting potential life rather than viability may be a compelling state interest but that the means used by the state to achieve that interest in *Roe* were fundamentally flawed.

a. Compelling State Interest Analysis

The state of Texas argued that it could treat the protection of fetal life as a compelling state interest; the Court rejected that argument unless the fetus was viable. Thus, the Court substituted its judgment for what it considered to be a compelling state interest—viability—for the state's assertion of what it considered to be a compelling state interest—potential life.

I find the Court's discussion of the potential-life argument inadequate in *Roe* and *Doe*, because the Court refuses to acknowledge the validity of the state's interest in increasing our valuation of life. The Court concludes that the constitutional text does not consider fetuses to be *persons*. Therefore, the Court concluded that they were not entitled to protection by the Court.

The absence of explicit constitutional protection for fetuses, however, does not mean that protecting their life cannot be a compelling state interest. Justifications can be important, or even compelling, without being explicitly mentioned in the Constitution. For example, an infant is not a full person for constitutional persons. She cannot vote, hold office, or even claim most of the protections contained in the Fourteenth Amendment. Yet, we would easily agree that a state can infringe a woman's liberty by criminalizing the killing of an infant. Similarly, adults are persons for constitutional persons. Yet, the courts have held that white adults' employment opportunities can be limited through affirmative action programs in order to protect the liberty interests of black adults, because the state has a strong interest in promoting affirmative action. The fact that white adults are constitutionally recognized persons does not prevent the state from infringing their liberties in order to protect the liberties of another group of persons. Thus, whether fetuses are constitutionally recognized as persons may affect whether fetuses can serve as *parties* in abortion cases, but that does necessarily resolve whether their protection can be a compelling state interest. By not recognizing the value in protecting fetal life, the Court did not engage in respectful dialogue about the interests implicated by its decision. It prevented dialogue on that interest in future cases by not laying a foundation for its consideration.

Professor John Hart Ely has recognized the weakness of the Court's assessment of the interest in protecting fetal life. He says:

> [I]t has never been held or even asserted that the state interest needed to justify forcing a person to refrain from an activity, *whether or not that activity is constitutionally protected*, must implicate either the life or the constitutional rights of another person. Dogs are not "persons in the whole sense" nor have they constitutional rights, but that does not mean the state cannot prohibit killing them: It does not even mean the state cannot prohibit killing them in the exercise of the First Amendment right of political protest. Come to think of it, draft cards aren't persons either.[12]

Although Ely is correct that the *Roe* decision is not sufficiently respectful of the state's interest in preserving fetal life, I do not think that Ely understands the real strength of the fetal life argument. In Stanley Hauerwas's terms, it is an argument about the kind of society that we want to be.[13] Many pro-life advocates use Holocaust imagery and love-based theology to argue that it is critical that we value all life, including all potential life, in order to avoid creating another Nazi Germany.[14] They are afraid of sliding down the slippery slope of terminating any life, even potential life, because it may move us toward a society that is callous toward life. The Court has never addressed that issue. It has not told us why we can feel secure that we are not moving toward a callous view toward life. The Court's silence neither promotes dialogue nor provides reassurance on that issue.

Nevertheless, the Court has chosen one point in a woman's pregnancy to protect potential life—that of viability. I do not, however, find that criterion supportable. Viability represents the time at which the fetus has a statistically significant chance of surviving outside the womb without substantial medical intervention. The fact of viability, however, is not relevant to the strength of the state's compelling interest. From a theological perspective, the purpose of restricting abortion is to protect our valuation of life generally in society, to make sure that we respect life in all of its various forms. It may be true that restricting abortion does not increase our valuation of life. If that is true, then the problem is the means used to achieve the state's objective. But the objective itself—increasing our valuation of life—is not tainted by the irrationality of the means chosen.

It is difficult to see how protecting viable fetuses is a more compelling state objective than protecting nonviable fetuses. The concept of viability refers to the ability (or statistical probability) of a fetus to survive outside a woman's womb. When the fetus's chance of survival outside the womb is above some figure, let's say 80%, then the fetus is considered to be viable.

All fetuses, however, are, statistically speaking, viable after implantation has occurred, because they have a greater than 80% chance of surviving if they are left inside a woman's womb. (The greatest risk to the fetus is spontaneous abortion or miscarriage which doctors estimate occurs 15% to 30% of the time.) The medical concept of viability refers to their ability to live outside the womb (with substantial medical intervention), but most fetuses are viable in a lay sense of the term in that they have a very high chance of survival if left inside the womb. Thus, if the state is concerned about protecting fetuses that have a significant chance of survival, then it could be properly concerned about all fetuses after implantation has occurred.

Protecting viable fetuses and protecting nonviable fetuses (so that they can become viable) are, therefore, indistinguishable objectives. A viable fetus is no more alive than a nonviable fetus. Both are dependent on pregnant women for their sustenance. The only distinction between them is that if removed from a pregnant woman's body, a viable fetus has a statistically significant chance of being able to continue its life. Both fetuses, however, are equally capable of ultimately sustaining personhood outside a woman's body if she chooses to carry her pregnancy to term. In other words, outlawing abortion would equally sustain the life of the nonviable as well as the viable fetus.

From a pregnant woman's perspective, a fetus is always viable if she chooses to keep it inside her womb. In other words, a fetus has a substantial likelihood of maturing into a person if a woman is willing to serve as its incubator for nine months. The term viability, as it is used in the abortion literature, refers to the ability of *medical science*, not the woman, to preserve a fetus's life if it is outside the woman's womb.

Viability is a significant moral distinction for the medical community, not the pregnant woman. At present, states use the viability distinction to impose a responsibility on a woman not to have an abortion after a certain period in her pregnancy. Because medical science could preserve the fetus's life *outside* the womb, states impose the responsibility on the pregnant woman to preserve the fetus's life *inside* her womb.

An alternative response to the fact of viability, however, would be to impose responsibility on the medical community, not the pregnant woman. We could say that when the fetus is viable, the pregnant woman should be permitted to terminate her pregnancy but not terminate the life of the fetus. Ironically, at the time in her pregnancy when she could have an abortion and not terminate the life of the fetus, we permit states to intervene and prevent the abortion. The more appropriate response would be for states to insist that a woman cooperate with a physician so that he or she could preserve the fetus's life. If a woman is unwilling to cooperate in preserving the fetus's life, then we could say that an abortion is not permitted. It would also be important for the state to be willing to bear the costs of preserving the fetus's life since, once again, it is not fair to impose all of the burdens on the pregnant woman.

The obvious problem with allowing women to abort the fetus in the third trimester, but to impose the duty on the state to sustain the fetus's life, is that it would probably make the abortion procedure more dangerous for women. That result would be unacceptable. But again, that result is unacceptable because of the limited state of medical science. If it became feasible to remove a live fetus from a woman's body in a way that would not jeopardize the woman's life or health nor the fetus's life then clearly that would be the most desirable result. Our present abortion analysis, however, does not move us to consider that superior alternative. Instead, it places all the burden on the pregnant woman rather than medical science to preserve fetal life.

To clarify my point about viability, I would like to emphasize that the viability issue cannot be a useful moral distinction about a woman's responsibilities unless the state is willing to bear some of the cost and responsibility of bringing a viable fetus to term. To say that a woman is morally compelled to carry a fetus to term because medical science could, but won't, bring the fetus to term makes no sense. Since viability is defined from the perspective of what medical science can do, then it can only be a distinction about what medical science should do. A woman has the capability of bringing a fetus to term from the moment of conception; it does not make sense for her moral responsibility to be dependent upon what an agent outside of her can but won't do.

Thus, the Court's choice of a compelling state interest—viability—is less logical than the state's choice of a compelling state interest—protecting potential life. Given the reasonableness of the state's asserted compelling interest, there is no constitutional justification for the Court's substituting its opinion for that of the state. Neither state interest is constitutionally mandated although the state should be free to articulate either objective. (It is important to remember that compelling state interests are never *required* to be protected; however, certain compelling state interests are available to states. Protecting potential life may be one such compelling state interest as it fits into the continuum of protecting the value of life generally.) The real problem with the state's statute, I would suggest, is the means used to achieve the objective rather than the compelling interest that was articulated Under existing constitutional doctrine, the Court had to determine whether the state had a compelling state interest and used necessary means to achieve that interest. The *Roe* Court struck down the Texas legislation under the compelling interest standard, finding that the state's interest in preserving fetal life could not be compelling in the first trimester. It never examined the means used by the state to achieve that interest. The more appropriate route, I would suggest, which would have been more respectful to the value of protecting life, would have been to strike down the legislation under the necessary means test.

b. Necessary Means Test

The necessary means test requires us to inquire how the availability of abortions affects a woman's valuation of life. Are women more likely to increase their valuation of life if abortion is made illegal? I will suggest that the Texas legislation should have failed the necessary means test because it was unlikely to cause women who are pregnant to value life more dearly.

The experiential literature suggests that the abortion decision is rarely easy for a woman, because she is often conflicted between her desire to protect her own life by not carrying a pregnancy to term and her desire to bring a life into the world.[15] It is apparently quite common for women who have had abortions to note mentally when the baby would have been born and to experience special sadness on the anniversary of the date that the baby would have been born. These women may value fetal life but also hold other values which lead them to choose an abortion. A woman who chooses an abortion does not necessarily want to have the fetus's life terminated. She says that she does not want to carry the fetus to term. Although I understand that some women who want an abortion might also object to extraordinary measures being taken to preserve the fetus's life, I do not believe that they have available an equality argument in favor of their position.

Even if we accept the premise that a woman who has an abortion wants to destroy the life of that particular fetus, she may still value fetal life. Many women, for example, choose abortions to defer childbirth. They do not bear a child now in order to bear a child later. It is *because* of their love and concern for the value of potential fetal life that they choose to defer child birth.

For example, one woman described the following life experience in a letter to NARAL:

> I had an abortion in 1949 because I could not go through with a loveless marriage for the sake of a child I did not want. . . . The benefits were incalculable. I was able to terminate the pregnancy, to complete my education, start a professional career, and, three years later marry a man I did love. We subsequently had three beautiful children by choice, children who were welcomed with joy, cherished always, and raised with deep pleasure because we attained economic security and the maturity necessary to provide properly for them.[16]

Such women want to have a child at a time in their life when they can best love and care for it. I understand that there are people who, in good faith, believe that such an action is unjustified murder or not in a woman's best interest. Nevertheless, I would expect that even those people would have to understand that the woman has not articulated an anti-fetal-life perspective. She does value and care for the fetal life, but she would make a different decision about this particular fetus than someone from a strict pro-life perspective.

In general, I find it ironic that society would try to treat pregnant women coercively in order to increase society's valuation of life. Women are already socialized to want to bear and raise children. Despite the economic, physical, psychological, and economic burdens of pregnancy and childbirth, women repeatedly sacrifice their lives to bear and raise children. Not surprisingly, women's socialization to value life has led them historically to be very active in the peace movement. To the extent that our society devalues life, as evidenced by a high homicide rate and the destruction of our environment, it is very difficult to say that women and their infrequent choice of abortion has been a cause of that devaluation of life. That our society would impose a disproportionate penalty on pregnant women who find themselves unable to carry a pregnancy to term is an expression of society's devaluation of women's lives rather than an honest attempt to increase our valuation of fetal life.

Thus, the state is not justified in using the coercive forces of the criminal laws to regulate the pregnant woman's conduct, because such regulation represents a substantial infringement of her liberty with only a highly speculative increased protection of the value of fetal life. Even if the state meets the compelling interest test, it cannot meet the necessary means test.

So far, I have argued that the state is not justified in criminalizing a woman's behavior in obtaining an abortion in order to protect our valuation of fetal life. The statute in *Roe*, however, did not only criminalize the woman's conduct; it also criminalized the conduct of the physician who performed the abortion. The result of such criminalization is still felt heavily on the pregnant woman. By effectively making abortion unavailable in her state, the woman is coerced into undergoing compulsory childbirth or unreasonable expenses to procure an abortion. Compulsory childbirth is a punitive measure on the mother and child without any increase in the mother's valuation of life. Nine months of physical discomfort itself is a drastic criminal penalty.

Although I would again conclude that the criminal law is not the way to achieve greater valuation of life under the necessary means test, I do think that the state has a valid interest in being concerned about healthcare workers' valuation of life when they perform repeated abortions. It is hard for healthcare workers to maintain an awareness that they are terminating a valuable entity, potential life, when they must perform a large number of abortions. In general, healthcare workers probably have to develop a callousness to death in order to perform their jobs. For example, healthcare workers who deal with AIDS patients must live with the reality that the life of their patients will generally be short.

I do not have empirical support for this argument, but it is an issue that I have discussed with my friends who perform direct-care services to persons with AIDS. They have reported to me that one of the most difficult aspects of their jobs is learning to deal with issues of life and death. I would like to suggest that the possibility of the devaluation of life is even more likely in the AIDS context than in the abortion context, because the person with AIDS is generally a child or an adult with whom the healthcare worker can develop a significant relationship over a period of time. I suspect that it is much more difficult to deal with death when one knows a person well than when one has a brief encounter with a fetus that has not yet matured into personhood.

We would hopefully never suggest that healthcare workers not deal with AIDS patients because they may develop a callous attitude about death. Yet, we might worry about the strain on the healthcare workers and try to develop programs to help them deal with this situation. Similarly, we might want to consider the effect on healthcare workers who perform numerous abortions and try to ensure that their work does not cause them to devalue life.

The strain on healthcare workers has been well documented in the abortion context. Doctor Bernard Nathanson describes it well:

> Curiously, abortion appears sometimes to have had a more profound effect on the people who were doing them than on those to whom they were being done. . . .
>
> . . . I also recall well being cornered by the wife of one doctor at the cocktail

party we gave when the 62nd Street [abortion] clinic opened. She drew me aside and talked in a decidedly agitated manner of the increasingly frequent nightmares her husband had been having. He had confessed to her that the dreams were filled with blood and children, and that he had literally become obsessed with the notion that some terrible justice would soon be inflicted upon his own children in payment for what he was doing. . . . Yet another doctor walked into my office after three weeks on the job and submitted his resignation. He declared that he had absolutely no feelings on the morality of abortion as such, but "when I'm up this close to it, it's just too much for me. Too bloody, too much pressure. You guys are turning out abortions here like an assembly line, and you expect us to work at this with no feelings at all."[17]

The question that these observations raise is what is a constitutional response to this problem by the state. Since I have already concluded that the state may not constitutionally criminalize the woman's conduct, it would not make sense to criminalize the physician, who is morally culpable in only a secondary sense. More fundamentally, however, the woman's liberty interest as defined above would be substantially implicated by criminalization of the physician's conduct. A state may not do indirectly what I have concluded it cannot do directly.

Nevertheless, the state's hands should not be tied in considering the well-being of healthcare workers. Although the *Roe* Court deferred to the judgment of the medical profession, it did not consider how performing abortions might affect the well-being of healthcare workers. Within the first trimester, a state is only permitted to regulate abortions to preserve and protect the health of the pregnant woman. Since the fetus is not yet viable, the state is not allowed to take steps to preserve the life of the fetus. Even accepting that the state may not take measures to preserve the life of the fetus, the state may want to take other steps to ensure that our society sufficiently values life. For example, it might want to create programs for healthcare workers to help them deal with the trauma sometimes associated with performing numerous abortions. Such programs would not increase the cost of abortion if the state paid for these programs. (I would also suggest generally that a state that institutes supposed pro-life policies but tries to pass the cost of those programs on to pregnant women rather than paying those costs themselves is insincere in its supposed pro-life position.) Under the Court's framework in *Roe*, I would expect such steps to be impermissible; yet, such steps might help protect our valuation of life while still permitting individual women to choose abortions. Thus, I would suggest that the Court spoke too broadly in ruling out any first-trimester regulations of abortion to protect our valuation of fetal life. Focusing on the means that the state used to achieve that interest, rather than invalidating the seriousness of the state's interest itself, would have resulted in a more respectful consideration of the fetal life issue. It would have promoted more dialogue on the abortion issue.

C. Activism Versus Restraint: Dialogue Revisited

So far, I have argued that the Court's privacy framework in *Roe* insufficiently promoted dialogue on abortion, because it was not sufficiently respectful of women's well-being and the state's interest in protecting potential life. Nevertheless, I have shown that the Court could have reached a similar holding, focusing on the means that the state used to achieve its protection of potential life. Those means, I have argued, demonstrated a fundamental lack of respect for women's well-being while not furthering the state's interest in increasing society's valuation of life.

Although my previous discussion concerning dialogue focused on the Court's decision-making framework, most discussions of the *Roe* decision have largely focused on the activist nature of the Court's decision. I believe that the Court's legal framework could have better promoted dialogue, but I do not believe that the activist nature of the Court's decision undermined societal dialogue about abortion. Thus, I will now discuss *Roe* from a different perspective: whether the Court's activism in *Roe* deterred societal dialogue about abortion.

In *Roe*, the Court did not simply hold that the Texas statute was unconstitutional. It also took the highly activist step of dictating the parameters of a constitutional abortion statute. It held that in the first trimester a state may not constitutionally regulate abortion, that it can only regulate abortion in the second trimester so as to protect the woman's health, and that it can regulate abortion in the third trimester so as to protect fetal viability but not if that protection interfered with the pregnant woman's health. By doing so, the Court arguably preempted much of the dialogue and consideration of the abortion issue that might occur in legislatures and the general public about abortion. Rather than permit the Texas legislature to enact a marginally different piece of abortion legislation, which would permit the plaintiff in *Roe* to have an abortion, and then have other women challenge the constitutionality of the new legislation, the Court suggested the general content of constitutional legislation. The question that the Court's activism raises is whether it inappropriately deterred dialogue on the important moral issue of abortion.

In assessing the consequences of the Court's judicial activism, I will consider the consequences for women's deliberations (or dialogue) about abortion and the consequences for legislative-judicial dialogue about abortion. Traditionally, when scholars discuss judicial activism, they talk about it entirely in terms of its consequences on democracy or legislative dialogue.[18] Rather than privilege legislative dialogue, I am going to consider the implications of judicial activism on all dialogue throughout society, not just in the legislature.

1. Background Observations

The issue of judicial activism raises the issue of the appropriate role for judges in our society. Although feminists traditionally advocate judicial activism, feminist jurisprudence must be cautious about judges' competence to render generally applicable *right answers* to difficult moral questions. To the extent that we question the existence of universally correct answers, we should hesitate before deferring to the judiciary on controversial social issues.

Although feminists routinely disclaim any interest in developing universal norms, their work, on close examination, reflects certain minimal universal aspirations. For example, Martha Minow criticizes our ability to speak from universal norms, yet she argues for the pursuit of the universal norm of compassion or respect when she encourages us to try to understand the world from the multiple perspectives of those who have been subordinated.[19] I call such attempts to define universal norms *minimalist* because they tentatively seek to attain universality but reflect the insight that norms may need to change as we gain greater wisdom. Under a Buddhist-feminist view, a minimalist conception of universality recognizes that, despite their differences, there is a fragile and subtle strand that connects all people to one another. By articulating certain minimalist aspirations such as love, compassion, and wisdom, feminist theory could have a confident, although often changing, set of universal aspirations.

From a minimalist perspective, feminist theory can sometimes support claims for judicial activism because sometimes there are right answers to difficult moral issues. Universal norms are possible, although not plentiful. However, the fact that there may be, on occasion, correct answers to difficult moral issues does not mean that judicial activism is always appropriate. A particular issue may not present a clear, right answer. Moreover, judges may not be sufficiently acting in good faith to acknowledge the right answer that does exist. Thus, we can only turn reluctantly to the courts to resolve disputes, recognizing that we are a long way from attaining the aspirations of love, compassion, and wisdom in our daily social lives which make good-faith dialogue possible.

Because I believe there are some universal ethical principles that shape our notion of justice, I believe judicial intervention can lead us closer to our aspiration of wisdom. Dialogue and contemplation, not rhetoric, however, are the vehicles by which we seek wisdom. Judicial activism is often criticized for being an imperial or rhetorical stance which does not promote dialogue throughout society. Nevertheless, I shall argue that in the abortion context, judicial activism can sometimes promote rather than deter dialogue.

2. Impact on Women's Deliberations About Abortion

The *Roe* decision is usually applauded as protecting women's deliberations about abortion by curtailing any regulation by the state of the woman's deliberative process during the first trimester. In general, that description is accurate because *Roe* prevents the state from imposing coercive measures on the woman's deliberative process, thereby promoting dialogue. Nevertheless, I would like to suggest that this aspect of the Court's decision was a little too activist, that the Court should have left open a bit more space for states to try to regulate the abortion decision-making process constitutionally.

The Court's control over the deliberative process can be seen vividly in *City of Akron v. Akron Center for Reproductive Health*, 462 U.S. 416 (1983), when the Court was asked to consider the constitutionality of regulations of the abortion decision-making process. One issue in *Akron* was the informed consent and waiting period requirements. In addition, no physician was permitted to perform an abortion until twenty-four hours elapsed from the time the woman initially consented to the abortion.

Turning first to the *informed consent* requirement, the Supreme Court struck it down because "it is fair to say that much of the information required is designed not to inform the woman's consent but rather to persuade her to withhold it altogether."[20] Thus, the Court appropriately rejected the informed consent requirement because it promoted coercion rather than deliberation. Nevertheless, in rejecting the informed consent requirement, the Court implied that a physician may only be required to impart *medical* information about the possible adverse consequences to a woman's health; it assumed that only medical consequences affected a woman's well-being. The Court's analysis of the informed consent issue in *Akron* paralleled the analysis in *Roe* by limiting itself to a discussion of how abortion decisions implicate women's physical well-being generally.

However, a state that is concerned about a woman's well-being should be concerned about far more than the possible physical consequences of abortion. It should also be concerned about the conflicting emotional and moral issues that a woman must resolve in deciding whether to have an abortion. The Constitution should permit a state to protect those aspects of a woman's well-being.

One problem with the *Akron* case is that it uses the wrong language to discuss how to produce more abortion dialogue. It talks about abortion restrictions in terms of informed consent requirements. Informed consent is a doctrine relating to the medical information that is disseminated before a medical procedure occurs. There is no reason to believe that physicians and nurses fail to provide adequate medical information before performing abortions. (The threat of malpractice gives them sufficient incentive to provide that information.) The problem is a lack of ethical discussions concerning abortion. Thus, as I discussed in the last chapter, I would like us to consider how we can facilitate more ethical discussions concerning abortion without using coercive, criminal laws which attempt to take the final decision away from the pregnant woman.

In order to understand how state regulation of the abortion decision could enhance women's liberty interests, we need to consider the process by which a woman makes an abortion decision. Considering the aspiration of wisdom, we would want to facilitate women's coming to an abortion decision which will move them towards their aspirations for their authentic self. Feminists often seem reluctant to permit the state to impose any requirements on how women make abortion decisions because many of these requirements have been coercive and would not facilitate real dialogue. Yet, it is important to keep in mind our aspirations when analyzing these measures. We know that the abortion decision can be very difficult for some women and that the wrong decision can create emotional trauma. Rather than being satisfied with any abortion decision made by a woman, we should consider ways that we can improve her qualitative judgment.

The Court should defer to state legislatures' judgment in regulating the abortion decision only if the regulations are founded on the fundamental premise that women's well-being must be dearly valued. So far, United States legislatures have not shown themselves capable of regulating the decision-making process in a way that promotes women's well-being. The most recent example of coercive rules with respect to women's decision-making process occurred in *Rust v. Sullivan*, 111 S. Ct. 1759 (1991). The Public Health Service Act specified that none of the federal funds appropriated under the Act's Title X program for family-planning services could be used in programs where abortion is considered to be a method of family planning. The Secretary of Health and Human Services interpreted this statute to forbid government-funded family-planning services from engaging in any counselling with respect to abortion. Thus, a doctor would be forbidden to discuss abortion even if the woman were experiencing severe complications from her pregnancy. Rather than being informed of the full range of medical options available to them, pregnant women would not be informed of the availability or desirability of abortion services. In *Rust v. Sullivan*, the Supreme Court ruled that that result was constitutionally permissible, thereby permitting the government to put its ideological position above a concern for the well-being of women and their fetuses.

Although the United States has not achieved good-faith regulations concerning the deliberation process, such regulations (although far from perfect) have been reached through legal-legislative compromise in France. The French resolution of the abortion problem recognizes the need for abortions, but regulates the woman's decision-making process. Under the French system, a woman has the right to choose an abortion during the first ten weeks of pregnancy if she is in "distress." Her claim of distress is not subject to review. The physician who receives the woman's initial request for an abortion must furnish her with a brochure that contains information about the public benefits and programs that are guaranteed to mothers and children, the possibilities for adoption, and a list of government organizations capable of providing her with assistance. In addition, the woman must attend an interview with a government-approved counselling service, which will furnish her with assistance and advice that will enable her to carry the fetus to term. At least one week must elapse between the time she initially requests an abortion and the performance of the procedure, unless the delay would place her beyond the ten-week period permitted for elective abortions.[21] Because the state funds medical care, women in France do not bear the financial cost of these measures. Mary Ann Glendon argues that this compromise between pro-life and pro-choice proponents protects the values held on both sides of the abortion debate without taking the abortion decision out of the hands of women.[22]

The French system is far from perfect, and I do not suggest it as the solution in the United States. That solution is only possible in a system with state-funded health care, including abortions, because it increases the costs of abortions. In addition, the French system would not work well in the United States because of our high rate of teenage pregnancy with late-term abortions for teenagers. We need to drastically improve sex education and the availability of contraceptives for teenagers before a ten-week limiting period could begin to seem the least bit reasonable. Unfortunately, we have made no progress with respect to poor teenagers over the last decade.

Finally, there are problems with the French use of the term *distress*. It suggests that pregnant women need to be hysterical to procure an abortion, harkening back to nineteenth-century images of pregnant women. While distress is not the ideal noun, we need to pick a noun that captures the idea that women and their partners ought to grieve about the need to have an abortion. Grieving is important for two reasons. First, the psychological literature suggests that women who grieve about their need to have an abortion may experience less post-abortion trauma.[23] Second, our respect for life and our aspiration to be loving and compassionate should lead us to grieve about terminating life. Some Buddhists therefore argue that women should be allowed to choose an abortion but that they should engage in a period of prayer and meditation concerning the abortion to maintain their respect for life.[24] Just as it is offensive when society celebrates the use of capital punishment, it is troubling when society fails to encourage women and their partners to be troubled by their decision to terminate fetal life. In fact, we should be troubled by the need for abortion to the extent that it signifies our failure to alleviate the social circumstances which result in unwanted pregnancy. Thus, we need to create societal mechanisms that will encourage all of society to grieve about the need for abortion. The French model takes a step in that direction, although not a perfect step that can be transported to the United States.

It is interesting to note the increasing evidence that the French system is built on respect for women's well-being. When drug manufacturers were reluctant to develop RU 486 (the abortion pill), the French government declared the drug to be the "moral property of women." It has taken aggressive steps to make a new form of abortion (RU 486) available to women which may, in the long run, prove safer because it avoids surgery. Interestingly, the French government must have realized that such a drug may ultimately make it extremely difficult for the government to regulate or monitor abortions because it could become widely available on the black market. Nevertheless, the government's commitment to protecting women's well-being and its trust in women were sufficiently strong that it insisted that the drug be developed. The contrast with the United States is extremely stark. RU 486 is not being developed in the United States and the government has certainly shown no trust in women nor concern for their well-being as it continues to restrict the availability of abortion. Good-faith dialogue is a two-way street. French women lived under some abortion restrictions that they may have disliked but soon were given the opportunity to procure abortions in a safer and easier manner. Unfortunately, such good-faith dialogue is rare on the abortion issue in the United States.

3. Impact of the Court's Activism on Legislative Dialogue

To the extent that commentators have considered the importance of dialogue in the abortion context, they have focused on legislative dialogue. They have argued that it is good for society to have legislatures engage in constructive dialogue; by ruling in an activist style, judges inappropriately preempt that dialogue. The former Solicitor General utilized this perspective in *Webster v. Reproductive Health Services* to argue for judicial restraint. He argued that the Court should overturn *Roe* and return the abortion issue to the legislature. He argued that it is important that a "constructive" rather than "inflammatory" dialogue take place in the legislature on the abortion issue and that judicial restraint is needed to facilitate that dialogue. He stated:

As long as the various factions continue to look to the courts, however, a con-structive dialogue will be impossible. 15n.15 The Court's continuing effort to oversee virtually all elements of the abortion controversy has seriously distorted the nature of abortion legislation. Because *Roe* and its progeny have resolved most of the central questions about the permissible scope of abortion regulation, leg-islative action in this area has been relegated to relatively peripheral issues. And because legislators know that whatever they enact in this area will be subject to de novo review by the courts, they have little incentive to try to moderate their positions. The result, all too often, has been statutes that are significant primarily because of their highly 'inflammatory' symbolic content—such as fetal description requirements and human disposal provisions. *Thornburgh*, 476 U.S. at 762 n.10. This process has undermined the accountability of legislative bodies, and has disserved the courts and the Constitution. As James Bradley Thayer once observed, the "tendency of a common and easy resort" to the power of judicial review "is to dwarf the political capacity of the people, and to deaden its sense of moral responsibility." J. B. Thay, *John Marshall* 106–07 (1901).[25]

Judicial restraint, he argued, would move us closer to constructive dialogue because it would force the legislature to respond to the abortion issue responsibly rather than through inflammatory legislation that it knows will be overturned by the courts.

The appellees in *Webster* did not dispute the importance of constructive dialogue on the abortion issue; they disagreed with the appellants about the effect the Court overturning *Roe* would have on that dialogue. They argued that overturning *Roe* would contribute to rather than abate inflammatory legislation in the abortion area:

The Solicitor General notes the tendency of some state legislatures to enact "inflammatory" abortion statutes and remarkably blames *Roe* for this phenomenon. S.G. Brief at 21 n.15. A more honest assessment would blame hostility in those legislatures to a woman's right to choose abortion. That assessment indicates that if *Roe* is eliminated, inflammatory legislation will not abate, but will flourish unchecked. Indeed, five states have announced their intention to criminalize abortion (except only to save the life of the mother) if and when this Court permits them to do so.[26]

They argued that judicial activism is needed to moderate the inflammatory dialogue of the state legislatures. I think it is clear that the appellees are correct as to the likely effect of the Court reversing *Roe* and leaving the abortion issue to the federal and state legislatures.

Looking first to the federal legislature, Congress's behavior can be traced through its coverage of abortion under Medicaid, an issue that was addressed in *Harris v. McRae*, 448 U.S. 297 (1980). The issue in *Harris* was the constitutionality of a federal amendment to the Medicaid statute that forbade Medicaid payment for abortions unless either the abortion was necessary to save the life of the pregnant woman or the pregnancy was the result of rape or incest. The plaintiff unsuccessfully challenged that result under the equal protection and privacy clauses. Thus, the Court acted with restraint, leaving it up to Congress to decide whether to fund abortions under Medicaid. The Court did not substitute its judgment for that of Congress.

According to the former Solicitor General, we should expect the post-*Harris* dialogue to be constructive in Congress since the courts were not interfering with it. Whether it was constructive can be determined by comparing that dialogue with the contemporaneous dialogue in other Western countries. In the former Solicitor General's own words, we can determine whether dialogue has taken place by seeing if the United States "is out of step with the legislative judgment of virtually every other country with which we share a common cultural tradition. . . . "[27] Thus, if the United States Congress responded to the legislative freedom created by *Harris* by moving closer to the other Western countries, then the Court's restraint facilitated dialogue; if Congress moved away from other Western countries, then the Court's restraint did not facilitate dialogue. The evidence from other Western countries is that nearly every one of them has decided that it is appropriate for the government to fund broad categories of therapeutic abortions for poor women. Western countries that provide for or subsidize all legally indicated abortions from public funds include: Australia, Austria, Britain, Canada, Denmark, France, Germany, Greece, Italy, Luxembourg, Netherlands, New Zealand, Norway, Portugal, Spain, Sweden, and Switzerland.[28] In sharp contrast, the United States Congress has responded to its legislative freedom by cutting back even further on the categories of abortions that would be funded by Medicaid—eliminating funding for pregnancies that result from rape and incest, and preventing the District of Columbia from using its own tax dollars to fund therapeutic abortions for poor women. The United States has moved well below the level of concern for poor women's well-being that has been established elsewhere in the Western world. Thus, under the Solicitor General's own test, I would say that our legislative experience with the abortion issue not only shows that we cannot trust the legislatures if *Roe* is overturned but that it is time to reconsider our confidence in Congress and overturn *Harris v. McRae* so that the United States can begin to move toward a humane level of healthcare. If the United States Congress proves itself to be incapable of engaging in constructive dialogue on the abortion issue, I find it hard to believe that legislatures, especially state legislatures that have already gone on record as saying that they would broadly criminalize abortion if *Roe* were overturned, would show themselves capable of engaging in constructive dialogue if the courts engaged in restraint.

It is true that Congress tried to expand Medicaid coverage for abortion to include rape and incest within the last couple of years, but President Bush vetoed that effort. Those efforts received lots of publicity and were heralded as an enormous victory for the pro-choice movement. But realistically, those efforts, even if they had been successful, would have still left the United States far behind the rest of the Western world and no further ahead than the United States was at the time of the *Harris v. McRae* decision. What is often forgotten about our Medicaid-funding rules is that they value fetal life over the woman's life, unless the woman's actual life is endangered. It is not sufficient for a woman to show, for example, that her health would be severely compromised by carrying a fetus to term. Thus, at eight weeks of pregnancy, when the fetus is at a very undeveloped stage and an abortion is a relatively safe and inexpensive procedure, a pregnant woman on Medicaid is not entitled to a state-funded therapeutic abortion. Congress seems relatively satisfied with that state of affairs unless her pregnancy was the result of rape or incest. The problems of rape or incest, however, are only a small part of the reasons why women may desire abortions to protect their own well-being. Congress has not even begun to think about abortions fully from the perspective of women's well-being. Congress's action to extend Medicaid-funded abortions to victims of rape or incest was therefore more symbolic than substantive, with the symbolism having little to do with real protection of women's well-being. It is hard to conclude from such a symbolic step, which still left the United States behind the rest of the Western world and was ultimately unsuccessful, that we should feel optimistic about congressional action on abortion.

Let me be clear that I am not insisting that the existence of dialogue can always be measured by substantive outcome. If the post-*Harris* history had been that Congress had decided to fund ten or fifteen categories of abortion, I would have trouble concluding on the basis of substantive outcome alone whether real dialogue about poor women's well-being and abortion funding had taken place. But when the post-*Harris* history is a step away from even the minimal funding that the Court approved before *Harris*, then I can conclude on the basis of substantive outcome alone that no dialogue has taken place.

If anything, we might fault *Roe* for being insufficiently activist in that it did not protect the lives and well-being of poor pregnant women by resting its holding on privacy rather than equal protection doctrine. The plaintiff in *Doe v. Bolton* became ultimately unprotected when the Court decided in *Harris v. McRae* that the state did not have to fund her abortion. Thus, we have been able to reach a legislative-judicial compromise on the abortion issue in the United States. But we have reached that compromise at the expense of indigent women's well-being. Indigent women's well-being has been unprotected since *Harris v. McRae*. Through that lens, one could therefore argue that Congress and the states are not capable of respectfully deciding when abortions are impermissible, since they have used that power to restrict the well-being of poor women beneath the level of human dignity.

That may be an unduly harsh criticism of the legislative response to legislative responsibility in the United States. Nevertheless, I find that harsh criticism necessary because there is no respectful justification for the abortion funding legislation—it doesn't save the taxpayer money because childbirth, which is funded, is far more expensive, and it doesn't value women's well-being. At a minimum, that legislative history should make us skeptical of the good faith of Congress and the states in considering women's well-being in the abortion area.

The United States is one of the few countries to be able to reach a compromise on abortion through the funding issue. Professor Mary Ann Glendon argues quite persuasively that legislative-legal compromise has occurred more effectively in other countries.[29] I agree with her conclusion but I would add to her observations that one reason that is the case is that those countries did not have available the United States funding compromise. They therefore were able to find more compassionate avenues for compromise which better respected women's well-being and the interest in fetal life.

Turning next to state legislatures, it is interesting to see that *Roe* has not been the imperial decision it is often described as. Despite the cries of judicial imperialism, an active and productive debate about abortion had occurred in the state legislatures before *Roe* was undermined by the *Webster* decision. Pro-life advocates had won many victories. They had been able to criminalize abortion activities by non-physicians, require spousal notification, require licensing of abortion facilities, require that abortions after the first trimester be performed in a hospital, prohibit nontherapeutic abortions after viability, require that physicians seek to preserve life and health of fetus, prohibit fetal research, require reporting, preclude perfor-mance of abortion after fetal viability except to preserve life or health of mother, apply restrictive zoning laws to abortion clinics, require physician to inform the woman of available social services to facilitate childbirth, require parental or judicial approval of abortions for minors, provide publicly financed services for childbirth but not for nontherapeutic abortions, and require the presence of a second physician during abortions performed after viability.

If the reasonableness of the dialogue can be judged by its balanced tone, it appears that the dialogue may have been fairly well balanced since many abortion restrictions were sufficiently reasonable to pass constitutional muster (despite *Roe*). If *Roe* were the imperial decision that some people claim, then it is unlikely that such a rich dialogue would have occurred. Thus, I do not find convincing the argument that the "imperialism" of *Roe* seriously impaired the judicial-legislative dialogue.

Unfortunately, our post-*Webster* experience demonstrates that many state legislatures are unlikely to use their opportunity to engage in abortion dialogue in a way that protects women's well-being if *Roe* is overturned. Louisiana, my home state, has been the most egregious in ignoring women's well-being. The male-dom-inated legislature (which includes only four women) passed an antiabortion statute which imposed a potential ten-year prison term and $100,000 fine on physicians who performed abortions. The only exceptions were either when the woman's life was in danger or if she were a victim of rape or incest and had reported the rape within five days of its occurrence. Louisiana's criminal abortion statute reflected the first time in the twentieth century that a state had passed an anti-abortion measure that did not even contain an exception for a pregnant woman's *health*. The state valued embryonic life at the moment of conception over a pregnant woman's health and well-being. The Republican Governor of Louisiana, Buddy Roemer, who describes himself as pro-life, vetoed the legislation claiming that it did not sufficiently respect the well-being of women in Louisiana. Within a few days, the legislature overturned the governor's veto—the first time a veto had been overridden in the twentieth century. Arguments that this legislation was highly insensitive to poor women who could not afford to travel to another state to have an abortion and who might now die from illegal abortions fell on deaf ears. Louisiana's benefits provided through the Aid to Families with Dependent Children program ranked forty-seventh of the fifty states with a maximum payment of $190 a month for a mother and two children. Louisiana's coercive abortion legislation left no reasonable alternatives to poor, pregnant women on AFDC. Even middle-class women were left unprotected by Louisiana's new legislation with the legislature refusing to modernize its antiquated day-care system, which provides little regulation of day-care providers. Thus, women were coerced into childbirth with no means of providing reasonable care for the children after birth.

Other states had similarly restricted abortions, but no state had gone so far as Louisiana in failing to consider women's health in restricting abortions. One pro-life advocate in the state aptly described the situation when she said that they decided to work with the "gentlemen" of the legislature and support whatever bill they wanted. They worked with an elite group of men in the legislature, who would never face an unwanted pregnancy, to penalize pregnant women. (As I vomited every day throughout the first trimester of my pregnancy, lost ten pounds, and slept twelve to eighteen hours per day, I wondered how many men in the legislature would be willing to put up with pregnancy to bear children.) To put it simply, women were not parties to a good-faith dialogue about their lives and health. Thus, twenty years after *Roe* and *Doe* were decided, some legislatures are picking up exactly where they left off in 1973—failing to protect the health and well-being of women. The vindicative legislature leaves the United States far behind the rest of the Western world, where such criminal measures have long disappeared in democratic societies.

The current spate of restrictive legislative activity with respect to abortion will create enormous geographic inequalities with respect to the availability of abortion and will have an enormous impact on the lives of poor women and teenage women who do not have the resources to travel for an abortion. It is important to insist on a uniform, respectful abortion policy that is available to protect the lives of all women, not just the women who have the economic resources to travel to a state which permits abortion. (From a religious-feminist perspective, we need to view dialogue from the perspective of the "least among us.") A uniform policy can only be achieved through Supreme Court or congressional action; it will not happen by delegating abortion responsibility to the state legislatures. And, unfortunately, it is unlikely to happen as a result of Supreme Court action.

Admittedly, there have been a few pro-choice victories, but we need not overemphasize the importance of these victories in assessing the relationship between judicial activism and dialogue. Judicial activism, which brought us sixteen years of a national, pro-choice climate, has played an important role in the present legislative climate. If we, as a society, had not been forced by the courts to live in a pro-choice regime for sixteen years, women would probably not be fighting so hard at the present moment to keep those rights through the legislative process. Women would not be taking for granted that they should be respected to make their own reproductive decisions. In other words, our historical experience of sixteen years of living in a pro-choice climate may have taught women the importance of reproductive freedom because they had a chance to experience how that freedom would dramatically improve the quality of their lives. Having experienced that freedom, they understand the importance of articulating those arguments to legislatures and courts. Judicial activism certainly can play an important role in adjusting social attitudes while it also preempts legislative decision-making for a lengthy period.

Thus, arguments for judicial restraint in the abortion area are unsatisfactory when they flow from an unqualified argument valuing legislative dialogue. An unqualified argument favoring democracy is insensitive to the need for courts to safeguard equal protection of the law when the legislature fails to respond to the needs of women and racial minorities. The purpose of strict judicial scrutiny and judicial activism under the Fourteenth Amendment is to protect insular minorities that do not have effective access to the political process from discriminatory state action. Our experience with abortion regulations suggests that women, especially poor women, do not have sufficient access to the political process to safeguard their well-being throughout the United States at the local or national level. Thus, I consider it important to construct equality-based arguments under the Fourteenth Amendment to demonstrate why it is that our democratic-constitutional regime should not tolerate state legislatures enacting abortion restrictions which disregard the well-being of women. Unqualified arguments for democracy fail to acknowledge the historical significance and importance of the Fourteenth Amendment.

III. CONCLUSION

In summary, courts should conclude that abortion restrictions violate women's constitutional rights because they substantially impact on women's ability to protect their well-being. Women's well-being is impacted both by the physical and socially created consequences of unintended and unwanted pregnancies if they are coerced into carrying the fetus to term through restrictions on abortion. Having concluded that abortion restrictions infringe women's constitutional rights, then the question becomes what state interests are sufficiently compelling to justify such an infringement. At this point, the best argument that the state can make is that it is trying to protect society's valuation of life. In assessing that argument, however, we should insist that the state value life in all of its forms, including the lives of the pregnant woman and her children. As Justice Marshall pointed out in *Harris v. McRae*, the government's decision not to fund abortions for poor women ensures "the destruction of both fetal and maternal life" rather than protecting potential life.[30] Until we, as a society, decide to protect life minimally by providing adequate prenatal care, postnatal care, childcare, and pregnancy leave, then it is hard to take seriously a government's claim that it is restricting abortion to protect its valuation of life. More likely, it is restricting abortion in order to display its disrespect for the lives of women.

Irrespective of how insincere one believes the government is when it restricts abortion, I am suggesting that the justificatory stage is where the heat of the argument should be occurring. Unfortunately, the Rehnquist Court is moving in the direction both of denying that the abortion restriction itself burdens women's lives and, therefore, of not requiring the government to justify the restriction. I am suggesting that a society that respects women's well-being may choose to restrict abortions but may not do so by denying that its actions do implicate women's well-being. That denial, itself, is a sign of disrespect of women's well-being. I will explain this framework further in later chapters.

Notes

1. Kathryn Kolbert, *Developing a Reproductive Rights Agenda* in Reproductive Laws for the 1990s: A Briefing Handbook 8 (Nadine Taub & Sherrill Cohen eds. 1988).

2. In fact, the Court was quite vague about what exact language within the Constitution justified its holding. I have focused on the liberty-due process clause because I consider that language to offer the strongest justification for the Court's holding. The liberty-due process clause states a state may not deprive a person of their liberty without due process of law.

3. *See* Marian Faux, Roe v. Wade: The Untold Story of the Landmark Supreme Court Decision That Made Abortion Legal 8 (1988). The plaintiff has since recanted her story that she was raped.

4. Roe v. Wade, 410 U.S. at 153.

5. John Hart Ely, *The Wages of Crying Wolf: A Comment on Roe v. Wade*, 82 Yale L.J. 920, 935 (1973).

6. 410 U.S. at 183 (quoting 1968 Ga. Laws 1249, 1277–80 § 26–1202 (a), repealed by 1973 Ga. Laws 635).

7. *Id.* at 185 (quoting Doe's allegations).

8. 410 U.S. at 192.

9. It is interesting to observe that, given the high rate of spontaneous abortion (or miscarriage) that occurs at that stage of a pregnancy (generally described as being between 15% and 30%), that it is hard even to describe the fetus as "*potential life.*" One might argue that the fetus is not potential life until nature has determined the true potentiality of that life by deciding whether to abort the fetus spontaneously. At a minimum, I would argue that a woman should have control over this period of spontaneous abortion (usually lasting until week thirteen or fifteen of the pregnancy) by deciding whether she wants to choose an elective abortion.

10. *See* N.Y. Times, Sept. 27, 1988, at 71, col. 4 & B7, col. 4. (Bush's spokesperson said, "Frankly he thinks that a woman in a situation like that [unwanted pregnancy] would be more properly considered an additional victim, perhaps the second victim. That she would need help and love and not punishment.").

11. 410 U.S. at 159.

12. Ely, *supra* note 5, at 926.

13. Stanley Hauerwas, *Abortion: Why the Arguments Fail* in Abortion Parley: Papers Delivered at the National Conference on Abortion held at the University of Notre Dame in October 1979 323, 327 (James T. Burchaell ed. 1980).

14. *See, e.g.*, James Burtchaell, *Die Buben sind unser Ungluck!: The Holocaust and Abortion* in Rachel Weeping and Other Essays on Abortion 141 (1982).

15. Carol Gilligan, In a Different Voice: Psychological Theory and Women's Development 70–103, 109–26 (1982); David Reardon, Aborted Women: Silent No More 179–84 (1987).

16. Lynn Paltrow, *Amicus Brief: Richard Thornburgh v. American College of Obstetricians and Gynecologists*, 9 Women's Rts. L. Rep. 3, 21 (1986).

17. Bernard N. Nathanson & Richard N. Ostling, Aborting America 141 (1979).

18. *See, e.g.*, Michael Perry, Morality, Politics and Law: A Bicentennial Essay (1988).

19. *See* Martha Minow, *Foreword: Justice Engendered*, 101 Harv. L. Rev. 10, 70–95 (1987).

20. *Id.* at 444.

21. Mary Ann Glendon, Abortion and Divorce in Western Law 16–17 (1987).

22. *Id.* at 18–20.

23. *See* Janet Mattison, *The Effects of Abortion on a Marriage* in Abortion: Medical Progress and Social Implications 169 (Ruth Porter & Maeve O'Connors eds. 1985).

24. *See* Buddhist Views on Abortion, 6 Spring Wind—Buddhist Cultural Forum 166, 170–71 (1986).

25. Brief of the United States as Amicus Curiae Supporting Appellants, at 21 & 21 n.15, Webster v. Reproductive Health Services, 492 U.S. 490 (1989) [hereafter Brief of the United States].

26. Brief for Appellants at 17–18 n.30, Webster v. Reproductive Health Services, 492 U.S. 490 (1989).

27. Brief of the United States in *Webster, supra* note 25, at 23.

28. *See* Rebecca Cook, *International Dimensions of the Department of Justice Arguments in the Webster Case*, 17 L. Med. & Health Care 384, 386–87 (1989).

29. Glendon, *supra* note 21.

30. 448 U.S. at 346.

CHAPTER SEVEN

Webster v. Reproductive Health Services

Where's the Feminist Argument?

Feminist litigation uses the insights and empowerment gained through consciousness-raising to
reform the law.[1]

I. INTRODUCTION

In the previous chapter, I have criticized the Court's treatment of the abortion issue, showing how the Court has not sufficiently protected women's well-being in considering the abortion issue under privacy doctrine. Unfortunately, the feminist legal strategies on the abortion issue are also often problematic. In the previous section, I pointed out some of the limitations of the privacy framework argued by the plaintiff. One might excuse the shortsightedness of the framework articulated by the plaintiff in *Roe* given the novelty of abortion-related legal protections. The problems that I observed in *Roe*, however, have persisted in our more recent abortion cases. To further describe the nature of this problem, I will focus on the briefs filed in the recent *Webster* decision. I will argue that virtually none of the briefs could be considered *feminist* and virtually none of them promote *good-faith dialogue* on abortion.

The issue in *Webster* was the constitutionality of a state statute which required "viability" testing before a woman could have an abortion after twenty weeks of pregnancy. The statute also prohibited public hospitals from performing abortions. The viability-testing requirement was particularly important because it seemed to be directly inconsistent with the Supreme Court's holding in *Roe* that second-trimester medical requirements could only be imposed to protect the health of the pregnant woman, not the fetus. Thus, the case provided the Court with the opportunity to reconsider *Roe* and, in particular, to reconsider *Roe's* trimester framework. Pro-choice feminists therefore defended *Roe* while pro-life advocates urged the Court to overrule *Roe* in the dozens of briefs filed with the Court.

Many readers might be surprised if they read the substantive arguments that were made in the briefs filed by feminists in *Webster*. Although many different briefs were filed on behalf of various feminist organizations, I will argue that very few of the briefs reflected the aspirations that I believe we should hold as feminists. In particular, the aspiration of good faith dialogue often seems to be absent. These briefs should instruct us, as feminists, in how we construct constitutional arguments in future cases.

In *Webster*, the appellants argued that *Roe* should be overturned. They therefore needed to demonstrate that abortion regulations do not infringe a woman's liberty or privacy interest and, to the extent that they do infringe that interest, the state's interest in preserving prenatal life overrides the woman's liberty interest. The appellees argued that *Roe* should be retained. They therefore needed to demonstrate that abortion regulations infringe women's liberty interests and that the state's interest in preserving prenatal life does not override that liberty interest.

The arguments in *Webster* could have been made in good faith. The appellants could have argued that they understood how abortion regulations do restrict women's liberty interest but that those restrictions are necessary because of the deep value we must give to protecting life. Similarly, the appellees could have both argued that they understood how important it is to value life and showed how restricting abortions does not achieve that result. Let us examine the briefs to see if the arguments were made in good faith. In addition, let us consider whether the style of constitutional argumentation corrupted the substantive concerns of each side.

II. APPELLANTS' BRIEFS

A. Women's Well-Being

In order to engage in a good-faith disagreement, the appellants needed to show that women's well-being would be protected if states were allowed to regulate abortion. Nevertheless, this issue was not discussed at all by the appellants or the Solicitor General, who submitted a brief on behalf of the appellants. The Solicitor General's silence on this issue is particularly interesting in light of the fact that the Government did ask the Surgeon General to conduct an evaluation of the impact of abortions on women's health. The Surgeon General's study concluded that there was no evidence demonstrating that abortions have adverse health consequences on women. The report stated: "Valid scientific studies have documented that, after abortion, physical health sequelae (including infertility, incompetent cervix, miscarriage, premature birth, and low birthweight) are no more frequent among women who experienced abortion than they are among the general population of women."[2] As to how women's psychological health is affected by having an abortion, the report stated: "Although numerous case histories attest to immediate or delayed psychological problems following abortions, the actual number of women who have suffered in this way is unknown."[3] Rather than respond to or acknowledge this evidence responsibly, the appellants and Solicitor General ignored it entirely. Because the Solicitor General and the appellants did not even recognize the necessity of discussing women's well-being in the context of abortion restrictions, I conclude that the chief briefs for the appellants did not reflect an attempt to engage in a good-faith dialogue.

In contrast, the brief filed by Feminists for Life of America on behalf of the appellants did consider women's well-being.[4] Moreover, this brief was feminist in its structure in that it contained lots of stories by individual women. In order to demonstrate the potential negative consequences of abortion, they provided extensive testimony from women who had abortions. For example, they claimed that many black women die during legal abortions that are performed by white men but that those deaths are not reported or are covered up.[5] They further tried to portray abortion as detrimental to the well-being of black women by describing Margaret Sanger, an early advocate of contraception and abortion, as racist.[6]

Feminists for Life agreed that it is important to protect women's well-being in relation to reproductive activity. However, they disagreed with pro-choice feminists as to how that protection should properly take place. They seemed to believe that women naturally want to protect fetal life and not have abortions and that it is only through the coercive and racist forces of our society that abortion becomes necessary. They therefore favored regulations of abortion that would provide women with more accurate knowledge of the consequences of having an abortion and the possibilities of bearing an unwanted child. Because Roe v. Wade arguably does not permit such regulations, especially when they would occur during the first trimester, these feminists therefore felt compelled to argue that Roe should be overturned to permit increased regulation of abortion. Because of their belief that women naturally do not desire abortions, they appear confident that the problem of abortion will largely disappear if women are more fully informed about reproductive matters.

From a feminist perspective, their argument is problematic because it represents gross stereotypes about women and is disrespectful to women's ability to assess their personal situation. The brief seems to assume that all women would choose to bring their pregnancies to term if their consciousness were raised. However, one integral aspect of consciousness-raising is the recognition that not all women need to respond to a life situation in the same way. Consciousness-raising tries to move women away from a monolithic programmed patriarchal response to one that better reflects consideration of their own well-being. In fact, when consciousness-raising results in women having a rather uniform view of society, it is sometimes criticized as not being good consciousness-raising; therefore, for women to move monolithically to a party line of always wanting to continue with their pregnancies is not a likely response to good consciousness-raising. It may be true that some women who have had abortions regret, with hindsight, that social circumstances forced them to make that decision. However, it is hardly feminist to let those individual stories speak for all women.

Thus, one must wonder if Feminists for Life really wanted women to be more informed before they made an abortion decision or, alternatively, whether they wanted women informed in a particular, coercive manner. As I argued in a previous chapter, it would be beneficial for women who seek to make reproductive decisions to have nondirective counselling available. *Roe v. Wade*, however, does not need to be overruled entirely for nondirective counselling to be made available to all pregnant women.

B. Preserving Prenatal Life

The second task for the appellants' briefs was to show that the courts need to provide the legislatures with more room to protect prenatal life by regulating abortion. Surprisingly, however, the briefs contained virtually no justification for why we should value prenatal life more than we do or how regulating abortion achieves greater valuation of prenatal life.

The brief by the Solicitor General did not explain why protecting prenatal life should be considered an important or compelling state interest.[7] The Solicitor General argued that the state's asserted interest in protecting prenatal life is not necessarily qualitatively different at different periods of pregnancy.[8] Even if it is, he asserted that the interest may still be sufficiently strong at all stages of pregnancy to constitute a compelling state interest. Interestingly, he argued in the negative; he did not offer any reasons why it should be regarded as compelling. He said:

> But even if there is a core of common sense in the notion that a State's legitimate interest in prenatal life "grows in substantiality" along with the development of the fetus, it does not follow that this interest should not be regarded as *compelling* throughout pregnancy. An interest may be sufficiently weighty to be compelling in the constitutional sense even if subsequently it takes on even greater urgency.[9]

The Solicitor General justified his argument that the interest is compelling with historical evidence that states in the mid-nineteenth century limited abortion because of "what was widely viewed as a moral evil comprehending the destruction of actual or nascent human life."[10]

The Solicitor General's historical argument, however, was not very supportive of the compelling interest test. As the Solicitor General recognized in *City of Richmond v. J. A. Croson*, 488 U.S. 469 (1989), the compelling interest test must focus on *contemporary* circumstances rather than historical circumstances. In *Croson*, the Supreme Court insisted that the City of Richmond produce contemporary evidence of discrimination against blacks in the construction industry to justify the city's minority set-aside program. It was not willing to rely upon a "generalized assertion" to meet the compelling interest test. It is inconsistent for the Solicitor General to argue in *Webster* that it can rely on historical evidence to support its claim that a state needs to protect prenatal life by restricting women's liberty interests but then reject such historical arguments in *Croson*.

The Solicitor General's historical argument appears especially inappropriate when one realizes that abortion, pregnancy, and childbirth have changed dramatically since the nineteenth century. As abortion has become a safer medical procedure for pregnant women, our moral evaluation about the procedure has changed. In the nineteenth century, abortion was a procedure that threatened the life of the pregnant woman and fetus; in the late twentieth century it is a procedure that preserves women's lives while terminating the life of the fetus. The Solicitor General is trying to freeze the Court at a nineteenth-century view of women's role in society.

In addition, the brief on behalf of Feminists for Life of America said not one word about why we should value prenatal life. It simply argued that some women will come to value prenatal life more after their abortion, so we should let the states decide how to protect their emotional health by regulating abortion.

Finally, the brief on behalf of the National Right to Life Committee was also silent about why we should value prenatal life.[11] They hid behind a state's-rights argument to support overturning *Roe*. They did not try to justify protecting prenatal life as a compelling state interest. Instead, after concluding that a rational basis test should be used to assess abortion restrictions, they summarily concluded that the statute should be affirmed because: "Given the states' historic interest in preserving life from the time of conception (an interest firmly rooted in the history and conscience of our nation), there is clearly a rational basis to uphold the Missouri statutes at issue herein."[12] This is the last sentence of their brief; they left the explanation for why protecting fetal life is important to a weak parenthetical phrase. Thus, the brief on behalf of the Right to Life Committee devoted only one sentence to discussing the importance of valuing life.

One obvious reason why these briefs failed to articulate in a systematic way why we should regulate abortion in order to show how much we value life was that the appellants did not hold a sustained position about the value of life. For example, the United States and various states that support regulation of abortion have defended capital punishment laws in the Supreme Court which place the United States alone in the Western world in its widespread use of the death penalty. It is hard to see how a consistent pro-life position could defend restrictions on abortion to protect a life that has not yet been born while defending death-penalty laws that exterminate the lives of juveniles and mentally retarded individuals. Feminists for Life may be the only organization that filed a brief on behalf of the appellants in *Webster* and opposes the death penalty. According to the Supreme Court in *Croson*, the Court has the obligation to examine asserted compelling interests closely to see if they are genuine or a camouflage for discriminatory attitudes. It does not take much scratching below the surface to see the disingenuousness of the chief briefs in *Webster* in supporting a state's interest in preserving prenatal life.

This discussion of the appellants' briefs suggests that their legal posturing has distorted their substantive arguments. They seem to have lost sight of why they want to regulate abortion and seem largely unable to respond to arguments about how abortion regulations affect women's well-being. The only exception to this pattern is the brief filed by Feminists for Life. The brief suggests that there are people who are trying to justify state regulation of abortion in feminist language.

Feminists who oppose abortion regulations might learn from the communitarian way in which this group tries to frame its argument. Its conclusion may be wrong but the structure of its argument may be correct.

III. APPELLEES' BRIEFS

The briefs filed by the appellees and the amici largely stood behind an individually based privacy argument to oppose abortion restrictions. Many of these briefs did not do a good job describing how women's well-being would be impacted by abortion restrictions; none of them acknowledged that it is important to value prenatal life.

The brief filed by the National Organization for Women represented the mainstream feminist position on abortion.[13] The brief solidly stood behind a privacy perspective which cannot acknowledge women's interconnectedness with the community or her responsibility to the community. The right to choose an abortion was couched entirely in privacy terms; no hint of a Fourteenth Amendment equal protection argument was ever made. An equal protection argument, however, would be superior to a privacy argument because a privacy argument is atomistic and not as woman-centered as an equal protection argument. An equal protection argument, by contrast, would permit us to discuss how abortion regulations are disrespectful of women's well-being, as members of the class of women. The NOW brief did seem to recognize the necessity of making an argument which is centered on consideration of women's well-being. Rather than use the Fourteenth Amendment for this purpose, however, the brief relied on a very brief Thirteenth Amendment argument. It stated that "Requiring women to surrender control of their bodies to the state during pregnancy is in a very real sense a form of involuntary servitude and thus is inconsistent with the letter and spirit of the Thirteenth Amendment."[14]

NOW's Thirteenth Amendment argument was brief and unconvincing. Moreover, it added an unnecessary requirement for showing an infringement of women's well-being—a requirement of proving an enslavement. That is a difficult requirement to establish because the state is not necessarily trying to enslave a woman during her pregnancy when it restricts abortion; it is trying to punish her for electing to choose an abortion after the abortion has occurred. That punishment constitutes an inequitable burdening of women's role in society since we take no steps to encourage men to avoid unwanted pregnancies and could therefore be described as a Fourteenth Amendment violation. By putting the argument in Thirteenth Amendment terms, NOW added the confusing issue of what it means to be enslaved and risked being disrespectful to the African-American experience of slavery; the Fourteenth Amendment equal protection argument would seem to be much more straightforward. In sum, by failing to make an equal protection argument, the NOW brief did not accurately discuss the implications of abortions regulations on women's well-being.

The NOW privacy perspective was also too atomistic because it failed to recognize women's responsibilities to others. It rejected arguments about women's responsibilities to society and said:

> There is no authority for the proposition that the state can compel an individual to give up the right to control his or her body to benefit another. The idea, for example, that the state could determine that a supposedly less worthy member of society must donate an organ to save the life of a pillar of the community is unthinkable. So too, is it far beyond the pale to suggest that a parent be ordered to undergo surgery and months of life-threatening activity in order to benefit a child.[15]

The obvious question that argument raises is why is it unthinkable for the state to compel us to donate an organ in order to save the life of another, especially another person with whom we are related. Patricia Beattie Jung, a religious feminist, agrees that the state should not compel organ donation yet she offers a more communitarian perspective on that issue than the NOW brief. Jung acknowledges that we should live in a society in which people are socialized to want to donate organs to sustain the life of another person. However, she rejects the idea that such values should be compelled.[16] Thus, one can reject the coercive features of abortion restrictions without also denying the importance of the values of donation.

The brief by Catholics for a Free Choice also fails the good-faith disagreement test by not focusing sufficiently on women's well-being and ignoring the state's interest in protecting prenatal life. It refuses to acknowledge that we may want to live in a world in which we have interconnected responsibilities to each other. It deals with the responsibility issue briefly in a footnote:

> Constitutional concerns of privacy protect bodily integrity of persons and do not require exceptional samaritanism. A parent cannot be compelled to save the life of a child by organ donation, transfusion or other invasive practice; nor could a fetus compel anyone (including the biological "father" of the fetus) to provide a blood transfusion in *utero* or after birth. There is no question that the individual's rights of privacy and physical integrity would prevail over the child's or the fetus' claim for assistance.[17]

This argument is especially surprising coming in a brief representing a religious viewpoint. One would expect many Catholics to support a Good Samaritan principle in thinking about the abortion issue. Catholics for a Free Choice attempted to avoid confronting this possibility by putting women on a pedestal, assuming that nearly all women do consider interests of other persons in making an abortion decision. They say: "A pregnant woman in the exercise of her conscience takes into account the many factors relevant to the decision, which may include the consideration of the needs and relations of persons (including the pregnant woman herself and her already born children)."[18] That argument is not especially feminist, smelling of biological essentialism and a stereotyped view of all women.

The brief for the appellees also relied entirely on a privacy argument. As an improvement over the two briefs discussed above, it tried to define the privacy right in a nonatomistic way. It stated:

> The Solicitor General's most serious error is his argument that a fundamental right to abortion does not flow logically out of the general right to privacy or personal autonomy which protects matters of procreation and family life, including contraception, because the woman is not "isolated in her privacy" in making the abortion decision. . . .
>
> This line of argument misconceives the nature of the "privacy" right. . . . That right is in no way dependent on whether an individual is "isolated" in his or her privacy. . . . Such decisions are best left to the individual rather than the state, not because of some abstract value in solitary decisionmaking, but because of the profound effect such decisions have on an individual's destiny. . . .
>
> Indeed, if this Court adopts the Solicitor General's proposed analysis of fundamental rights, according to which the countervailing state interest undercut the nature of the right itself rather than guiding the extent to which it can be abridged, it will have set itself on a course which reaches far beyond the narrow issue of proscription of abortion.[19]

This brief tried to salvage privacy theory by making it appear less atomistic. We're told that women are not isolated in their privacy and yet the state is supposed to protect their decisionmaking capacity when that decision-making has a profound effect on the individual's destiny. However, this argument failed to address how the decision may have a profound effect on others. The appellees did not allow at all for the possibility that a pregnant woman may ever have obligations to others, including the fetus, citing with approval cases in which pregnant women were found not to be liable for tortious prenatal injuries and criticizing cases in which courts tried to compel women to modify their behavior in order to protect fetal well-being.[20] Substantively, the appellees may be correct that states act unconstitutionally when they attempt to control women's behavior during pregnancy. However, I do not see how we can be convinced of that fact, as feminists, without being offered a communitarian, woman-centered perspective that considers a woman's responsibility to her fetus in a nonatomistic way. We would need to *let in* the fetus in order to achieve that argument. Thus, I do not find the attempt to salvage privacy theory to be an effective argument.

More powerful feminist briefs were filed in *Webster* by groups representing women of color, juvenile women, international women's health organizations, as well as a coalition of organizations committed to women's equality.[21] Unlike the briefs discussed above, they starkly portrayed the implications to poor women and juveniles of reversing *Roe*. They did not discuss the abortion issue entirely as a privacy issue; they discussed it as an issue jeopardizing the well-being, and very life, of women.

The brief filed by the National Council of Negro Women and other organizations representing women of color argued that with abortion illegal, women of color were disproportionately represented among those who died or were left sterile by illegal abortion. For example, in New York in 1965, before abortion became legal, there were 4 abortions deaths for every 100,000 live births for white women, 56 abortion deaths for every 100,000 live births for nonwhite women, and 61 abortion deaths for every 100,000 live births for Puerto Rican women.[22]

In contrast, they argued that the legalization of abortion has helped save the lives of women of color. After New York legalized abortion, for example, the maternal mortality rate for women of color fell by 51%.[23] Nevertheless, the brief made it clear that it is not enough to make abortion legal if we want to protect the well-being of poor women of color. Even with abortion legal, women of color continue to seek illegal abortions because they cannot afford legal abortions. Between 1975 and 1979, for example, 82% of the women who died after illegal abortions were African-American and Latina.[24] Any increase in the cost of abortion, they argued, acts to force some poor women to choose illegal abortions which are not performed by licensed health care practitioners. From these facts, they concluded:

> This data, and data on health complications from illegal abortions among the poor, even after legalization, suggest that access to abortion must be very broad to ensure against unconscionable discrimination. Any dilution of Roe v. Wade spells a return to an era when women seeking abortions had to risk their lives in order to obtain one.[25]

One important theme from the brief by women of color is that the abortion issue is one about the cost of abortion, not simply about the legality of abortion. They argued that abortion is already too expensive for poor women to be able to protect the health of themselves and their children. Even without Roe being reversed, poor women's lives are already endangered when they need an abortion. If the Court permits the state to raise the cost of abortion a little more through hospitalization and testing requirements, the health of poor women would be compromised even further. The brief stated that Medicaid-eligible women had abortions two to three weeks later than other women; nearly half of them reported that financial reasons caused their delay. This delay caused 22% of Medicaid-eligible women in 1982 to have second-trimester rather than first-trimester abortions, increasing substantially the healthcare risks and costs of having an abortion.[26] Every incremental cost in abortion means either fewer abortions for poor women or delayed abortions at significant health risk to poor women.

The women of color's nondiscrimination argument was deeply feminist because it asked the court to protect all women, not just middle-class, adult, white women. The Roe privacy argument easily allowed the result in Harris v. McRae to occur, because it was embedded in an individualistic rather than communitarian framework. The brief showed that we need to make abortion arguments in anti-discrimination terms, not only so that Roe can be retained, but so that Harris can be overturned.

Nevertheless, one shortcoming of their brief is that they devoted little space to translating their observations about the impact of reversing Roe on the well-being of women of color into legal argument. They never directly told the Court that it would need not only to uphold *Roe* but to reverse *Harris v. McRae* to accept the full implications of their argument. I can understand their reluctance to make such a bold argument to this Court, because the Court seems so hostile to radical, class- or race-based arguments. Nevertheless, they might have written a more powerful brief which could have formed the basis of a strong dissenting opinion if they had translated their argument more directly into equal protection terms. The briefs of the appellants attacked the privacy justification for *Roe* as unprincipled. By offering a cogent equal protection perspective, the women of color could have provided the progressive members of the Court with an opportunity in *Webster* to begin to reweave our abortion legal argumentation in more radical and communitarian language, even if that step had to first occur in a dissenting opinion. As the dissent in *Plessy v. Ferguson*, 163 U.S. 537 (1896) served as the foundation for *Brown v. Board of Education*, 349 U.S. 294 (1955), the dissent in *Webster* could have served as the foundation for the overturning of *Harris v. McRae* at a future time.

The brief representing juvenile women also made powerful arguments about the implications of reversing *Roe* on the well-being of adolescent women. Before abortions were legal and relatively accessible to adolescents, the brief observed that a large proportion of teenage girls who attempted or succeeded in suicide thought they were, or actually were, pregnant.[27] For teenagers who do carry the fetus to term, the mortality rates from continued pregnancy and childbearing are much higher than for women aged twenty to twenty-four.[28]

However, the brief on behalf of juveniles also failed to translate its substantive observations into an equal protection framework; instead, the brief relied entirely on the right to choose as a liberty interest. As I have argued above, when we use individualistic liberty arguments, we do not fully protect the interests of poor women and women of color. To borrow a term from Mari Matsuda, we can learn a lot about good constitutional argumentation by "looking to the bottom."[29] The evidence from the bottom—women of color, poor women, and teenagers—is that abortion regulations harm the well-being of both women and their children. Our legal arguments need to reflect that fact.

Both the women-of-color brief and the juvenile-women brief let in the fetus somewhat. The brief on behalf of women of color did not portray the abortion issue as a contest between women and prenatal life. They noted that illegal abortions cause women of color to disproportionately become sterilized. The brief on behalf of juvenile women focused on protecting prenatal life more directly. It observed that teenage girls are approximately half as likely to receive prenatal care as other pregnant women and that the children of teenage mothers are twice as likely to die in infancy than those born to women in their twenties.

The brief by International Women's Health Organizations related the issue of maternal health to fetal well-being even more directly.[30] They noted that the United States ranks nineteenth in the world in infant mortality, a statistic that is largely attributable to the high infant mortality rates among poor women. They stated that "It has been established that the increase in the legal abortion rate is the single most important factor in reductions in both white and nonwhite neonatal mortality rates."[31] In addition, they noted that other countries take a more communitarian approach to the abortion issue by recognizing how a woman's pregnancy can affect the well-being of other family members. Thus, many Western countries, such as Britain, permit lawful abortion when continuation of a woman's pregnancy involves risk of injury to the physical or mental health of any existing children of her family. This approach protects a woman's right to have an abortion while not pretending that the woman is isolated in her pregnancy.

Thus, the briefs on behalf of women of color, juvenile women, and the international women's health organizations portrayed the issue as one about how we can help poor women to bring healthy children into this world. They made it clear that the United States stands alone in the world in its disrespect for the well-being of both women and children.

Nevertheless, not one of these briefs did a sufficient job discussing the state's interest in valuing life. Most of the discussions about the effect of abortion on the lives around women were made in footnotes. No brief had an entire section which acknowledged the importance of valuing life but then showed how regulating abortion does not achieve that value. We can make a much more powerful feminist argument that is also more open to the state's interest in protecting prenatal life within existing constitutional discourse.

IV. THE COURT'S OPINION

Not surprisingly, neither the majority nor dissenters' opinions in *Webster* reflected a feminist perspective or encouraged good-faith dialogue on the abortion issue. I will now discuss the various opinions written by the Court in *Webster*.

Chief Justice William Rehnquist wrote the opinion for the Court. His opinion was joined by four other Justices—Byron White, Sandra Day O'Connor, Antonio Scalia, and Anthony Kennedy—with respect to the prohibition against using public employees or facilities to perform or assist an abortion not necessary to save the pregnant woman's life. Rehnquist's conclusion that this part of the statute was constitutional was an extension of the Court's earlier decision in the Medicaid abortion-funding cases. He concluded that the state's refusal to allow public employees to perform abortions in public facilities leaves a pregnant woman with the same choices as if the state had chosen not to operate any public hospitals at all. As in *Harris v. McRae*, Rehnquist acknowledged that a state was permitted to make a value judgment favoring childbirth over abortion and to implement that judgment in allocating public funds and facilities.

Justice Harry Blackmun's dissent, which was joined by Justices William Brennan and Thurgood Marshall, argued that Missouri's public facilities provision could be easily distinguished from *Harris v. McRae* because of the sweeping scope of Missouri's definition of a public facility. Under Missouri's broad definition, any institution that was located on property owned, leased, or controlled by the government was considered to be public. Thus, the essentially private Truman Medical Center, which performed 97% of abortions in the state after sixteen weeks of pregnancy, would be prohibited from performing abortions under the state statute. Despite

Harris v. McRae, Justice Blackmun concluded that the funding provision should be held unconstitutional because it unduly infringed a woman's opportunity to procure an abortion in the second trimester of pregnancy.

Justice Blackmun's discussion of the public-facility provision comes only in a footnote and is not the primary focus of his decision. He largely ignored the powerful briefs provided by women of color and adolescent women that demonstrated the dramatic consequences of this provision on their lives. These briefs noted that poor women and teenage women are more likely than other women to seek abortions at public health facilities because they do not have access to private physicians. They are also more likely to have second-trimester abortions because they delay having abortions until they save the necessary amount of money or find out how to get an abortion. When Blackmun noted that the healthcare provider that performs nearly all of the second-trimester abortions will not be able to do so, he could have observed that poor women and teenagers would be disproportionately unable to procure legal abortions. Given the relationship between teenage pregnancy and the cycle of poverty, the inability to procure an abortion often has dramatic consequences in the life of a poor, teenage woman. Although Justice Blackmun was certainly correct to note that the public facility ban "leaves the pregnant woman with far fewer choices, or, for those sick or too poor to travel, perhaps no choice at all,"[32] it would have been better if he had described the impact of this regulation in the race-, class-, and age-based way in which it is most likely to operate. Then, we would have been provided with a fuller and more accurate description of the impact of this regulation in women's lives.

Justice Blackmun's discussion of the public-facility provision skirted the question whether *Harris v. McRae* should be overturned. He tried to distinguish *Harris* from *Webster* rather than call for its reconsideration. He therefore did not challenge the Court's privacy case law, which permitted compromise on abortion through the funding issue. As such, he did not challenge the lack of real dialogue about the impact of our current abortion policies on the lives of all women.

The amicus brief filed by women of color was not so subtle. They implicitly argued that *Harris* must be overturned, although, as discussed above, they did not sufficiently put their arguments in an equality framework. They often used exactly the same information that they had provided the Supreme Court in *Harris* to argue that the well-being of poor women cannot be protected unless the government ensures that legal abortions are available to poor women on the same basis as middle-class women. The brief on behalf of International Women's Organizations showed that the United States stands alone in the Western world in permitting abortion to be lawful but not funding any abortions for poor women unless their very lives are endangered. These comparative data showed that the United States fails to respect the lives and well-being of poor women. Unlike other Western countries, the United States fails to fund prenatal care, postnatal care, pregnancy leave, and childcare but then tries to tell poor women that it prefers childbirth to abortion. The most logical explanation for this position of both the United States government and the state of Missouri is that government officials have not bothered to educate themselves on the impact that funding and public-facility restrictions have on the lives of poor women. And, as long as poor women have virtually no political power, it seems unlikely that government officials will focus on their needs. Thus, as I have stated above, an equality argument was available from the data supplied by various amicus briefs but no member of the Court pursued that route.

Both the majority and dissenters in *Webster* did focus on the viability-testing provision although not from a feminist perspective. Chief Justice Rehnquist's discussion of this provision only received the support of Justices White and Kennedy, but the separate concurrences of Justices O'Connor and Scalia made a majority for the conclusion that the provision was constitutional. The provision presented both technical and substantive difficulties. Technically, the provision appeared to require physicians to perform viability tests that were contrary to accepted medical practice. If that had been the actual meaning of the statute, most of the Justices would have been compelled to find it unconstitutional, even under a lenient standard of review, because the statute would have rationally served no public purpose. In order to avoid that conclusion, Rehnquist offered a somewhat strained interpretation of the statute so that a physician would have the discretion to perform only tests that were medically appropriate.

Having overcome this technical hurdle, Rehnquist then turned to the substantive difficulties posed by the provision. Under the Court's prior doctrine, as articulated in *Roe v. Wade*, a state was permitted to impose abortion restrictions to protect fetal life only after viability. Because the viability-testing requirement took effect as early as twenty weeks, four weeks before the beginning of viability, Rehnquist faced a seeming conflict with *Roe*.

Rehnquist concluded that the *Roe* trimester framework was too rigid and that if the state has an interest in preserving potential human life after viability, it also has an interest in preserving that potential life before viability. Although Rehnquist's statement about preserving potential human life may be read to mean that states could outlaw abortions before the twenty-fourth week of pregnancy and thereby overturn *Roe*, he refrained from reaching that conclusion, because that question was not before the Court.

The problem with Rehnquist's analysis, as I have discussed above, is not that he challenges the viability distinction. That distinction is quite vulnerable. The problem is that he ignores the means that the state used to achieve its interest in protecting viable, potential life. Rather than demonstrate its commitment to life by bearing some of the costs of viability testing, the state passed all of those costs along to pregnant women. Moreover, by limiting the facilities at which second-trimester abortions were available, it made it quite difficult for a pregnant woman to find a healthcare provider who could perform the necessary tests. Finally, the tests that were required served little or no purpose. Virtually no doctor who has a patient who he or she believes is twenty-weeks pregnant will be off in their estimate by more than four weeks. Yet that remote likelihood is the rationale underlying the previability-testing requirement. If the Court would have treated women's liberty interest in choosing an abortion as a serious liberty interest, then it could not have upheld such sloppy means under the necessary means test.

Justice Blackmun wrote a blistering opinion for the dissenters. He accused Justice Rehnquist of being deceptive in not acknowledging that he was really overturning *Roe*. Moreover, he chided Rehnquist for not giving the Court a usable framework to evaluate future abortion cases. Blackmun said that he feared "for the liberty and equality of the millions of women who have lived and come of age in the sixteen years since Roe was decided" and "for the integrity of, and public esteem for, this Court."[33] Substantively, he accused the Court of offering no rationale for its rejection of the trimester framework, saying that the Court used an "it is so because we say so" jurisprudence.[34] The trimester framework, he argued, does make sense because it reflects the developmental view that one is more entitled to the rights of citizenship as one increases one's ability to feel pain, to experience pleasure, to survive, and to react to one's environment.

Although Justice Blackmun wrote his dissent in strong language and even mentioned that the majority's opinion would have a dramatic effect on the *liberty and equality* of women's lives, there is no specific discussion of that effect. Blackmun spent most of his opinion explaining why there was no good reason to change the course of using the right of privacy on which the Court had commenced in his opinion in *Roe*.

One of the most disappointing parts of Blackmun's opinion was his conclusion that if the majority's technical interpretation of the provision were correct, he "would see little or no conflict with *Roe*."[35] In other words, he seemed to agree with Justice O'Connor's argument that such a provision would not constitute an undue burden on women's lives. Blackmun dissented from the majority because he disagreed with its technical interpretation of the viability-testing provision, not because he fundamentally disagreed about the impact that requirement (as understood by the majority) would have on women's lives and well-being.

If Justice Blackmun had truly considered the liberty and equality interests of women, he would not have been so easily satisfied. As the briefs that were presented to the Court by women of color and teenage women dramatically showed, raising the cost of abortion, even marginally, has a marked impact on the ability of poor women to purchase abortions. And because women of color and teenage women are more likely to delay abortion decisions, they will be hit harder by the viability-testing requirement than are other women. For poor women, even the requirement that they pay for their own abortions is an undue burden on their reproductive decision making. Raising the cost of abortion presents an even greater—and even more undue—burden.

From the perspective of protecting the well-being of women, *Webster* is doubly discouraging. Not only did the majority of the Court not seem to understand the meaning of abortion regulations in women's lives, but even the dissenters did not display much understanding or sensitivity. They seemed more determined to protect the integrity of their prior decisions than to consider the reality of new abortion restrictions on women's lives.

Ironically, both the majority and dissenters in *Webster* focus on the legitimacy of the state's interest in protecting previable fetuses. That issue, however, was the least troubling issue in the case from a feminist perspective. A much more troubling issue was how the state sought to achieve its interest—by not taking women's healthcare needs seriously and by imposing all of the costs and burdens on pregnant women.

The only way for the Court to promote good-faith dialogue on abortion is for it to take the lives of women seriously as well as the state's interest in protecting life. It must insist that the state protect life respectfully—by safeguarding women's lives as well as prenatal life. The means used by the state of Missouri in *Webster*, like the means used by the state of Texas in *Roe*, reflect a profound disrespect for the lives of pregnant women, and they do not further the state's interest in promoting the value of life generally.

Notes

1. Naomi Cahn, *Defining Feminist Litigation*, 14 Harv. Women's L.J. 1, 9 (1991).

2. Surgeon General's Report on Abortion, 135 Cong. Rec. E906, E908 (daily ed. Mar. 21, 1989).

3. *Id.*

4. Brief of Feminists for Life of America, Women Exploited by Abortion of Greater Kansas City, The National Association of Pro-Life Nurses, Let Me Live, and Eliot Institute for Social Sciences Research, as Amici Curiae in Support of Appellants, Webster v. Reproductive Health Services, 492 U.S. 490 (1989) [hereafter Brief of Feminists for Life of America].

5. *Id.* at 17–18.

6. *Id.* at 18–19 n.35.

7. Brief for the United States as Amicus Curiae Supporting Appellants, Webster v. Reproductive Health Services, 492 U.S. 490 (1989) [hereafter Brief for the United States].

8. *Id.* at 15.

9. *Id.*

10. *Id.* at 16.

11. Brief Amicus Curiae of the National Right to Life Committee, Inc. in Support of Appellants, Webster v. Reproductive Health Services, 492 U.S. 490 (1989).

12. *Id.* at 26.

13. Brief for the National Organization for Women as Amicus Curiae Supporting Appellees, Webster v. Reproductive Health Services, 492 U.S. 490 (1989) [hereafter Brief for NOW].

14. *Id.* at 13.

15. *Id.*

16. Patricia B. Jung, *Abortion and Organ Donation: Christian Reflections on Bodily Life Support* in Abortion & Catholicism: The American Debate 141 (Patricia B. Jung & Thomas A. Shannon eds. 1988).

17. Brief for Catholics for a Free Choice, Chicago Catholic Women, National Coalition of American Nuns, Women in Spirit of Colorado Task Force, et al., as Amici Curiae in Support of Appellees, at 31 n.6., Webster v. Reproductive Health Services, 492 U.S. 490 (1989).

18. *Id.* at 32.

19. Brief for Appellees, at 9–10, Webster v. Reproductive Health Services, 492 U.S. 490 (1989).

20. *Id.* at 12.

21. *See* Brief Amici Curiae of the National Council of Negro Women, Inc., National Urban League, Inc. et al. in Support of Appellees, Webster v. Reproductive Health Services, 492 U.S. 490 (1989) (filed March 29, 1989) [hereafter Brief of the National Council of Negro Women]; Brief Amici Curiae in Support of Appellees by Center for Population Options, The Society for Adolescent Medicine, The Juvenile Law Center, and the Judicial Consent for Minors Referral Panel (filed March 30, 1989) [hereafter Brief of the Center for Population Options]; Brief of Amici Curiae International Women's Health Organizations in Support of Appellees (filed March 30, 1989) [hereafter Brief for International Women's Health Organizations]; Brief of Amici Curiae American Public Health Association, et al. in Support of Appellees (filed March 30, 1989) [hereafter Brief of American Public Health Association]; Brief of Seventy-Seven Organizations Committed to women's Equality in Support of Appellees (filed March 30, 1989). *See also* Brief of Canadian Women's Organizations, Amici Curiae in Support of Appellees (undated) (discussing abortion issue in terms of the right of a woman to control her reproductive capacity to live as full and equal participants in society).

22. Brief of National Council of Negro Women, *supra* note 21, at 17–18.

23. *Id.* at 17–18.

24. *Id.* at 21.

25. *Id.* at 22.

26. *Id.* at 22.

27. Brief of the Center for Population Options, *supra* note 21, at 9.

28. *Id.* at 7.

29. Mari Matsuda, *Looking to the Bottom: Critical Legal Studies and Reparations*, 22 Harv. C.R.-C.L. L. Rev. 323 (1987).

30. Brief for International Women's Health Organizations, *supra* note 21.

31. *Id.* at 16.

32. 109 S.Ct. at 3068 n.1.

33. *Webster*, 109 S. Ct. at 3067.

34. *Id.* at 3075.

35. *Id.* at 3070.

CHAPTER EIGHT

Maternity Cases

In the previous two chapters, I applied a group-based equality perspective to abortion cases. In this chapter, I will apply this perspective to *maternity cases*—cases involving women who decide to go to term. These women, as we will see, have also been subjected to state coercion. These stories, as well as the stories of women who desire to abort their fetuses, are important and need to be part of our discussion of choice and reproductive health.

I. COERCED MEDICAL TREATMENT DURING PREGNANCY

A. Susan Taft

Susan Taft was a married woman who had borne four children. In addition, at least one of her pregnancies resulted in a miscarriage at the seventh month with the fetus not surviving. She became pregnant in July 1982 and wanted to give birth to a child.

For three of her four successful pregnancies, she had had an operation known as a "purse string," which involved suturing so that the cervix would hold during pregnancy. Ms. Taft's physician apparently recommended that she have the operation for her 1982 pregnancy; however, she objected on religious grounds. Her husband disagreed with her decision.

Her husband went to court to compel her to have the operation. No testimony was introduced in court other than the testimony of Susan Taft and her husband, Lawrence Taft. Although Ms. Taft was only four months pregnant and legally entitled to have an abortion without the consent of her husband, the trial court judge ordered her to have the operation. On October 18, 1982, the trial court entered its decision; on October 29, 1982, the Court of Appeals stayed the judgment pending appeal. Ultimately, on March 4, 1983, presumably at the eighth month of her pregnancy, the Supreme Court affirmed the Court of Appeals and vacated the trial court's judgment in *Taft v. Taft*, 388 Mass. 331 (1983). Had the original trial court decision not been stayed by the Court of Appeals, Ms. Taft would have been coerced to have the operation despite the Supreme Court's ultimate decision.

Unfortunately, the trial judge never published an explanation for his decision but one can readily speculate that he saw a maternal-fetal conflict and decided to resolve that conflict on behalf of the fetus. He was able to make that judgment solely on the basis of the husband's testimony, apparently finding it more credible and persuasive than the wife's.

From an equality perspective, I would ask two central questions: First, were the judge's and husband's actions predicated on respect for Ms. Taft? Second, would coercing Ms. Taft to undergo the surgery contribute to her or society's valuation of life?

It seems quite apparent that the trial court's decision (and the husband's actions) were based on extreme disrespect for Ms. Taft, the person who would bear the physical and emotional consequences of a miscarriage if one would occur. She apparently wanted to bring a baby into the world based on a set of religious principles that were quite important to her. Given that the case was not rendered moot, one must presume that she was able to bear that child successfully soon after the Massachusetts Supreme Court handed down its decision. The trial judge credited the husband's wishes and ignored the strong emotional equities on the woman's behalf. Not only was the trial judge able to credit the husband's views but he was able to rely on the husband for expert medical opinion that was most likely well beyond his competency. The judge, too, then became a medical expert on the basis of this male, lay witness.

As for Ms. Taft's valuation of life, what seems to have been lost on the trial court is that she did want this pregnancy to be successful. She had already experienced four successful pregnancies, three of which occurred with the benefit of the operation. She also had experienced a very late miscarriage which must have been very painful for her emotionally. By having four children already, she had made quite a substantial contribution to bringing children into this world. It is hard to imagine that Ms. Taft could be made to value life more. Her religious principles apparently led her to believe that the lives of all of us would benefit if she were not coerced into undergoing the surgery in question.

I have no idea whether the operation was necessary for Ms. Taft, nor do I know how uncomfortable was the operation that would be performed. Ms. Taft was the person with the most information. She knew how difficult she would find another miscarriage; she knew how painful would be the operation; and she knew the strength of her religious convictions. It is only in a society in which women's views are devalued and ignored that a trial-court judge could compel Ms. Taft to undergo surgery on that scanty record.

Ms. Taft's choice was a choice that was based on respect for herself as well as a valuation of fetal life. Reasonable people may disagree about the wisdom of her decision; however, there is no clear right answer which a court should feel free to impose upon Ms. Taft. Society does not gain by interfering with her expression of choice and life. It is only through profound disrespect for her life that a court could interfere with her decision.

B. Santiago X

Santiago X was a single mother of ten children who was also a Jehovah's Witness. She was eighteen-weeks pregnant when she admitted herself to the hospital due to bleeding from esophageal varices. Her doctor informed her that she needed a transfusion in order to save the life of her fetus, but she refused to have one on religious grounds. Her pregnancy was apparently wanted; she was in the second trimester of her pregnancy when she was admitted to the hospital and could have lawfully obtained an abortion.

Upon learning of this situation, the hospital's lawyer tried to telephone a judge to get a court order permitting them to perform a transfusion against the patient's wishes. After trying a couple of different judges, the lawyer finally located Justice Lonschein who agreed to come to the hospital to hear the case. Ms. Santiago was provided with no counsel and no notice to her family. No stenographic record was kept of the conversation that transpired. The doctors testified that a transfusion was necessary to save the life of the fetus and, presumably, the life of the pregnant woman (although the court did not specifically mention this fact). Ms. Santiago informed the judge that she objected to a transfusion on religious grounds.

In *In the Matter of the Application of Jamaica Hospital*, 128 Misc.2d 1006, 491 N.Y.S.2d 898 (Supreme Court 1985), the New York State Court ordered Ms. Santiago to undergo the transfusion. The court decided that the fetus could be considered a "human being" even though it was not yet viable and could have been lawfully subjected to an abortion. Therefore, the court found that it had an obligation to protect the fetus's life. The judge appointed the doctor as special guardian of the fetus and ordered him to exercise his discretion to do whatever was medically necessary to save the fetus's life, including the transfusion of blood to Ms. Santiago.

At first glance, this may seem like a wise decision, because the court apparently acted in a way that was preservative of the health and well-being of the pregnant woman and the fetus. On closer examination, however, enormous problems become apparent.

First, one must ask what evidence of respect toward Ms. Santiago was present in the case. Very little. Although the hospital was able to locate a judge and get him to travel to the hospital, the hospital did not manage to notify Ms. Santiago's next of kin. The court had no information regarding Ms. Santiago other than her statement that she was a Jehovah's Witness and did not desire a transfusion. In addition, the court never mentioned how Ms. Santiago's health would be affected by the transfusion. Even if it is true that the transfusion would have saved Ms. Santiago's life, that was never specifically stated. Moreover, the risks associated with a transfusion were not mentioned, such as the risk of HIV infection. Admittedly, this case was decided in 1985 before we had as much information about HIV, but that fact makes the danger of the court's decision even more apparent.

In 1985, we knew that AIDS could be spread through HIV infected blood but we hadn't yet taken significant steps to make the nation's blood supply safe. Ms. Santiago lived in a part of the country with a high incidence of HIV infection. There was, unfortunately, some chance that the blood transfusion would transmit HIV to her. In addition, the court assumed that it would be best for Ms. Santiago's ten children for her to undergo the transfusion. That is quite a substantial assumption which ignores how the well-being of the other children might be negatively implicated by the addition of another person to the household. A true pro-life perspective would have had to consider all of the lives involved in the case rather than focus on one eighteen-week-old previability fetus. Finally, the court never considered what level of damage may have already occurred to the fetus. The court noted that the fetus was in "mortal danger," which would seem to suggest that serious impairment had possibly already occurred. Again, one must inquire as to what was best for Ms. Santiago and her family. How would they support a potentially handicapped child? The court's single-minded focus on the nonviable fetus made it ignore entirely the risks to Ms. Santiago of undergoing a transfusion as well as the complete effects on the family. There is, therefore, no evidence of respect for Ms. Santiago's life, health, or well-being.

One also must consider the public-policy implications of this case. Will future Jehovah's Witnesses who are pregnant refuse to seek any prenatal care out of fear that they will be coerced into having a transfusion? Isn't it better for Ms. Santiago to bleed in a hospital setting where she can get an IV rather than to stay at home (with her ten children) to bleed to death? The court's assumption that it is acting on the behalf of fetal life is shortsighted. Other fetuses may be deprived of prenatal care due to the court's sloppy intervention. Respecting Ms. Santiago's choices would have preserved both choice and life. Unfortunately, the court did not examine the entire context of the case to see that fact.

II. COERCED CESAREANS

A. Angela Carder

Angela Carder was a poor, white woman who became pregnant in her late twenties. She had married at age twenty-seven, at which time her leukemia, with which she had struggled her entire life, had been in remission for three years. She had not undergone chemotherapy for over a year. Before she became pregnant, she realized that her pregnancy would be high-risk due to her medical history. Nevertheless, she and her husband decided to have a child together, and she soon became pregnant.

At the twenty-fifth week of pregnancy, Ms. Carder saw a physician when she experienced shortness of breath and back pains. She was diagnosed as having a tumor on her lungs. She was admitted to the hospital on June 11, 1987, and her condition was diagnosed as terminal. At first, she was told that she would die within weeks; on June 15, 1987, she was told that she might die much sooner.

Ms. Carder could have insisted on passive treatment, in which case she and her fetus would have died relatively quickly. Instead, she agreed to life-sustaining treatment so that a cesarean section could be performed at the twenty-eighth week of her pregnancy and the fetus could be given a reasonable chance to live. To the extent that her wishes could be ascertained, it appeared that she did not want the cesarean section performed before the twenty-eighth week because of the strong likelihood that the fetus might be severely disabled, if it could live at all. She also wanted her own health and comfort to receive primary consideration. She apparently believed that it would be in everyone's interest for her to stay alive for two more weeks and have the cesarean section performed at that time. Ms. Carder's husband and mother—the people who would most directly feel the loss of Ms. Carder's life as well as the effects of the loss or survival of the fetus—apparently agreed with her resolution of this difficult moral and ethical dilemma.

Despite Ms. Carder's and her family's expression of their opinions, the hospital sought a declaratory order from the Superior Court "as to what it should do in terms of the fetus."[1] A "hearing" was convened at the hospital, without Ms. Carder present. The judge then decided to order a cesarean section so that the fetus would have an opportunity to live; he did not discuss the action's consequences on Ms. Carder's life. The judge was informed shortly thereafter that Ms. Carder was awake and had clearly communicated that she did not want a cesarean section performed at that time. However, after reconvening the court, the judge reaffirmed his original order, saying that the order was appropriate even if she refused to consent. The entire hearing apparently took about an hour.

A ten-minute appeal took place in a telephone conversation with a three-judge panel. The panel denied the request for a stay.

Doctors performed the cesarean section on Ms. Carder, and the nonviable fetus died approximately two hours later. Ms. Carder died approximately two days later; her death was most likely hastened by the operation. Five months later, the court of appeals issued its opinion, which was premised on the assumption that Ms. Carder's and her family's wishes could be discounted as selfish. More than a year later, the court of appeals reconsidered the case and overturned its earlier decision.[2] By then, however, Ms. Carder and the fetus were dead.

Two questions should be asked in this case: First, were the hospital's and court's actions predicated on an unconstitutional disrespect for Ms. Carder's well-being as a woman? Second, did judicial intervention better serve the state's interest in protecting life than Ms. Carder's own decision?

Only institutions that do not respect Ms. Carder's well-being could act as did the trial court and hospital, whose collective actions actually *hastened Ms. Carder's death* without expressing concern for that eventuality. Similarly, the court of appeals failed to respect Ms. Carder's well-being by ignoring the shortening of her life and not attempting to prevent future repetition of such coercive actions, except quite belatedly. Ms. Carder received far fewer procedural protections than we would ever permit in the case of a criminal sentenced to death. Her wishes expressed before the hearing were ignored, and the judges did not bother to talk with her despite the fact that she regained consciousness during the legal wrangling. The court had to treat Ms. Carder, a live and conscious person, as if she was already dead to justify this extraordinarily coercive action.

In addition, the court's assumption that Ms. Carder was acting selfishly was disrespectful of women's well-being. The entire context of Ms. Carder's life showed that she was a woman who had been diagnosed with leukemia fifteen years earlier, gone into remission, become pregnant, and now wanted to defy predictions that she and her fetus would die in a couple of days. By stereotyping her as a selfish woman, the court could not see the context in which Ms. Carder was acting to protect her own and others' well-being. A group-based equality approach could bring that context to the forefront by bringing Ms. Carder's entire life, rather than the relatively momentary period of pregnancy, to the court's attention. It is only through sexist stereotypes about pregnant women that the court could justify its actions. Such sexist predicates to state action should be unconstitutional under the equal protection clause.

Having established that the hospital's decision and the court's action were predicated on an unconstitutional disrespect for Ms. Carder's well-being, we can deal with the asserted justification for this action—the protection of fetal life. Society does benefit by valuing life in all of its various forms, including fetal life. From a public policy perspective, however, judges must face the question of whether judicial intervention into these kinds of cases serves any productive function. Is there reason to believe that life would be more valued if judges rather than pregnant women were responsible for making difficult reproductive decisions? I believe the answer is clearly no. In my view, Ms. Carder, for example, demonstrated an extremely high valuation of life in all of its various forms. As I see it, her valuation of potential life led her to become pregnant and decide to bear the enormous burdens of pregnancy and childbirth. It also led her to conclude that a cesarean section should occur at the twenty-eighth week of her pregnancy rather than the twenty-sixth week. Her valuation of the quality of the life of her husband and mother led her to want not to impose upon them the burdens of raising a severely disabled child. The valuation of her own life led her to conclude that she should be permitted to live as comfortably as possible for the last weeks of her life. By contrast, a superior court judge's clumsy one-hour intervention and an ineffectual fifteen-minute appeal were predicated on enormous disrespect for the length and quality of Ms. Carder's life and did not further the length and quality of the fetus's life.

A major problem underlying the court's analysis is its insistence on viewing the case as one of competing rights: the rights of the pregnant woman versus the rights of the fetus. By suggesting an equality approach which *lets in* the fetus, I am trying to remove us from a bipolar, oppositional way of thinking about pregnant woman's interests and the fetus's interests. My approach shows how these interests may coincide rather than conflict. By showing how women generally make difficult reproductive decisions *because of* rather than *in spite of* their valuation of life in its various forms, I believe we can see that pregnant women are the people most likely to protect life in all of its forms. It is they, therefore, who deserve decision-making responsibility for reproductive choices, rather than judges who are accustomed to thinking about pregnant women and fetal life as oppositional.

More generally, we can conclude from the Carder case that judicial intervention serves no productive function in this type of case. Judges are no more likely to protect the interest in life, in all of its various forms, than the pregnant woman who is facing a highly contextualized ethical dilemma. In addition, the possibility of judicial intervention stalls our healthcare system because risk managers feel compelled to turn to a state court and say "what should we do?" rather than communicate directly with the people involved. Judges need to understand that they perform no productive function by trying to act as God in these kinds of cases, pretending that there is an ultimately right ethical answer that they can determine abstractly in a brief time period. All they demonstrate is their disrespect for family members by substituting their abstract judgment for the highly contextualized judgment of the people who are dealing with a difficult ethical dilemma.

The ultimate irony in the Carder case is that Ms. Carder was *not* choosing an abortion; she was choosing to continue her pregnancy in the hope that she might live for a few more weeks. She had planned her pregnancy and looked forward to the birth of a healthy child. That the state could intervene to abort her nonviable fetus through a cesarean section and hasten her death should offend our valuation of life and choice.

B. Jessie Mae Jefferson

Jessie Mae Jefferson presented herself to the Griffin Spalding County Hospital at about the thirty-sixth week of her pregnancy to receive prenatal care. Her husband was a minister, and apparently both she and her husband objected to surgery or transfusions on religious grounds. She apparently did not object to nonsurgical medical care and had therefore voluntarily presented herself at the hospital to receive prenatal care.

When the physician examined her, he concluded that she had a complete placenta previa which meant that the placenta was blocking her birth canal. The physician then advised her that there was a 99% certainty that the fetus could not survive a vaginal delivery. In addition, the physician advised her that she had no better than a 50% chance of surviving a vaginal delivery. Finally, the physician indicated that it was virtually impossible for the condition to correct itself. On the basis of her religious beliefs, Ms. Jefferson refused to consent to a cesarean section or a blood transfusion, even though the action purportedly put both herself and her fetus at risk.

Unable to obtain Ms. Jefferson's consent, the hospital sought a court order requiring Ms. Jefferson to undergo both a cesarean section and blood transfusion, if necessary. On the day that the petition was filed against Ms. Jefferson, the superior-court judge ordered her to undergo the requested procedures even though neither she nor her husband were available to testify. Temporary custody of the unborn child was given to the state of Georgia to make all medical decisions until the birth of the child. The Georgia Supreme Court affirmed the holding on February 3, 1981 in *Jefferson v. Griffin Spaulding County Hospital Authority*, 247 Ga. 86, 274 S.E.2d 457 (1981), and Ms. Jefferson was escorted to the hospital to receive the appropriate medical treatment. During tests at the hospital, it was determined that the placenta had moved, clearing the way for natural childbirth. The baby was born through natural childbirth on February 9, 1981.

As in the above cases, the court imposed its hasty judgment for that of the pregnant woman's even though she was the person most directly affected by the consequences of her actions. The woman's well-being was considered sufficiently unimportant that a court order could be issued in her absence, although all of the parties agreed that the birth of her child was not imminent.

In thinking about the consequences of this case on the valuation of life, one must realize what incentive it gives to a woman with regard to prenatal care. Ms. Jefferson was under no legal obligation to receive prenatal care although it is generally considered beneficial to both the pregnant woman and fetus for her to receive prenatal care. By subjecting her to extraordinary coercion (in essence putting her under house arrest and taking the custody of her child from her), the court gave her an enormous incentive not to seek prenatal care during any future pregnancy. It is through *dialogue* and *cooperation* with women that we can expect them to take the best possible care of themselves during their pregnancies. Ms. Jefferson, however, was confronted with enormous disrespect that served no ultimately beneficial purpose. Looking at the previous cases together, one gets a clear picture of the arrogance of trial-court judges who believe that they should decide what is in the best interest of pregnant women and their fetuses. It is amazing how frequently their conclusions are exactly the opposite of what is best for all concerned. It should not surprise us that a woman who desires to be pregnant and has experienced many months of that pregnancy will generally be in a much better position to make a so-called correct decision than a judge who is called in on an emergency basis. Choice is preservative of life.

C. Discussion

Forced cesarean sections seem to occur most frequently on poor, minority women who are already often outside the healthcare system. A recent survey found that court orders for cesarean sections were sought against fifteen women in eleven states.[3] Of those fifteen women, seven were black, five were African or Asian, and only three were white. Four of fifteen did not speak English as their primary language. It is quite likely that the vast majority of women were of a low socioeconomic status, given their race and language skills.

The court orders were rendered in a very brief amount of time. In 88% of the cases, they were obtained within six hours.[4] In 19% of the cases, they were obtained in one hour or less, usually by telephone. The prediction of harm to the fetus was inaccurate in at least six cases in which these court orders were sought.

This data provides further support for the analyses that I offered above. Coerced cesarean sections are part of the subordination of minority women. Society provides them with virtually no prenatal care or assistance after delivery of a child, yet society wants to intervene and force these women to undergo major surgery in order to bring a child into the world.

Michelle Harrison has provided an excellent description of the surgical procedure involved in a cesarean section:

> The surgeon takes a scalpel from the nurse and with one strong and definite motion creates a crescent-shaped incision along the woman's pubic hairline. . . . With scalpel and forceps—delicate tweezers—the surgeon cuts deeper beneath the subcutaneous tissue, to a thick layer of fibrous tissue that holds the abdominal organs and muscles of the abdominal wall in place. Once reached, this fibrous layer is incised and cut along the lines of the original surface incision while the muscles adhering to this tissue are scraped off and pushed out of the way. . . . The peritoneum is lifted away from the uterus and an incision is made in it, leaving the uterus and bladder easily accessible. The bladder is peeled away from the uterus. . . .
>
> The obstetrician extends the initial cut either by putting two index fingers into the small incision and ripping the uterus open or by using blunt-ended scissors and cutting in two directions away from the initial incision. If the membranes are still intact, they are now punctured by toothed forceps, and the fluid spills out onto the table. . . .
>
> The rest of the surgery is more difficult for the woman. There is more pain and women often vomit and complain of difficult breathing as we handle their organs and repair the damage. . . .
>
> The placenta separates from or is peeled off the inside of the uterus. Then, since the uterine attachments are all at the lower end, near the cervix, the body of the uterus can be brought out of the abdominal cavity and rested on the outside of the woman's abdomen, thus adding both visibility and room in which to work.
>
> With large circular needles and thick thread a combination of running and individual stitches is used to sew closed the hole in the uterus. A drug called pitocin is added to the woman's IV to help the uterus contract and to decrease the bleeding. Small sutures are used to tie and retie bleeding blood vessels. The "gutters," spaces in the abdominal cavity, are cleared of blood and fluid. The uterus is then placed back in the abdominal cavity. The bladder is sewn back onto the surface of the uterus, and then finally the peritoneum is closed. . . .
>
> Muscles overlying the peritoneum are pushed back into place, and are sometimes sewn with loose stitches. . . . [The fascia] is closed with heavy thread and many individual stitches so that, even if a thread breaks, the stitches won't all come out. The subcutaneous tissue, most of which is fat, is closed in loose stitches that mainly close any air spaces which might become sites for infection. Skin, the final layer, is closed with either silk or nylon thread or metal staples. . . .
>
> A dry bandage is placed over the woman's incision and then taped to her skin. The drapes are removed. A baby has been born.[5]

One must wonder, in the hour or so that the judges spent deciding these cases, if they considered the trauma to the woman of having a cesarean section. After a child is born, a court would not feel entitled to require a parent to have a blood transfusion or a bone marrow transplant to save the life of an existing child. Yet, somehow, the woman's life becomes invisible when the question is whether to force her to undergo a cesarean section in order for a child to be born.

The opportunity for real dialogue and understanding about these women's lives is virtually nonexistent. Many of these women did not even speak English and a major medical decision was made by a judge in a relatively brief period of time. Not surprisingly, these judges' medical decisions were often based on erroneous medical assumptions.

The ultimate irony in these cases is that they encourage a woman who opposed a cesarean section to have an abortion rather than risk childbirth. A woman who fears that the state may intervene harshly into her life during her pregnancy— ranging from the detention of a sixteen-year-old pregnant female in Wisconsin who the judge felt lacked "motivation or ability" to seek prenatal care to a suit against a mother whose son's teeth were discolored because she had taken tetracycline during pregnancy[6]—may abort her fetus rather than risk society's punitive judgments concerning her pregnancy.

III. COERCED BLOOD TRANSFUSIONS DURING DELIVERY

A. Stacey Paddock

Stacey Paddock was pregnant. She was willing to have the hospital perform all required surgical procedures during her delivery except for a blood transfusion. Because she was anemic, Rh negative, and a cesarean section was deemed necessary, her physicians wanted permission to give a blood transfusion to Ms. Paddock. For religious reasons, neither Stacey nor Scott Paddock would consent to blood transfusions. The hospital went to court to compel Ms. Paddock to accept a blood transfusion to save her own life. In *Crouse Irving Memorial Hospital, Inc.*, 127 Misc.2d 101, 485 N.Y.S.2d 443 (Sup. 1985), the court ordered Ms. Paddock to accept a blood transfusion, which was expected to occur in a few days.

This case is quite interesting, because the court treated it as if there was a maternal-fetal conflict where none was evident. Ms. Paddock consented to all of the medical care that would be needed to assist the infant, including a cesarean section. What she did not consent to was a blood transfusion for herself, which the doctors believed was necessary to protect her life. Thus, whether she obtained a blood transfusion had nothing to do with the baby's ability to survive, according to the record presented by the court.

Nevertheless, applying the doctrine of the best interest of the child, the court compelled Ms. Paddock to undergo a transfusion. The court acknowledged that adults are generally permitted to make their own decisions with respect to medical treatment. An adult can therefore not normally be compelled to undergo a particular surgical procedure to save his or her life. On the other hand, parents are compelled to authorize medical treatment for their children that is necessary to sustain the life of their children. In order to reach its conclusion, the court treated Ms. Paddock as if she were trying to withhold a medically necessary transfusion for the child. There was no statement in the record, however, that a blood transfusion for the child was contemplated.

In order to reach its result, the court had to treat Ms. Paddock as if she were a child over whom the court had authority. In fact, Ms. Paddock was an adult who was competent to decide whether her religious principles were more important than a blood transfusion. Whether the child lived was irrelevant to her decision in this matter. Treating Ms. Paddock as if she were a child, I would argue, was indicative of the court's fundamental disrespect for her. It was the same kind of disrespect that permitted the Carder court to, in essence, kill Angela Carder so that the fetus could have an insignificant chance of surviving. In both cases, the women's sole role was seen as sustaining the life of a fetus. The fact that they had needs and interests of their own became irrelevant.

Ironically, the Paddock court concluded that she had to consent to the blood transfusion because she had authorized the cesarean section. In other words, if Ms. Paddock had chosen to stay home and not seek medical assistance that would save the life of the fetus, then the court would not have intervened. But since she sought medical treatment to save the life of the fetus, her own right to refuse to consent to a blood transfusion was waived. Once again, the public-policy implications make no sense. We are encouraging women like Ms. Paddock not to seek medical treatment at all rather than to seek medical treatment for the fetus while maintaining her own religious principles. Ms. Paddock's actions were more preservative of fetal life, as well as more protective of her own self-respect, than the actions of the court.

IV. FETAL ABUSE CASES: DRUG USE DURING PREGNANCY

A. Jennifer Johnson

Jennifer Johnson was a poor black woman who lived in Florida. She was addicted to crack cocaine. During her pregnancy, she attempted to get help for her addiction because she was concerned about its effect on her fetus. After Florida law-enforcement officials discovered that her two children tested positively for cocaine at birth, she was convicted of passing a metabolite from her body to her newborn infants during the sixty-second period after birth and before the umbilical cord was cut. She was prosecuted under a statute designed to punish the distribution of drugs to children under eighteen.

The government learned of her crack addiction because she confided her addiction to the obstetrician who delivered the baby at a public hospital. The government used the fact that she had sought treatment during the pregnancy as evidence that she had the necessary intent to pass drugs to the fetus. (Her knowledge of the potential harm gave her intent.)

Women like Jennifer Johnson who seek public assistance for their drug addiction or who trust their obstetricians sufficiently to confide in them are most likely to be prosecuted for drug use during pregnancy.[7] Thus, our policy of prosecuting such women acts as a deterrent to their getting adequate prenatal care and treatment for their drug addiction. Neither deterrent is beneficial to the pregnant woman or fetus.

B. Discussion

Although I acknowledge that it is appropriate and important for society to encourage women not to use drugs during their pregnancies, the coercive ways in which society has often responded to women's use of drugs has not been in the best interest of the pregnant woman or fetus. We need to find ways to intervene into women's lives while they are pregnant that are modeled on compassion and dialogue rather than on punishment and coerciveness. The ways in which society has chosen to intervene into the lives of women who use drugs, in particular, reflects both a racist and sexist mentality.

Despite the fact that much more evidence exists about the impact on the fetus of a pregnant woman's drinking alcohol or smoking marijuana than on her using crack cocaine, society has responded to the crack-cocaine problem much more vigorously than it has responded to the alcohol problem. Warnings by the Surgeon General on alcohol containers stating that drinking alcohol may be harmful to the fetus are generally considered sufficient with respect to the alcohol problem. Prosecutions and incarcerations under state drug statutes, however, are considered necessary in response to the crack-cocaine problem. Interestingly, a 1989 study of 2,278 highly educated women found that 30% consumed more than one drink per week while pregnant.[8] Another study found that black women were more likely to test positively for cocaine use during pregnancy than white women (7.5% versus 1.8%) but that white women were more likely to test positively for use of marijuana during pregnancy than black women (14.4% versus 6.0%). Thus, overall, alcohol and marijuana use are much more prevalent practices that may harm the fetus than crack-cocaine use yet virtually all of the prosecutions for fetal abuse during pregnancy have been against women who allegedly use crack. Furthermore, the women prosecuted are disproportionately poor and black.

Dorothy Roberts does an excellent job summarizing the perspective that underlies these selective prosecutions:

> Focusing on Black crack addicts rather than on other perpetrators of fetal harms serves two broader social purposes. First, prosecution of these pregnant women serves to degrade women whom society views as undeserving to be mothers and to discourage them from having children. If prosecutors had instead chosen to prosecute affluent women addicted to alcohol or prescription medication, the policy of criminalizing prenatal conduct very likely would have suffered a hasty demise. Society is much more willing to condone the punishment of poor women of color who fail to meet the middle-class ideal of motherhood.
>
> In addition to legitimizing fetal rights enforcement, the prosecution of crack-

addicted mothers diverts public attention from social ills such as poverty, racism, and a misguided national health policy and implies instead that shamefully high Black infant death rates are caused by the bad acts of individual mothers. Poor Black mothers thus become the scapegoats for the causes of the Black community's ill health. Punishing them assuages any guilt the nation might feel at the plight of an underclass with infant mortality at rates higher than those of some less developed countries. Making criminals of Black mothers apparently helps to relieve the nation of the burden of creating a health care system that ensures healthy babies for all its citizens.[9]

The prosecution of poor, African-American women for cocaine use therefore is consistent with the empirical statistics that I provided in an earlier chapter. As those empirical statistics show, society does not value the lives of poor women and their children. It provides no social policy which would substantially improve the quality of their lives. And then, in the name of a pro-life mentality, the state prosecutes poor pregnant women rather than affirmatively solving the high infant-mortality rate in poor communities in the United States. It is only with a group-based equality perspective that is sensitive to class and race, as well as gender, that one can see the values underlying these prosecutions.

V. CONCLUSION

The mentality behind many of the cases that I have reported above is *fetal life at any cost*. Women as well as other children in the family are invisible. In addition, the future life of the fetus that may be born is invisible. The courts and doctors often have a tunnel-vision perspective on the importance of sustaining fetal life irrespective of the consequences on other lives in our community. Throughout this book, I have emphasized that we are each many selves, that there is an inter-connectedness among all of us. It is time to take fetal life out of its isolated tunnel and put it in the interconnected web of life to see what are the consequences of particular reproductive decisions. It is also time for society to consider how to truly sustain life—by providing prenatal care, childcare, health benefits, meaningful education, proper nutrition, and affordable housing. The money that is wasted on lawsuits to coerce women to undergo certain medical treatments could be much more fruitfully spent on the living persons among us—women, men, and children who desperately need basic sustenance to survive.

In the final analysis, intervening coercively in women's lives in order to possibly sustain fetal life seems to be more of an indication of society's subordinate attitude toward women, especially poor minority women, rather than an indication of a true pro-life mentality. We need to be creating incentives and opportunities for women to seek prenatal care rather than scare them from doctors by intervening coercively in their lives when they seek medical care for their pregnancies. More fundamentally, we need to create social policies which will get them out of the poverty that leads to crack-cocaine addiction. It is time that we looked at our own responsibility as a society to others rather than always blaming poor women for the socioeconomic conditions in which they have been born.

Notes

1. 533 A.2d at 612.

2. 533 A.2d 1235 (D. C. App. 1990).

3. Veronika E. B. Kolder, Janet Gallagher, and Michael T. Parsons, *Court-Ordered Obstetrical Interventions*, 19 New England J. of Medicine 1192 (May 7, 1987).

4. *Id.* at 1195.

5. Michelle Harrison, A Woman in Residence 81–84 (1982) (as quoted in Janet Gallagher, *What's Wrong with Fetal Rights*, 10 Harv. Women's L.J. 9, 36 n. 137 (1987)).

6. *Id.* at 1195–96.

7. See Berrian, Pregnancy and Drug Use: The Dangerous and Unequal Use of Punitive Measures, 2 Yale J.L. & Feminism 239, 247 (1990).

8. Rosenthal, When a Pregnant Woman Drinks, N.Y. Times, Feb. 4, 1990, section 6 (Magazine), at 49.

9. Dorothy Roberts, Punishing Drug Addicts Who Have Babies: Women of Color, Equality, and the Right of Privacy, 104 Harv. L. Rev. 1420, 1435–36 (1991).

Afterword

Toward Choice and Life

As I finish writing this book, my mind is full of the stories of women that I have read. These women are frequently poor, young, and subject to considerable sexual coercion in their lives. I want to maintain the aspirations of love, compassion, and wisdom for these and all other people but also know how far we, as a society, are from making those aspirations possible for everyone. I realize that society is not an *other*; society is us, our many selves. Thus, I, like everyone, am part of the fabric that has made the social conditions in which we live. We have each helped create a world in which neither choice nor life are truly meaningful for most women. That is our responsibility.

The rhetoric of the abortion movement is so often a we-they mentality with the objective, on both sides, of using the law instrumentally to achieve change. The law, however, is no more an other than are we. The law is a reflection of the society in which we live. How we use it is a reflection of who we are. As pro-choice advocates, many of us have called for private individualism and we have, in return, received the selfishness that accompanies that private individualism through our reproductive health policies. It is time, I believe, for us to shape the reproductive health conversation in a way that is consistent with our highest aspirations for our authentic selves. Let's talk about the meaningful choice and life that we want to be a part of all women's lives. Let's try to create the social conditions in which those choices and lives may be possible.

At the time that I began writing this book, I tended to see the federal courts as our savior from coercive state legislatures. For a while to come, that result seems unlikely. We can no longer count on a handful of men on the Supreme Court to protect us from state legislatures. Instead, we need to have productive dialogues at all levels of society and government in order to protect the lives of women and children. I do not welcome the enormity of that task nor do I expect it to be entirely successful, especially in my own community of Louisiana. But I do believe that to the extent we succeed in having meaningful dialogue on all reproductive health issues at all levels of society that we will benefit tenfold as a society. We would then have respectful and effective reproductive health policies which the majority of society would understand rather than policies supported by a privileged few. I hope to live to see such a transformative dialogue in my lifetime.

Nevertheless, we cannot unfortunately abandon the courts during these conservative times. For example, the women of Louisiana presently face the potential enforcement of a statute which will absolutely forbid nearly all abortions. If we entirely avoid the court system, then women are left with virtually no recourse to protect their lives and well-being. When women are attacked by hostile state legislatures, they unfortunately must respond in self-defense even when that self-defense is not as dialogic as we may ultimately desire. Thus, I am presently working on an amicus brief in the Fifth Circuit on behalf of the appellees, which will represent the women who will be the most disadvantaged by the Louisiana legislation—principally, poor, female adolescents and handicapped women. (The brief is attached as an appendix.) In working on this litigation, I will try to be as true to my ideals as possible. I will argue from an equality perspective rather than a privacy perspective. I will be willing to acknowledge the importance of protecting life but will argue that the absolute criminalization of abortion does not actually protect life or increase our valuation of life. I will try to expose the hypocrisy of a state that criminalizes abortion in the name of protecting life while also having one of the highest capital-punishment rates in the United States and while also refusing to provide adequate welfare benefits or childcare to poor women with children. I hope that even a conservative judiciary which has pronounced itself so hostile to *Roe v. Wade* can see the inhumanity of Louisiana's law.

Unfortunately, the tone that I will be forced to use in this brief will be argumentative and rhetorical; it is not likely to meet my aspirations for dialogue. But as I have said in previous chapters, we must work to create the preconditions in society whereby dialogue is possible while we also work to facilitate dialogue. Those preconditions are so woefully absent with respect to women's well-being in Louisiana that one is foolish to speak in a voice that assumes that the preconditions for dialogue exist. What I do not yet know is how one can engage in dialogue while also waiting for the preconditions for true dialogue to exist. I shall try to answer this question as I continue to practice law.

Even at the earliest stages of this litigation, I can see ethical dilemmas. In the brief, I will pretend that I am *representing* various groups which serve disadvantaged women in my community. I have talked to or met with the leaders of these organizations and tried to explain generally what will be the focus of this brief. But the people I am talking to are not lawyers. They may not understand the subtle distinctions between a privacy and equality approach; and they certainly will not be able to appreciate the doctrinal difficulties with each approach. Moreover, I will have virtually no contact with their client population. Would the women they represent agree with the perspective that I articulate in the brief? Essentially, the brief represents *my* perspective. Even the students assisting me on the brief will not see the big picture. Am I therefore acting instrumentally to impose my view on others? Is there any way that, as lawyers, we can really represent our clients in grand constitutional cases? Somehow, the writing of a brief has never struck me as a relational exercise even when I work with others to produce the final product.

Working on the Louisiana abortion case has already made me painfully aware of the devastation that a legislature can bring to women's lives when it does not respect those lives. In the last few pages of this book, I would like to share with the reader some of the specifics about the Louisiana statute so that we can remember the need to be constantly vigilant to protect women's well-being in society. Irrespective of what the courts have to say on this issue, we have to see fully the society in which we live.

The Louisiana statute states in its preamble that the "public policy of the state of Louisiana [is to protect] the life of the unborn from the time of conception until birth."[1] Unfortunately, their concern for life did not extend to the period *after* birth. Conception is defined as the "contact of spermatozoan with the ovum."[2] Thus, the state claims that it wants to protect the life of the unborn even in those cases when the "conception" does not result in implantation and no possible live birth can result.

The statute then forbids all abortion procedures except self-induced abortions. In other words, the state does not criminalize a woman's taking her own life into her hands or seriously jeopardizing the fetus's life by trying to induce an abortion; it only criminalizes the physician's conduct if he or she tries to perform a safe and effective abortion. Safe abortions are made illegal whereas unsafe abortions are made lawful. (And that is supposed to represent a pro-life mentality?)

Somewhat ambiguously, the statute defines an abortion as the performance of various acts "with the specific intent of terminating a pregnancy."[3] Nowhere in the statute, however, is *pregnancy* defined. Based on the preamble, it would seem to be the case that pregnancy is defined as conception, thereby making it unlawful for a doctor to prescribe more than a dozen contraceptive devices such as the IUD, morning-after pill, NORPLANT, low-dose contraceptive pill, and menstrual extraction. The statute would ban no contraceptive used by men but would ban the most popular devices used by women, increasing women's dependence upon men. Interestingly, the defendants themselves can't seem to agree on what the term "pregnancy" was intended to mean. One defendant, the Attorney General, states that pregnancy was intended to mean implantation.[4] By contrast, an amicus brief filed by state representatives who voted in favor of the statute does not dispute that pregnancy means conception.[5] By contrast, they try to argue that contraceptive devices do not try to prevent implantation (a futile argument).

This ambiguous definition of abortion would seem to suggest that a physician cannot perform a D & C on a woman who has had a spontaneous miscarriage until he or she can demonstrate that the fetus is entirely dead. Moreover, a physician who prescribed the morning-after pill or menstrual extraction to a rape victim would also be subject to liability under the statute. At least, the statute would chill their behavior given its ambiguity.

The statute does purport to contain a few abortion exceptions. These are: (1) the termination of a pregnancy either to preserve the life or health of the unborn child or to remove a dead unborn child from the pregnant woman, (2) the termination of a pregnancy to save the life of the pregnant woman, and (3) the termination of a pregnancy which is the result of rape or incest when various requirements have been met. On its face, the statute explicitly puts the health of the "unborn child" over that of the pregnant woman, since a pregnancy can be terminated to protect the unborn child's health but not to protect the pregnant woman's health. Louisiana is the only state to pass an anti-abortion measure in the twentieth century that does not contain an exception for the pregnant woman's *health*.

The rape and incest exception, however, is the most outrageous in its meaninglessness. A victim of rape must see a physician within five days of being raped, and report the rape to law enforcement officials within seven days *if* she wants to retain her right to have an abortion within thirteen weeks of conception. And, if she chooses to have an abortion, then the abortion must be performed by someone other than the first physician whom she saw. Thus, the woman must see a strange physician either to report the rape or to have the abortion—an absurd situation for a victim of rape who is already traumatized. Incest victims are also subject to the seven-day and thirteen-weeks requirements although they are not subject to the five-day physician requirement.

Not only must a rape victim see a physician, but the physician is required to determine if she is already pregnant and to treat her for venereal disease. The costs of both procedures, of course, are to be borne by the rape victim even if she knows that she could not already be pregnant or subject to venereal disease. And, of course, depending upon when the woman last had consensual, unprotected intercourse, it may not be possible to know whether she is already pregnant. As with most reproductive matters, however, the statute is based on biological fiction rather than fact.

Finally, the physician is only allowed to terminate a pregnancy if it was the result of rape or incest. Whether the pregnancy was truly the result of rape or incest, however, will not be known until a prosecution is sought. Since very few rape or incest prosecutions occur within thirteen weeks of the rape, it would seem that physicians have little legal protection if they believe a woman who has alleged rape or incest and perform an abortion. Is the physician supposed to act as judge and jury? One can well imagine what this statute will do to the reporting of rape when women realize that the cost of such reporting has just risen and that her physician will have to assess her credibility. But the response of "why bother?" is probably exactly what the Louisiana legislature had in mind. Rape prosecutions were clearly secondary to preserving the life of a fetus which was created through the act of rape.

It is easy to feel sarcastic when closely examining the Louisiana statute. The reality, however, is that the federal courts will probably let the statute stand. I expect that the statute's only real chance of defeat is in the hands of the Louisiana state courts, which must stand for election before the women and men of Louisiana. Although the election booth does not seem to have deterred the entrenched state legislature, I suspect that it may influence the state-court judges who are increasingly under attack for not representing the diversity of our community. My optimistic side refuses to believe that such an egregious statute could truly be allowed to go into effect. Somehow, I believe that women's voices will be heard and some good-faith dialogue will occur. Unfortunately, the women of Louisiana may have to endure many months or even years of rhetorical dialogue before the voices of good faith do emerge.

The experiential and empirical literature about women's reproductive lives can be very depressing. While reading this literature, I often wondered why I didn't just crawl into bed and pull the covers over my face and fall asleep forever. The world can look so, so bleak through the eyes of women. It is only by being a hopeless optimist that I can persist in my life work and struggle. And, for me, that optimism comes from the combination of feminism and theology. I hope that this book will inspire others to be optimistic in face of the reality of our lives so that they, too, can join in the journey to help us all achieve our aspirations for our authentic selves.

Notes

1. House Bill 112, Act No. 26 Regular Session (1991) § 1 (passed subsequent to gubernatorial veto).
2. *Id.* at § 2 (D)(4).
3. *Id.* at § 2 A(1).
4. Memorandum in Support of Motion for Judgment on the Pleadings by Defendants Buddy Roemer and William J. Guste, Jr., Sojourner T. v. Buddy Roemer, No. 91–2247 (filed Aug. 5, 1991) at 5–6.
5. Brief of Representative Sam Theriot, Senator Allen Bares, et al., as Amici Curiae in Support of Defendants' Rule 12(c) Motion for Judgment on the Pleadings and in Opposition to Plaintiffs' Rule 12(c) Motion for Judgment on the Pleadings, Sojourner T. v. Buddy Roemer, No. 91–2247 (filed Aug. 5, 1991) at 15–18.

Appendix

Sojourner T., et al.,

Plaintiffs-Appellees,

—versus—

Buddy Roemer et al.,

Defendants-Appellants,

No. 91-3677

On Appeal From The United States District Court
For The Eastern District of Louisiana

Brief for Black Women for Choice et al.,
as Amicus Curiae Supporting Appellees

STATEMENT OF THE ISSUE

Whether Act 26 of the 1991 Louisiana Legislature ["the Act"], criminalizing abortion and many forms of contraception, violates the equal protection clause of the Fourteenth Amendment to the United States Constitution by discriminating against women?

INTEREST OF THE AMICUS CURIAE

BLACK WOMEN FOR CHOICE is a New Orleans based organization founded to encourage participation by women of color in the effort to protect the right of women to choice in all aspects of life, especially regarding the choice to bear children. We are particularly concerned with educating adolescent women on reproductive issues so that they can make informed decisions about their bodies. It is clear that such decisions have long-lasting, and potentially adverse effects, on future opportunities in education, employment, and other important phases of life. This is especially true for women of color. We agree with the other *amici* that the legislation enacted by the Louisiana state legislature, which severely curtails choice, should be struck down.

THE COMMUNITY RELATIONS COMMITTEE, JEWISH FEDERATION OF GREATER NEW ORLEANS, is an umbrella organization representing all major Jewish organizations and synagogues in Greater New Orleans. It is committed to having abortion be a safe and legal procedure, free of government interference, for all women consistent with their own private religious beliefs.

LOUISIANA CHOICE, NEW ORLEANS CHAPTER is committed to working with electoral and legislative processes to ensure a woman's right to safe and legal abortion.

Because the Louisiana legislature has refused to protect womens lives and well-being, LOUISIANA CHOICE joins the other *amici* in requesting this court to overturn the Louisiana criminal abortion statute.

THE LOUISIANA NATIONAL ORGANIZATION FOR WOMEN is the state affiliate of the National Organization for Women, an organization of over 250,000 members committed to taking action to secure equal rights for women, including the right to safe and accessible birth control and abortion. It joins this brief, because it believes that Louisiana's abortion law violates the equal rights of women.

THE LOUISIANA PSYCHIATRIC ASSOCIATION, whose membership consists of over 450 psychiatrists, affirms its position that abortion is a medical procedure and that the early termination of pregnancy is a matter to be decided by the patient and the physician. Because of the potentially adverse emotional consequences of unwanted pregnancy on families and society, the Louisiana Psychiatric Association opposes all constitutional amendments, legislation, and regulations curtailing family planning and abortion services to any segment of the population.

THE NATIONAL COUNCIL OF JEWISH WOMEN, GREATER NEW ORLEANS CHAPTER, is a community service organization committed to the advancement of human welfare through the activities of volunteers engaged in a multifaceted coordinated program of education, advocacy and services. It joins this brief in an effort to protect the welfare of the women of Louisiana, consistent with their own religious values.

THE NEW JERSEY WOMEN LAWYERS ASSOCIATION ["NJWLA"] is a non-profit bar association formed for the purpose of identifying issues of concern to women attorneys, and to study and advise the public and its membership on issues affecting the legal status of women. As such, the attention of the NJWLA membership has been called to the issue before the Court, namely Louisiana's criminal abortion statute and its negative impact on the legal status of women. The NJWLA therefore joins in the brief of *amicus curiae* in support of equality for women.

THE WOMEN OF COLOR REPRODUCTIVE HEALTH FORUM is sponsored by the Council on the Concerns of Women Physicians of the National Medical Association. The National Medical Association represents approximately sixteen thousand African-American Physicians nationwide. A major goal of the Women's Council is to improve the health status of African-American women, particularly the underserved and underrepresented.

The state of Louisiana has been chosen as one of the states of focus for the project given the poor reproductive health indices in the areas of teenage pregnancy, cancer, sexually transmitted diseases, and infant mortality. The REPRODUCTIVE HEALTH FORUM Project's task is to increase the quantity and quality of reproductive health care services to African-American women, and to empower African-American women to adopt more preventive health behaviors.

The new abortion law negatively impacts the major goal of the projects as it *worsens* the health status of African-American women. Prior to *Roe v. Wade*, 70% of all abortion-related deaths were African-American women. Whenever reproductive rights are abrogated, women of color die first, and disproportionately. We join the other *amici* in urging this court to strike down the discriminatory anti-abortion legislation in issue.

SUMMARY OF ARGUMENT

The Act, which criminalizes abortion and contraception, discriminates against women. It therefore violates the equal protection clause of the Fourteenth Amendment, as well as the right to privacy. This brief focuses on the equality issues.

The Act would cause a devastating, disparate impact *only* against women. It would shorten women's lives, harm their reproductive capacities, as well as sharply reduce their standard of living. Although the Louisiana legislature was made aware of this impact, it consistently refused to pass any amendments to the Act that would lessen this impact.

Appellants cannot justify this impact against women, because the means chosen do not substantially serve the state's purported objective of protecting life. Virtually no other geographical unit in the western world has passed such a restrictive measure in the twentieth century. Louisiana has unconstitutionally disregarded the value of women's lives in its radical attempt to protect embryonic life from the moment of conception.

The Act reflects an out-moded view of women as compulsory bearers and caretakers of children that is drawn from Louisiana's nineteenth century civil law tradition. The equal protection clause requires Louisiana to move its civil law tradition into the twentieth century by respecting the lives and well-being of women.

ARGUMENT

I. THE ACT DISCRIMINATES AGAINST WOMEN

A. Introduction

In the complaint filed in this case, plaintiffs alleged that the Act, which criminalizes abortion and many forms of contraception, discriminates against them as women. The Act violates their sex-based equal protection rights as guaranteed by the Fourteenth Amendment, because it:

> imposes burdens upon women's reproductive choices and bodily integrity that are not imposed upon the reproductive choices of men, contributes to negative stereotypes about women, and prevents women from becoming full and equal participants in society. (Amended Complaint § 118)

Because the district court decided the case on the basis of plaintiffs' privacy claim, it did not reach the equal protection claim. The court stated: "I recognize that if the Supreme Court overrules *Roe v. Wade*, one or more of these issues may have to be considered on remand." (opinion, p. 4) Appellants Roemer and Guste have not challenged that conclusion by the district court. (Brief of Appellants at 3 n.1.)

The Supreme Court has never considered the applicability of sex-based equal protection doctrine to an abortion and contraception case, because it has decided those cases on privacy grounds. Although the parties represented by this brief agree with appellees that the Act violates the right to privacy, they believe that the Act also violates the equal protection clause. Thus, this Court should instruct the lower court, in the event of a remand, to conclude that the Act discriminates against the plaintiffs as women, because it violates the Fourteenth Amendment.

When a plaintiff challenges a measure on the ground that it constitutes gender discrimination, the Court first determines whether the plaintiff has established a prima facie case of gender discrimination. To establish a prima facie case, the plaintiff can establish that the legislature created a per se gender-based classification. See, e.g., *Mississippi University for Women v. Hogan*, 458 U.S. 718 (1982). Alternatively, the plaintiff can establish that the legislature intentionally created a gender-based disparate impact. See, e.g., *Personnel Administrator v. Feeney*, 442 U.S. 256 (1979).

In the present case, plaintiffs can establish a prima facie case of gender discrimination under either method of proof. The Act constitutes a per se gender-based classification, because it classifies on the basis of a trait—pregnancy—that, as a matter of biology, only women possess. Alternatively, the plaintiffs can demonstrate that the legislature intentionally harmed women by passing the Act, because the legislature knowingly created the maximum impact against women while regulating abortion and contraception.

If the plaintiffs can meet the intentional standard for disparate impact then they have necessarily met the per se standard. Accordingly, this brief will focus on the impact-intent standard while recognizing that the more lenient per se standard is also available in the present case.[1]

B. The Act Produces Disparate Impact Against Women

A gender-based impact occurs in a pregnancy-related case when the government's policy *burdens* women rather than simply fails to *benefit* them. Thus, in *Nashville Gas Co. v. Satty*, 434 U.S. 136 (1977), the Court was able to conclude that the plaintiffs established a disparate impact, because the employment policy substantially burdened women's reproductive lives.[2] As then-Justice Rehnquist stated for the Court in *Satty*, a gender-based impact is established when the government "has not merely refused to extend to women a benefit that men cannot and do not receive, but has imposed on women a substantial burden that men need not suffer." *Id.* at 142.

The Act, criminalizing abortion and many forms of contraception, produces a devastating, disparate impact against women. Women are the only group that will be substantially impacted by the Act. The purpose of the Act is to preclude the women of Louisiana from being able to terminate a pregnancy from the moment of conception. The statute intends to coerce nearly 17,000 women, who otherwise would choose to terminate their pregnancies through lawful and safe abortions, to undergo compulsory childbirth, self-induce an abortion, or seek an illegal abortion. Each of these alternatives would be very detrimental to the lives and well-being of the women in the state of Louisiana. In addition, the effect of the statute will be to ban many forms of contraception; each of the banned contraceptives are ones presently available to women, not men. More importantly, it is women, not men, who will face the burden of compulsory pregnancy that is the result of banning contraceptives.[3]

In *Webster v. Reproductive Health Services*, 492 U.S. 490 (1989), Chief Justice Rehnquist recognized that abortion regulations can have a dramatic negative impact on women's lives.

---

1. To the extent that *Geduldig v. Aiello*, 417 U.S. 484, 496–97 n.20 (1974) can be interpreted as rejecting the per se standard, it was wrongly decided and has been sharply criticized. *See generally* Law, *Rethinking Sex and the Constitution*, 132 U. Pa. L. Rev. 955, 984 nn. 107–09 (1984) (citing dozens of articles criticizing *Geduldig*). Reproductive issues are basic to women's well-being in society. Congress recognized this fact when it amended Title VII of the Civil Rights Act of 1964, 42 U.S.C. §2000 e *et seq.*, (1991) to state explicitly that pregnancy-based discrimination constitutes sex discrimination. *See* 42 U.S.C. § 2000e(k) (1991). This Court should defer to Congress' interpretation of sex-based equality, because section 5 of the Fourteenth Amendment explicitly gives Congress the power to enforce the Fourteenth Amendment.

2. Although *Satty* involved an alleged violation of Title VII of the Civil Rights Act of 1964, 42 U.S.C. § 2000e *et seq.*, (1991) rather than the Constitution, the Court used the same analysis to determine whether a gender-based impact had been established as it would have in a constitutional case.

3. Although amici agree with Appellees that the Act unconstitutionally bans many forms of contraception, this brief will focus on the impact to women of banning nearly all abortions. As this brief will demonstrate, banning abortion coerces many women to undergo compulsory childbirth, seek illegal abortions, or self-induce abortions with serious negative consequences. By also banning many forms of contraception, the Act greatly magnifies the impact on women.

Yet, he predicted that states would never again impose nearly absolute abortion restrictions on women:

> The dissent's suggestion . . . that legislative bodies, in a Nation where more than half of our population is women, will treat our decision today as an invitation to enact abortion regulations reminiscent of the dark ages not only misreads our views but does scant justice to those who serve in such bodies and the people who elect them.

Id. at *521.*

Despite Chief Justice Rehnquist's prediction, the Louisiana legislature has responded to *Webster* by re-enacting its nineteenth century abortion statute. The nineteenth century is the dark ages for the women of Louisiana. Because the legislative process has consistently failed to protect the women of Louisiana, judicial intervention is needed to protect them. In particular, the women who are least well represented by the political process and who will be most impacted by the statute—adolescent females, women with handicaps, and poor and minority women—need to be protected.

1. Adolescent Females

The Act would disproportionately coerce pregnant adolescent females to undergo compulsory childbirth, self-induce an abortion or seek an illegal abortion, because they are unlikely to have the economic resources and knowledge to travel out of state to obtain a legal abortion. These results would effect large numbers of females, because, at present, females aged 18–19 years old have the highest rate of abortions of any age group. *See* Henshaw et al., *A Portrait of American Women Who Obtain Abortions,* 17 Family Planning Perspectives 90 (1985).

Studies have found that illegal abortion, rather than childbirth, is the most likely result in countries in which safe or legal abortions are not available. *See* Mashalaba, *Commentary on the causes and consequences of unwanted pregnancy from an African perspective,* 3 Int. J. Gynecol. Obstet. 15, 17 (1989). The negative health consequences of illegal abortions would be dramatic for pregnant adolescents. "Complications include hemorrhage, puerperal infection, and abdominal perforations, which can lead to death, chronic morbidity, or secondary infertility." *Id.*

For those pregnant adolescent females who "choose" compulsory childbirth over illegal abortion, the negative health consequences would also be dramatic. They would be at an increased risk of developing gallstones, *see* Buiumsohn et al., *Cholelithiasis and Teenage Mothers,* 11 J. of Adolescent Health Care 339 (1990); of suffering the effects of an ectopic pregnancy, *see* Gale et al., *Tubal Pregnancy in Adolescents,* 11 J. of Adolescent Health Care 485 (1990); and of aggravating common pre-existing conditions such as asthma, *see* Apter et al., *Outcomes of Pregnancy in Adolescents with Severe Asthma,* 149 Archives of Internal Medicine 2571 (1989). Pregnant adolescents are also at a disproportionate risk of dying from a hemorrhage or miscarriage, and have a relatively high maternal morbidity and mortality rate. *See* Barnett, *Factors that Adversely Affect the Health and Well-Being of African-American Adolescent Mothers and their Infants* in Teenage Pregnancy: Developing Strategies for Change in the Twenty-First Century 101, 105 (eds. Jones and Battle 1990). The risk of health problems and medical complications are even higher for African-American adolescents. *Id.* at 106.

The long-term negative consequences of adolescent childbearing for young women include reduced educational attainment, lower earnings, increased risk of welfare dependency, greater marital instability, a more rapid pace of childbearing, and lower perceived personal efficacy.

See Brazzell & Acock, *Influence of Attitudes, Significant Others and Aspirations on How Adolescents Intend to Resolve a Premarital Pregnancy,* 50 J. of Marriage & Family 413 (1988).

Female adolescents, themselves, are minors who do not have the right to vote. The Louisiana legislature has sacrificed their lives for the lives of embryos from the moment of conception.

2. Women with Handicaps

Coerced childbirth would substantially harm the health of many women with handicaps. Therapeutic abortions are routinely recommended for women with congestive heart failure, cyanotic congenital heart disease, primary or secondary hypertension, renal failure, kidney disease, or Eisenmenger Syndrome, because these conditions threaten a pregnant woman's health. *See* Elkayam & Gleicher, *Cardiac Problems in Pregnancy,* 25 JAMA 2838 (1989). Similarly, therapeutic abortions are generally recommended for pregnant women with breast cancer in Stage IV or V, so that they can receive the necessary treatment. *See* Onion, *Breast Cancer with Pregnancy,* 84 Amer. J. of Nursing 11–26 (1984).

Coerced childbirth would also worsen the medical condition of pregnant HIV-positive women, because it would depress cell-mediated immunity, and thereby cause more rapid progression of HIV infection. *See* Koonin et al., *Pregnancy-Associated Deaths Due to AIDS in the United States,* 258 JAMA 2714-17 (1987). Women in the later stages of HIV infection are more likely to experience severe pregnancy complications such as breech presentation or their own death. *See* Selwyn et al., *Prospective Study of HIV Infection and Pregnancy Outcomes in Intravenous Drug Use,* 261 JAMA 1289-94 (1989). Thus, the Centers for Disease Control recommends that HIV-infected women not become pregnant. *See* Grimes, *The CDC and Abortion in HIV-Positive Women,* 259 JAMA 1176 (1987).

Finally, pregnant women with pre-existing major psychiatric illness would not be able to receive adequate medical care if abortion were criminalized:

> Psychiatrists are confronted with patients who have suffered major postpartum psychiatric decompensations after previous deliveries and who, at serious risk of recurrence, consult them for advice. Other patients suffer from chronic psychiatric diseases that make them unable to care for children. . . . The administration of psychotropic medication is another complicating clinical issue. Psychiatrists may, in emergency situations, prescribe agents with unknown or adverse effects on embryonic development before a patient's pregnancy can be diagnosed.

Stotland, *Psychiatric Issues in Abortion, and the Implications of Recent Legal Changes for Psychiatric Practice* in Psychiatric Aspects of Abortion 1, 13 (Stotland ed. 1991)[4]

Like adolescents, women with handicaps are a group that is poorly represented by the political process and needs protection from the courts to avoid being sacrificed for the lives of embryos from the moment of conception.

3. Poor and Minority Women

The Act would have a dramatic, negative impact on the lives of poor and minority women. At present, the highest legal abortion rate is among unmarried women under 30 who are nonwhite, nonHispanic, and who have a family income under $11,000 per year. *See* Goldsmith, *Researchers Amass Abortion Data,* 262 JAMA 1431 (1989). Few abortion-related deaths presently occur. By contrast women of color accounted for 64% of the deaths

---

4. The Louisiana legislature was made aware of these adverse effects on women with preexisting mental illness through the testimony of Dr. Helen Ullrich. *See* Testimony by Dr. Ullrich before Louisiana Senate Committee on Health and Welfare 38–39 (May 29, 1991).

associated with illegal abortions in this country in 1972. *See* Cates & Rochat, *Illegal Abortions in the United States: 1972–1974*, 8 Fam. Plan. Persp. 86,87 (1976). Mishandled criminal abortions were the principal cause of maternal deaths in the 1960's. *See* Niswander, *Medical Abortion Practices in the United States*, in Abortion and the Law 53 (Smith ed. 1967). The mortality rates for African-American women were nine times higher than for white women. *See* Gold, *Therapeutic Abortions in New York: A 20 Year Review*, 55 Am. J. Pub. Health 964–65 (1965).

Poor and minority women, like female adolescents and women with handicaps, have been consistently ignored by the Louisiana legislature. This Court should not tolerate the callous indifference to their lives reflected by the Act.

C. The Louisiana Legislature Knowingly Caused Harm to Women in Passing the Act

Because the Act would have a dramatic gender-based impact on women's lives and well-being, this Court should conclude that this impact violates the Constitution so long as the adverse effects reflect an "invidious" purpose. *Personnel Administrator v. Feeney*, 442. U.S. 256, 274 (1979). As the Supreme Court said in *Feeney*, the "dispositive question, then, is whether the appellee has shown that a gender-based discriminatory purpose has, at least in some measure, shaped the [legislation]." *Id.* at 276.

Although the Supreme Court in *Feeney* did not find that the plaintiffs established a record of purposeful discrimination,[5] such evidence is readily available in the present case. The Louisiana legislature, unlike the legislature in *Feeney*, was repeatedly informed of the impact of this Act on women in the state of Louisiana at the time of its enactment. Yet, time and time again, the state refused to modify its absolute abortion ban to minimize the impact on women. It soundly rejected an amendment to provide an exception when a woman's health was endangered by her pregnancy, *see* Addendum A-1 (amendment rejected by a vote of 8–30); rejected an exception for women with AIDS, *see* Addendum A-2 (amendment rejected by a vote of 12–26); and rejected an amendment to increase welfare benefits to pregnant women, *see* Addendum A-3 (amendment tabled by a vote of 23–14). No justification except for an indifference to the lives and well-being of women could explain such actions. The state knowingly imprisoned these women to compulsory childbirth while shortening their lives.

II. APPELLANTS CANNOT CONSTITUTIONALLY JUSTIFY THEIR DISCRIMINATION AGAINST WOMEN

A. Introduction

If the plaintiff establishes a prima facie case of gender-based discrimination then the statute is unconstitutional unless the defendants can meet their burden of justification. The Supreme Court has held that the defendants must "carry the burden of showing an 'exceedingly persuasive justification' " in a gender-based equality case. *Mississippi University for Women v. Hogan*, 458 U.S. at 724 (quoting *Kirchberg v. Feenstra*, 450 U.S. 455, 461 (1981)). In

---

5. In *Feeney*, the Massachusetts legislature originally passed the veteran's-preference statute when men and women did not routinely compete for the same jobs. *Id.* at 255 n.14 (noting the standard practice of having jobs listed on a gendered basis until 1971). The legislature therefore conceived of its intent as assisting one group of men, veterans, over another group of men, nonveterans. Thus, the Court was not able to conclude from the facts in *Feeney* that the legislature consciously harmed women when it originally enacted the veterans preference statute.

assessing the stated justifications, the Court undertakes a "searching analysis", *Id.* at 728, of whether the restriction is, in fact, "substantially related to the statutory objective." *Craig v. Boren*, 429 U.S. 190, 197 (1976). That statutory objective must be "important." *Id.*

Exacting as it is, this scrutiny escalates to the highest level where, as here, legislation that discriminates on the basis of gender also intrudes on bodily integrity, procreation, health, family, and life itself. *See, e.g., Skinner v. Oklahoma*, 316 U.S. 535 (1942) (applying strict scrutiny under the equal protection clause to a compulsory sterilization law); *Zablocki v. Redhail*, 434 U.S. 374 (1978) (applying strict scrutiny under the equal protection clause to a marriage restriction that discriminated against persons with outstanding child support obligations). *See also Thornburgh v. American College of Obstetricians & Gynecologists*, 476 U.S. 747, 772 (1986) (recognizing importance of extending "private sphere of individual liberty" to "women as well as to men.") Because plaintiffs can prevail in the present case under the more lenient intermediate scrutiny, this brief will argue under that standard.

B. The Act is Not Substantially Related to Its Purported Objective of Protecting Life

If the state's objective were to protect life, then that objective would meet the requirement of being an "important state interest." However, the state did not have a genuine interest in protecting the lives of children or women. Instead, it was trying to coerce women to return to their nineteenth century exclusive roles of childbearer and caretaker of children.

Louisiana ranks nearly last in the United States in regard to the health and well-being of its children—a situation that would be greatly exacerbated if the Act would go into effect. Senator Cleo Fields understood this problem and tried to persuade the legislature to modify the Act so that it would be able to better serve the women and children of Louisiana. He informed the legislature that Louisiana's infant mortality rate was 11.9% in 1987, one of the highest in the United States; that 8.7% of all babies that were born were low birth weight as compared to 6.9% nationally; and that 36% of Louisiana women received late prenatal care or no prenatal care at all, a condition that leads to high infant mortality and low birth weight. *See* Statement of Senator Fields before Louisiana Senate Committee on Health and Welfare at 49 (May 29, 1991).

Based on this testimony, Senator Fields was able to convince the Senate Committee on Health and Welfare to amend the Act so as to allow it to go into effect only when Medicaid eligibility for pregnant women and children was expanded. The Senate, however, stripped the bill of that amendment. *See* Official Journal of the Senate of the State of Louisiana 48–49 (June 3, 1991) (tabled by a vote of 34–14). *See also* Addendum A-3 (language of rejected amendment). Senator Field tried to reintroduce the amendment on June 4, 1991, when it was again tabled by a vote of 23–15. *See* Official Journal of the Senate of the State of Louisiana 14–15 (June 4, 1991).[6]

The Louisiana legislature was willing to shift the burden of compulsory childbirth on to women, as well as the enormous expenses of childrearing, but it was not willing to do anything meaningful to assist the children who would be born or to relieve women of childcare responsibilities. Those means are not pro-child or pro-life.[7] When stripped of their

---

6. In addition, the legislature refused to improve the state's regulation of day care centers so that children could receive adequate day care and mothers could avoid some childcare responsibilities while maintaining employment or education. *See* La. H.B. 15 (1991) and La. S.B. 3 (1991). *See also Day-care bill dealt a blow in the House*, The Times-Picayune 1, col. 5 (August 1, 1991).

7. The legislature also rejected an amendment that would have eliminated capital punishment in the state. *See* Official Journal of the Senate of the State of Louisiana 15 (June 4, 1991). (Tabled by a vote of 29–8). *See also* Appendix A-4 (language of amendment).

rhetoric, they are means designed to coerce women into resuming their traditional role of motherhood.

The irrationality and ineffectiveness of the Act becomes more apparent when one compares it to legislation passed elsewhere. Other states and other countries have sought to protect life, yet virtually no other jurisdiction in the western world has considered it necessary or appropriate to pass such a stringent anti-abortion measure in this century.

Within the United States, even before *Roe v. Wade* was decided, states were moving in the direction of liberalizing their abortion laws and breaking with the nineteenth century tradition of restrictive abortion laws. These more liberal laws contained numerous abortion exceptions and reflected an increasing respect for women's well-being.[8] See *Doe v. Bolton*, 410 U.S. 179, 182–83 (1973).[9] Louisiana, however, has never been willing to consider the importance of women's lives when regulating abortion.

Since *Webster* was decided, the overwhelming majority of states have not restricted abortion at all. Of the few states that have passed measures restricting abortion, they have created numerous exceptions.[10] If the means chosen under the Louisiana Act were closely tailored, then one must inquire why *no other state in the last century* has considered it necessary or appropriate to enact such a stringent measure even before *Roe v. Wade* was decided.

Although the appellants claim that the purpose of the Act is to protect the unborn child, it is not codified as part of Louisiana's Crimes Against Persons statutes. Instead, it is a part of the code that deals with public morality—the part of the code that has historically restricted both abortion and contraception. As such, it reflects an attempt to resurrect nineteenth century views on public morality and women's place in society rather than a genuine concern for the person.

C. The Act is Based on Out-Moded and Stereotypical Views of Women

Appellants argue that their absolute prohibition of abortion stems from their civil law tradition. Brief of Appellant Connick at 25–28. That civil law tradition, however, is unconstitutionally based on out-moded and stereotypical views of women.

Under the Civil Codes of 1808, 1825, and 1870, women could not exercise political rights, vote or hold any elective office. In addition, they could not exercise any civil function unless specifically capacitated. See Saunders, Lectures on the Civil Code of Louisiana 14 (1925). Married women had little capacity to act without the authority of their husbands. *Id.* at 33. It was not until 1979, under judicial mandate, that Louisiana drafted an equal management act to eliminate the "head and master" rule. See 1978 La. Acts No. 627, *repealed by* 1979 La. Acts No. 709 § 5 *replaced by* 1979 La. Acts Nos. 709, 710, 711. *See also Kirchberg v. Feenstra*, 450 U.S. 455 (1981) (finding Louisiana's "head and master" rule to be unconstitutional).

Most of western Europe shares this same civil law tradition. Yet, Europe has managed to adapt that tradition to the twentieth century by respecting women's well-being along with

---

8. Amici do not suggest that these laws were constitutional. Nevertheless, they reflected *more* consideration of women's well-being than Louisiana's virtually complete ban on abortion.

9. The statute considered in *Roe* was not passed in the twentieth century. Like the Louisiana statute, it represents a nineteenth century understanding of women's role in society.

10. The most *restrictive* post-*Webster* measure passed by a state has been the Utah statute which provides for an abortion exception in the event of rape or incest, grave damage to the woman's health, or grave fetal defects. Utah Code Ann. @ 76-7-302(2) (1991). Guam, which is a territory subject to the United States Constitution, has passed an abortion measure that is less restrictive than Louisiana's. *See* 9 Guam Code Ann. § 31.20 (1991). Amici do not suggest that these statutes are constitutional. Nevertheless, they reflect *more* respect for women's well-being than the Louisiana statute.

fetal well-being. See Cook, Abortion laws and policies: challenges and opportunities, 3 Int. J. Gynecol. Obstet. 61, 62–65 (1989). France, Louisiana's civil law ancestor, has a much less restrictive abortion law than Louisiana.[11] In addition, France has been the world leader in providing publicly funded abortion and contraception through the development of RU 486.

One obvious indication of the Louisiana legislature's stereotypical views of women reflected in the Act is its exemption of women who self-induce abortions from the statute's coverage. La. Rev. Stat. Ann. § 14:87 (A) (2) (1991). No justification consistent with the statute's purported objective can explain this exception. Self-induced abortions are likely to destroy both women and fetus' lives. On the other hand, such an exception supports a nineteenth century "pedestal" view of women by leaving them free from the criminal law.

Louisiana's traditional ideology that supports the Act is reflective of the ideology that has been found elsewhere to support abortion restrictions. Support for laws banning abortions have been found to be an outgrowth of stereotypical notions that women's only appropriate roles are those of mother and housewife; in many cases, such laws have emerged as a direct reaction to the increasing number of women who work outside the home. See generally Luker, Abortion and the Politics of Motherhood 192–215 (1984).

Louisiana cannot hide behind its civil law tradition to remain in the dark ages. The equal protection clause requires it to move its civil law tradition into a twentieth century understanding of women's rights and well-being.

The women of Louisiana would prefer to be represented by their legislature rather than turn to the courts for protection. Woman after woman testified before the Louisiana legislature about the dramatic negative consequences that would follow if the Act were enacted. Unfortunately, their efforts did not result in the legislature approving one meaningful exception to the Act. Until the women of Louisiana can gain access to the responsible state legislature that Chief Justice Rehnquist described in Webster, they will have to seek protection from the courts.

11. French law permits a woman to choose an abortion without restriction in the first ten weeks of her pregnancy; after ten weeks, an abortion is permitted when the pregnancy would seriously endanger a pregnant woman's health or the fetus is suffering from a particularly serious disease or condition. See 26 Intl Digest of Health Leg. 351–54 (1975). At no time during her pregnancy, does a woman in France need to demonstrate that her life was threatened by the continuation of her pregnancy in order to obtain an abortion.

CONCLUSION

For the foregoing reasons, Amicus Curiae Supporting Appellees urge this Court to affirm the district court. Alternatively, this Court should instruct the district court, in the event of a remand, that the Act violates the equal protection clause of the Fourteenth Amendment.

Respectfully submitted,

RUTH COLKER (Counsel of Record)
WENDY BROWN
Tulane Law School
6801 Freret Street
New Orleans, LA 70118
(504) 865-5968

Attorneys for Amicus Curiae
Supporting Appellees

The assistance of twenty-five students in the Tulane Law School Community Service Program is gratefully acknowledged.

Addendum: Text of Selected Rejected Amendments

PHYSICAL OR MENTAL HEALTH EXCEPTION

The physician terminates a pregnancy when the physical or mental health of the mother is seriously threatened by the pregnancy and prior to such termination, the physician prepares a report, and obtains the written concurrence of another physician, stating each reason which warrants the termination of the pregnancy.

Official Journal of the Senate of the State of Louisiana 19 (June 4, 1991) (rejected by a vote of 8–30).

HIV EXCEPTION

The physician terminates a pregnancy when the mother has tested positive for the presence of the human immunodeficiency virus (HIV), which result has been confirmed by the second test, with each test being conducted by a laboratory approved by the Department of Health and Hospitals for such purposes, and prior to such termination, the physician prepares a report stating the reason which warrants the termination of the pregnancy.

Official Journal of the Senate of the State of Louisiana 14 (June 4, 1991) (rejected by a vote of 12–26).

AMENDMENT TO INCREASE MEDICAID ELIGIBILITY

A. Upon receipt of the necessary waivers from the appropriate federal agency, which the secretary of the Department of Health and Hospitals shall request, the department shall amend the Medicaid state law to provide for:
(1) Eligibility for Medicaid services for all pregnant women with an income up to one hundred eighty-five percent of the federal poverty income guidelines.
(2) Medicaid eligibility for any pregnant woman who qualifies based on preliminary financial information indicating that her income and resources fall within the eligibility criteria and guarantee of payment for her services.
(3) Eligibility criteria for Medicaid services for pregnant adolescents based on the income of the pregnant adolescent and not on the income of her parents.
(4) A program of care coordination for all eligible pregnant women. . . .
B. In accordance with the Administrative Procedure Act, the department shall promulgate regulations requiring that all public health programs which render prenatal care services shall provide, at a minimum, for the following:
(1) Expanded or flex-time hours of operation so that health care services are available to pregnant women during evening and weekend hours.

(2) An initial appointment within two weeks of request and minimal waiting time to receive services after entering a health care facility.

(3) Procedures to assure that pregnant women are receiving and continue to receive prenatal services.

. . . .

Sections 2, 3, 5, and 6 of this Act shall become effective only if, as, and when the program provided in Section 4 of this Act is funded and implemented and in such event shall become effective on the first day of the calendar month after the department certifies to the governor and the legislature that the program is implemented.

Official Journal of the Senate of the State of Louisiana 48–49 (June 3, 1991) (tabled by a vote of 23–14).

Capital Punishment Amendment

to remove the imposition of capital punishment for the commission of any criminal offense

Official Journal of the Senate of the State of Louisiana 15 (June 4, 1991) (tabled by a vote of 29–8).

Table of Cases

Index

RUTH COLKER is Professor of Law at Tulane University. She has written widely on the topics of feminist theory and abortion in the *Yale Law Journal*, the *Duke Law Journal*, the *California Law Review*, and the *Harvard Women's Law Journal*. She has also worked on the Louisiana abortion case *Sojourner T. v. Buddy Roemer*.